P9-AZX-212

How to Be Idle

How to Be Idle

TOM HODGKINSON

HarperCollins*Publishers*

Originally published in the United Kingdom in 2004 by Hamish Hamilton, an imprint of Penguin Books Ltd.

FIRST U.S. EDITION

Printed on acid-free paper

Library of Congress Cataloging-in-Publication Data
Hodgkinson, Tom.
     How to be idle / Tom Hodgkinson.—1st ed.
         p.   cm.
     Originally published: London : Hamish Hamilton, 2004.
     Includes bibliographical references (p.).
     ISBN 0-06-077968-3
     1. Laziness. I. Title.
  BF485.H53 2005
  158—dc22   2004059932

05 06 07 08 09   ❖/RRD   10 9 8 7 6 5 4 3 2 1

For Gavin Hills,
who knew how to live

Contents

Preface

The idea that idleness is good goes against everything we have ever been taught. Industry, hard work, duty, self-sacrifice, toil: surely these are the virtues that will lead to success in life?

Well, no. In the West, we have become addicted to work. Americans now work the longest hours in the world. And the result is not health, wealth and wisdom, but rather a lot of anxiety, a lot of ill health and a lot of debt.

This book seeks to recover an alternative tradition in literature, poetry and philosophy, one that says not only is idleness good, but that it is essential for a pleasurable life. Where do our ideas come from? When do we dream? When are we happy? It is not when staring at a computer terminal worrying about what our boss will say about our work. It is in our leisure time, our own time, when we are doing what we want to do.

These are the truths that the great loafing poet Walt Whitman knew. Instead of working, he preferred to wander and observe. These wanderings gave us *Leaves of Grass*. Mark Twain never liked work much. He preferred fun. And Thoreau turned his back on the busy rushing of the commercial world to seek freedom in the woods.

It's time to say no to jobs and yes to fun, freedom and pleasure. It's time to be idle.

Tom Hodgkinson
AUGUST 2004

8 a.m.

Waking Up Is Hard to Do

Let us be lazy in everything, except in loving
and drinking, except in being lazy.
Gotthold Ephraim Lessing (1729–81)

I wonder if that hard-working American rationalist and agent of industry Benjamin Franklin knew how much misery he would cause in the world when, back in 1757, high on puritanical zeal, he popularized and promoted the trite and patently untrue aphorism "early to bed and early to rise, makes a man healthy, wealthy and wise"?

It is a sad fact that from early childhood we are tyrannized by the moral myth that it is right, proper and good to leap out of bed the moment we wake in order to set about some useful work as quickly and cheerfully as possible. In my own case, it was my mother whom I remember very clearly screaming at me to get out of bed every morning. As I lay there in blissful comfort, eyes closed, trying to hang on to a fading dream, doing my utmost to ignore her shouting, I would start to calculate the shortest time it would take me to get up, have breakfast and go to school and still arrive with seconds to spare before assembly started. All this mental ingenuity and effort I expended in order to enjoy a few more moments of slumber. Thus the idler begins to learn his craft.

Parents begin the brainwashing process and then school works yet harder to indoctrinate its charges with the necessity of early rising. My own personal guilt about feeling actually *physically incapable* of rising early in the morning continued well into my twenties. For years I fought with the feelings of self-hatred that accompanied my morning listlessness. I would make resolutions to rise at eight. As a student, I developed complex alarm systems. I bought a timer plug, and set it to turn on my coffee maker and also the record player, on which I had placed my loudest record, *It's Alive* by The Ramones. 7:50 a.m. was the allotted time. I had set the record to come on at an ear-splitting volume. Being a live recording, the first track was prefaced by crowd noise. The cheering and whooping would wake me, and I'd know I had only a few seconds to leap out of bed and turn the volume down before Dee Dee Ramone would grunt: "one—two—three—four" and my housemates and I would be assaulted by the opening chords of "Rockaway Beach," turned up to 11. The idea was that I would then drink the coffee and jolt my body into wakefulness. It half worked. When I heard the crowd noise, I would leap out of bed and totter for a moment. But what happened then, of course, was that I would turn the volume right down, ignore the coffee and climb back to the snuggly warm embrace of my duvet. Then I'd slowly come to my senses at around 10:30 a.m., doze until twelve, and finally stagger to my feet in a fit of self-loathing. I was a real moralist back then: I even made a poster for my wall which read: "Edification first, then have some fun." It was hip in that it was a lyric from hardcore punk band Bad Brains, but the message, I think you'll agree, is a dreary one. Nowadays I do it the other way around.

It wasn't until many years later that I learned that I was not alone in my sluggishness and in experiencing the conflicting emotions of pleasure and guilt which surrounded it. There is a wealth of literature on the subject. And it is generally written by the best, funniest, most joy-giving writers. In 1889, the Victorian humorist Jerome K. Jerome published an essay called "On Being Idle." Imagine how much better I felt when I read the following passage, in which Jerome reflects on the pleasures of snoozing:

Ah! how delicious it is to turn over and go to sleep again: "just for five minutes." Is there any human being, I wonder, besides the hero of a Sunday-school "tale for boys," who ever gets up willingly? There are some men to whom getting up at the proper time is an utter impossibility. If eight o'clock happens to be the time that they should turn out, then they lie till half-past. If circumstances change and half-past eight becomes early enough for them, then it is nine before they can rise. They are like the statesman of whom it was said that he was always punctually half an hour late. They try all manner of schemes. They buy alarm clocks (artful contrivances that go off at the wrong time and alarm the wrong people) . . . I knew one man who would actually get out and have a cold bath; and even that was no use, for afterward he would jump into bed again to warm himself.

Self-confessed slumberer Louis Theroux, writing in the magazine which I edit, the *Idler*, recalls one such stratagem, developed by his friend Ken. "It went like this: keep a cold mug of coffee and two Pro Plus pills by your bedside. Set the alarm for 8:20 a.m.—half an hour before you actually want to get up—and when it goes off, in the instant of lucidity that the alarm clock triggers, knock back the coffee and the pills, then go back to sleep. Half an hour later you spring awake in the grip of a massive caffeine rush."

Sleep is a powerful seducer, hence the terrifying machinery we have developed to fight it. I mean, the alarm clock. Heavens! What evil genius brought together those two enemies of the idle—clocks and alarms—into one unit? Every morning, through-out the Western world, happily dreaming individuals are rudely thrust from sleep by an ear-splitting ringing noise or insistent electronic beeping. The alarm clock is the first stage in the ungodly transformation that we force ourselves to endure in the morning, from blissed-out, carefree dreamer to anxiety-ridden toiler, weighted by responsibility and duty. What is truly amazing is that we buy alarm clocks voluntarily. Is it not absurd to spend our own hard-earned cash on a device to make every day of our lives start as unpleasantly as possible, and which really just serves the employer to whom we sell our time? Yes, there are some alarm clocks that dispense with the alarm and instead wake us with the chatter of early-morning radio DJs, but are these any better? The oppressive cheerfulness of the DJs is designed to get us into a good mood for the day ahead, or to distract us from our deep woes with daft jokes. I find it simply irritating. There's nothing worse than the banal chirpiness of another human being when you are in a state of deep, heavy, existential reflection. As my friend John Moore, the laziest man in the world, says when his wife tries to wake him up: "I'll get up when there's something worth getting up *for*."

In the UK, the highbrow version of this national wake-up call is Radio 4's *Today* programme, which discusses the calamities of the day with great seriousness and concern. Most countries have a serious news show first thing in the morning. This has the effect of stimulating such emotions as anger and anxiety in the listener. But a certain type of person feels it is their *duty* to listen to it, as if the act of merely listening is somehow going to improve the world. Duty, oh, what a burden you are! Isn't there room for a news-free radio station? When I listen to classical music on the radio, for example when driving, there is nothing worse than having my reverie and dream-flow interrupted by the tedious reality of news headlines.

So: for most of us the working day begins in torment when, wrenched from the nectar of oblivion, we are faced with the prospect of trying to become dutiful citizens, ready to serve our masters in the workplace with gratitude, good cheer and abundant energy. (Why are we all so desperate for "jobs," by the way? They're horrible things. But more on this later.)

After the alarm clock, it is the turn of Mr. Kellogg to shame us into action. "Rise and Shine!" he exhorts us from the Corn

Flakes packet. The physical act of crunching cornflakes or other cereals is portrayed in TV advertising as working an amazing alchemy on slothful human beings: the incoherent, unshaven sluggard (bad) is magically transformed into a smart and jolly worker full of vigour and purpose (good) by the positive power of cereal. Kellogg himself, tellingly, was a puritanical health-nut who never had sex (he preferred enemas). Such are the architects of our daily life.

For all modern society's promises of leisure, liberty and doing what you want, most of us are still slaves to a schedule we did not choose.

Why have things come to such a pass? Well, the forces of the anti-idle have been at work since the Fall of Man. The propaganda against oversleeping goes back a very long way, over two thousand years, to the Bible. Here is Proverbs, chapter 6, on the subject:

6 Go to the ant, thou sluggard; consider her ways, and be wise:

7 Which having no guide, overseer, or ruler,

8 Provideth her meat in the summer, and gathereth her food in the harvest.

9 How long wilt thou sleep, O sluggard? when wilt thou arise out of thy sleep?

10 Yet a little sleep, a little slumber, a little folding of the hands to sleep:

11 So shall thy poverty come as one that travelleth, and thy want as an armed man.

In the first place, I would seriously question the sanity of a religion that holds up the ant as an example of how to live. The ant system is an exploitative aristocracy based on the unthinking toil of millions of workers and the complete inactivity of a single queen and a handful of drones. The voice of God goes on to admonish the poor "sluggard" for sleeping and then warns that poverty and hunger shall be his rewards if he continues to lie in bed. Idleness is sin, and the wages of sin is death (and the wages of hard work are £22,585 p.a. with London weighting).

Christianity has promoted bed-guilt ever since. This passage from the Bible is used as a bludgeon by moralists, capitalists and bureaucrats in order to impose upon the people the notion that God hates it when you get up late. It suits the lust for order that characterizes the non-idler: don't waste time! Better to be busy than doing nothing!

In mid-eighteenth-century London, Dr. Johnson, who had nothing to be ashamed of as far as literary output goes, is to be found lacerating himself for his sluggardly habits. "O Lord, enable me . . . in redeeming the time I have spent in Sloth," he wrote in his journals at the age of 29. Twenty years later, things haven't improved, and he resolves "to rise early. Not later than six if I can." The following year, having failed to rise at six, he adapts his resolution: "I purpose to rise at eight because though I shall not yet rise early it will be much earlier than I now rise, for I often lye till two." Johnson, deeply religious and of a melancholic temperament, felt ashamed of his sloth. But did his sloth cause any pain to others? Did it kill anyone? Did his sloth force people to do things they would rather not? No.

In the late eighteenth and the nineteenth centuries, it suited new avatars of Progress to promote a culture of early rising among the working classes. In 1755, the Rev. J. Clayton published a pamphlet, "Friendly Advice to the Poor," in which he argued that early rising would keep troublemakers off the streets: "The necessity of early rising would reduce the poor to a necessity of going to Bed betime; and thereby prevent the Danger of Midnight revels." The Methodist John Wesley, who himself rose every morning at 4 a.m., wrote a sermon called "The Duty and Advantage of Early Rising" (1786), in which he claimed that lying in bed was physically unhealthy, and used comically quasi-scientific terms to drive home his argument: "By soaking so long between warm sheets, the flesh is as it were parboiled, and becomes soft and flabby. The nerves, in the meantime, are quite unstrung." In 1830, the original "bluestocking," Hannah More, published the following lines on "Early Rising":

> Thou silent murderer, Sloth, no more
> My mind imprison'd keep;
> Nor let me waste another hour
> With thee, thou felon, Sleep.

This is very strong language. More sees Sloth, the seventh deadly sin (although the original seventh was sadness), as a murderer of time, who keeps the lazy man's mind imprisoned. He must be fought against; there must be a manly battle of wills. This is, of course, palpable nonsense: sleep is a friend, not a felon. Everyone knows that the mind, far from being imprisoned, is actually at its freest when we are lying in bed dozing in the morning, and we will come back to the creative benefits of that delicious in-between state later. Creativity, though, was definitely not a buzzword for the new capitalists. The architects of the

Industrial Revolution needed to convince the masses of the benefits of tedious, disciplined toil. And the best-selling Victorian author Samuel Smiles's books were titled *Self-Help* (1859), *Thrift* (1875) and *Duty* (1880), and were packed with homilies like the above. Cleanliness, order, good housekeeping, punctuality, self-sacrifice, duty and responsibility: these self-denying "virtues" were communicated by a sophisticated network of moralists, writers and politicians.

If we think we are free of this sort of thing today, then look at our magazines and the "sort your life out" features which proliferate. Patronizing self-help books regale us with various bullet-pointed strategies to become more productive, less drunk and more hard-working. Many of these strategies involve spending a lot of money. Men's and women's magazines employ body anxiety to send us to that modern torture chamber we call the gym. We toil all day and then *pay for the pleasure of running on a treadmill!* Adverts for electronic personal organizers imply that the gadget will help us to achieve robotic perfection; the writer Charles Leadbetter recently noticed that the fantasy schedules which appear in ads for "Organizers" (as if the mere purchase of the device will magically organize your life) invariably start with the line: "7 a.m. Gym."

Not only is early rising totally unnatural but I would argue also that lying in bed half-awake—sleep researchers call this state "hypnagogic"—is positively beneficial to health and happiness. A good morning doze of half an hour or more can, for example, help you to prepare mentally for the problems and tasks ahead. This was the view of one of my favourite philosophers, Lin Yutang. A Chinese-American writer of the early twentieth century, he spent much of his time trying to persuade striving

Americans of the validity of the laid-back philosophy of ancient China, which, he says, encouraged "freedom and nonchalance," and a "wise and merry philosophy of living." In his book *The Importance of Living*, published in 1938, he devoted a whole chapter to the art of lying in bed. Here he advises the student of good living to resist early rising:

> What does it matter even if [a man] stays in bed at eight o'clock? A thousand times better that he should provide himself with a good tin of cigarettes on his bedside table and take plenty of time to get up from bed and solve all his problems of the day before he brushes his teeth . . . in that comfortable position, he can ponder over his achievements and mistakes of yesterday and single out the important from the trivial in the day's programme ahead of him. Better that he arrive at ten o'clock in his office and master of himself than that he should come punctually at nine or even a quarter before to watch over his subordinates like a slave-driver and then "hustle about nothing," as the Chinese say.

This idea that lying in bed half awake could actually make the idler's life more efficient came up when I interviewed the poet John Cooper Clarke. He uses his morning slumber time, he said, to plan what he is going to wear that day. His mind ranges freely and pleasurably through his wardrobe, weighing up various combinations of styles, colours and materials. Dressing after this little mental workout, therefore, is a doddle, nowhere near as tedious and burdensome as the prospect first appears.

The humane, truculent and brilliant journalist G. K. Chesterton was another writer who attacked the notion that early rising is morally good and staying in bed is morally bad. He instead took a libertarian view: the time we rise should be a matter of personal choice. "The tone now commonly taken towards the practice of lying in bed is hypocritical and unhealthy," he writes in his 1909 essay "On Lying in Bed." "Instead of being regarded, as it ought to be, as a matter of personal convenience and adjustment, it has come to be regarded by many as if it were a part of essential morals to get up early in the morning. It is upon the whole part of practical wisdom; but there is nothing good about it or bad about its opposite."

Greatness and late rising are natural bedfellows. Late rising is for the independent of mind, the individual who refuses to become a slave to work, money, ambition. In his youth, the great poet of loafing, Walt Whitman, would arrive at the offices of the newspaper where he worked at around 11.30 a.m., and leave at 12.30 for a two-hour lunch break. Another hour's work after lunch and then it was time to hit the town.

So what can we do? In my own case, my life improved dramatically when I got rid of the alarm clock. I found that one can train oneself to wake up at roughly the correct time—if, indeed, you are unlucky enough to have a "correct time" to wake up at—without it. This way, one wakes slowly, naturally and pleasurably. One leaves one's bed when one is ready, and not when someone else wants you to. Gone is the daily agony of being wrenched from delicious sleep by the mechanical noise of the bell. It helps also, of course, not to have a job and to be one's own master. But even if you are yoked to employment, I suggest you try it. It works. And it could be your first step to idleness.

Of course, it's not always easy to tower into sublimity from the comfort of your own bed when the people around you are toiling. Sometimes the dedicated slugabed is rudely awakened by the yelling of builders, the bustle of housemates, the entreaties of toddlers or even dawn's rosy fingers coming in at the window. These impediments to sleep must be blocked out if you are to enjoy your morning doze. So may I offer another practical tip? Simply invest in earplugs, black-out blinds and eyeshades. With these simple devices, you can extend your doze time. In the case of young children, the earlier they can be trained to get themselves up and prepare their own breakfast, the better.

I asserted at the beginning of this chapter that Benjamin Franklin's "early to rise" dictum was not only misery-making but also false. How so? Well, when I think of people who are healthy, wealthy and wise, I see amongst their ranks artists, writers, musicians and entrepreneurs. It is well known that none of these types are early risers. In order to have ideas and then to plan how to realize those ideas, creative people need thinking time, away from the desk, away from the telephone, away from the myriad distractions of everyday and domestic life. And morning snoozing is one of the best times to do this.

As to how on earth going early to bed could automatically guarantee riches and happiness, I suppose nothing can be proved, but I'm with Dr. Johnson who confidently asserted: "Whoever thinks of going to bed before twelve o'clock is a scoundrel."

No, the early risers are not healthy, wealthy and wise. They are frequently sickly, poor and stupid. They serve the late risers. If you don't believe me, look at the drawn, desperate faces around you on the underground systems in the major cities of our great industrialized nations—London, Tokyo, New York— between eight and nine in the morning. Healthy? Certainly not.

Wealthy? No, or they would not be on the underground trains at that time. In fact, the lowest-paid workers tend to be the ones who are travelling the earliest. Wise? How can they be, if they choose to commute in this way? If you want health, wealth and happiness, the first step is to throw away your alarm clocks!

9 a.m.

Toil and Trouble

> I wander through each charter'd street,
> Near where the charter'd Thames does flow,
> And mark in every face I meet
> Marks of weakness, marks of woe.
>
> William Blake, "London" (1794)

Nine a.m. is surely the most brutal and feared of all the hours in the idler's day, for it is the time when someone, somewhere, decided that work should start. Just before 9 a.m., buses, trains, trams and roads heave with grim-faced toilers as they lug themselves from one part of town to another. Lifts sigh with large-jeaned marketing executives, office girls with lots of make-up clatter through reception, recent immigrants with hard hats arrive at the building sites, city boys charge up on coffee, retail workers wait outside the shop for the boss to arrive with the keys, escalators take us from an airless underworld and deposit us in equally airless offices. We read newspapers and become anxious. We have a job. A job! Our reward after years of education! We worked hard in our youth in order to work hard again in our adulthood. A job! The summit of our lives! The answer!

The idea of the "job" as the answer to all woes, individual and social, is one of the most pernicious myths of modern society. It is promoted by politicians, parents, newspaper moralists and leaders of industry, on the left and on the right: paradise, they say, is "full employment." One key index to the success of a country is the size of its unemployed population. The more people have jobs, the better, we are told. "Job" is rarely defined with any precision to the teenager or to the student as they make their journey towards it, but the myth suggests to us that a "good job" will offer us ample money, a social life, status and work which we will find "rewarding." It's actually astonishing how little we pause to reflect on these terms when at school or college. And even though, as children, we hear our parents complaining every night about their bosses or co-workers, it doesn't put us off the world of work. We think it will be different for us.

As is commonly the case with such controlling ideas, there is a vast gap between the promise of the job and its reality. When we enter the ignoble world of work, we are soon shocked at the humiliations we encounter there. The worst job I had was working as a researcher on a tabloid magazine, near Chancery Lane in London. Two years previously, at university, I had been reading novels, running magazines, playing in a hardcore punk band and getting up when I felt like it. On the whole, I had been master of my own time and had done things I wanted to do. I was now calling the press office at Asda to check the price of baked beans eight hours a day. I was habitually late in the morning, my friends all seemed to be more successful, and I resented being asked to go to the garage to collect the editor's car or go on the—accursed term—"coffee run." The master at 21 had turned into a slave at 22.

So: no fun. It was certainly not rewarding, financially, emotionally or intellectually. The only true pleasure it provided was the negative one of sitting in the pub at the end of the day with co-workers complaining about the bosses. The money was lousy, so I did not even have the compensation of spare cash. I seemed to have only enough money to get to work and back, buy a cheese sandwich at lunchtime and pay my rent. I was there for nearly two years and I would say that the whole experience was a complete waste of my time, apart from revealing to me how grindingly dull and joyless an office can be. I learned that far from fun, satisfaction and money, my only reward for being a slave was misery, penury and resentment. And the terrible irony is that when our current job turns out to provide neither much money nor much fun, we think we can solve the problem by getting a better job. So it goes on: an endless cycle, a miserable set-up, as satirized brilliantly in the UK sitcom *The Office*.

In defence of our strictly regimented work life, people will say, "Oh, but people enjoy work for the social interaction." There is the persistent myth of the lottery winner, who, despite never having to work again, keeps their minimum-wage factory job. I have never believed this. No, people enjoy the social interaction *despite* the unpromising conditions in which that social interaction takes place: the dismal grey surroundings, the people you have not chosen to be with, the dispiriting canteens, the laws against smoking and drinking, the patronizing "mission statements" on the walls. Does anyone really suppose that if we didn't have jobs, all social interaction would cease? Most human beings are sociable creatures; we are quite capable of seeking out interaction without the help of an employer. Do we not have family, friends, the pub, the café, the bar, the market?

And in any case, pleasure at work is often frowned upon. My boss at the magazine used to tell us off for talking to each other. In *Nickel and Dimed* (2001), her superb undercover study of low-wage life in America, Barbara Ehrenreich reports that workers in cheap restaurants and cleaning companies were frequently admonished for what they called "gossip," for idle chit-chat.

The English historian E. P. Thompson, in his classic book *The Making of the English Working Class* (1963), argues that the creation of the job is a relatively recent phenomenon, born out of the Industrial Revolution. Before the advent of steam-powered machines and factories in the mid eighteenth century, work was a much more haphazard and less structured affair. People worked, yes, they did "jobs," but the idea of being yoked to one particular employer to the exclusion of all other money-making activity was unknown. And the average man enjoyed a much greater degree of independence than today.

Take the weavers. Before the invention in 1764 of the spinning jenny by the weaver and carpenter James Hargreaves, and of the steam engine in the same year by James Watt, weavers were generally self-employed and worked as and when they chose. The young Friedrich Engels noted that they had control over their own time: "So it was that the weaver was usually in a position to lay by something, and rent a little piece of land, that he cultivated in his leisure hours, of which he had as many as he chose to take, since he could weave whenever and as long as he pleased," he wrote in his 1845 study *The Condition of the Working Class in England*. "They did not need to overwork; they did no more than they chose to do, and yet earned what they needed."

In addition to this autonomous and leisure-filled life, the weavers were also in control of the whole manufacturing process: they produced the cloth and sold it to a travelling merchant. It was a simple, unsophisticated existence; Engels maintains that they had little knowledge or even interest in what was going on in another village say five miles away. But they were not enslaved to a job; they were task-orientated, rather than being bound by a nine-to-five (or its yet more brutal ancestor, the dawn-to-dusk). They worked as much as they needed to and no more. Time was not money, as Benjamin Franklin was later to assert. E. P. Thompson, in *Customs in Common* (1991), quotes from a description of Mexican mine-workers of the early twentieth century to give a sense of pre-industrial work patterns. These strong-willed Mexicans were "willing to work only three or four days a week if that paid for necessities." They preferred to work on the basis of a project rather than on the hours they put in: "Given a contract and the assurance he will get so much money for each ton he mines, and that it doesn't matter how long he takes doing it, or how often he sits down to contemplate life, he will work with a vigour which is remarkable." Presumably because the quicker they got the work done, the sooner they could go to the pub.

Our happy pre-industrial Mexicans and pre-1750 peasants did

not see the need to work longer hours than were necessary to furnish them with meat and ale. Thompson writes: "The work pattern was one of alternate bouts of intense labour and of idleness, wherever men were in control of their own working lives."

Work and life were intertwined. A weaver, for example, might weave eight or nine yards on a rainy day. On other days, a contemporary diary tells us, he might weave just two yards before he did "sundry jobs about the lathe and in the yard & wrote a letter in the evening." Or he might go cherry-picking, work on a community dam, calve the cow, cut down trees or go to watch a public hanging. Thompson adds as an aside: "The pattern persists among some self-employed—artists, writers, small farmers, and perhaps also with students [idlers, all]—today, and provokes the question of whether it is not a 'natural' human work-rhythm."

England, then, before the invention of the dark satanic mills, was a nation of idlers. But this chaotic approach troubled contemporary moralists, who believed that people must be kept busy to keep them out of mischief. In 1820, the middle-class observer John Foster noted with horror that agricultural labourers, having finished their work, were left with "several hours in the day to be spent nearly as they please . . . They will . . . for hours together . . . sit on a bench, or lie down on a bank or hillock . . . yielded up to utter vacancy and torpor." And early architects of the Industrial Revolution such as Matthew Boulton and Josiah Wedgwood are often to be found in letters complaining of the laziness of their workers.

But the new Protestant work ethic was successful. The Industrial Revolution, above all, was a battle between hard work and laziness, and hard work won. Machines stole the process of production from hands and minds. Workshops became "manufactories"; the self-employed became the employed; families began to live on wages alone and to buy in the groceries that perhaps they had grown themselves in previous generations. They might have been earning more money, but a terrific blow was dealt to their quality of life. Joyful chaos, working in tune with the seasons, telling the time by the sun, variety, change, self-direction; all this was replaced with a brutal, standardized work culture, the effects of which we are still suffering from today.

In other words, the job was invented in order to make things easier for those at the top. The people were stripped of their independence in order to service the grand dreams of a socially aspirational mill-owner who believed in hard work—for other people. As G. K. Chesterton put it in *What's Wrong with the World* (1910):

> The rich did literally turn the poor out of the old guest house on to the road, briefly telling them that it was the road of progress. They did literally force them into factories and the modern wage-slavery assuring them all the time that this was the only way to wealth and civilization.

For what is Progress? Clint Eastwood's preacher in *Pale Rider* puts the matter elegantly. When told by a local town fat cat that a group of independent gold miners who refuse to move off their land to make way for his company are "standing in the way of Progress," Clint simply asks: "Yours or theirs?"

The ascendancy of the clock and the machine tore us from nature. This is how the contemporary French academic Thierry

Paquot, author of *The Art of the Siesta* (1998), mourns the loss of the natural way of life:

> The wandering countryman, given to siestas and dreams but also ready to work, will no longer be able to organize his daily activities according to his mood. He will have to obey an externally imposed regime, completely foreign to his way of life. Work in the fields has for a long time evaded the ticking of the clock, permitting country dwellers to harmonize their time with that of nature . . .

How did the bloody-minded and freedom-loving Brits allow themselves to become servants of capitalism, a "Slave State" as Bertrand Russell put it, in his 1932 essay "In Praise of Idleness"? The great problem of the Industrial Revolution was how to transform a population of strong-willed, independent-minded, heavy-drinking, party-orientated, riot-loving, life-loving Englishmen into a docile, disciplined, grateful workforce. In 1835, a prominent moralizing philosopher—today we call them management gurus—called Andrew Ure wrote a book called *Philosophy of Manufactures*, aimed at the new bosses, in which he wrote of the difficulty of dealing with a nation of idlers and gave advice on brainwashing. He spoke of the problem in terms of a conversion:

> . . . it is found nearly impossible to convert persons past the age of puberty, whether drawn from rural or from handicraft occupations, into useful factory hands. After struggling for a while to conquer their listless or restive habits, they either renounce their employment spontaneously, or are dismissed by the overlookers on account of inattention . . . [there is] a need to subdue

the refractory tempers of work-people accustomed to irregular paroxysms of diligence . . . it is excessively in the interest of every mill-owner to organize his moral machinery on equally sound principles with his mechanical, for otherwise he will never command the steady hands, watchful eyes, and prompt cooperation, essential to the excellence of product . . . there is, in fact, no case to which the Gospel truth, "godliness is great gain," is more applicable than to the administration of an extensive factory.

God was ruthlessly brought in by the capitalists to control the minds of the masses. Crucially, the new, joyless creed of Methodism was preached to the labouring poor in church on Sunday. At church, they were bombarded with the idea that they were sinful, that all pleasure was wrong, and that the path to salvation lay in quiet suffering on this earth. God was reinvented as a sort of Big Brother figure, and it was His will that you worked hard. Thompson writes: "Not only the 'sack' but the flames of hell might be the consequence of indiscipline at work. God was the most vigilant overlooker of all. Even above the chimney breast 'Thou God Seest Me' was hung."

The founder of Methodism, John Wesley, was particularly keen on terrifying and controlling small children. "Break their wills betimes," he wrote. "Let a child from a year old be taught to fear the rod and to cry softly; from that age make him do as he is bid . . ." Children were assaulted by terrifying images of the burning flames of hell, of the evil demons who would pursue you if you were naughty. These images were burnt into the imagination of the small child, and would help to forge the cowed, obedient mindset of the later adult.

A good reserve weapon, if fear of God failed to convert the rural slackers into urban drudges, was hunger. Another management philosopher of the nineteenth century, the Rev. Andrew Townsend, argued that to use mere force of law to impress the new work ethic on the workers "gives too much trouble, requires too much violence and makes too much noise." Better and easier, he maintained, to keep them hungry. "Hunger, on the contrary, is not only a pressure which is peaceful, silent and incessant, but as it is the most natural motive for work and industry, it also provokes the most peaceful efforts." The philosophy of low wages was also enthusiastically followed: the lower the wage, the harder the proletariat would toil. The same philosophy is today followed in the fast-food industry, where the production of food has been industrialized and deskilled in the same way that the production of cloth was industrialized in the nineteenth century. Fast-food workers suffer the lowest wages in the US and perform the same tedious tasks all day. Again, the dogma of hard work—which is deeply embedded in contemporary notions of what it means to be American—is what keeps us toiling and keeps us happy to be exploited in this way.

Around the same time, the thundering polemicist Thomas Carlyle did much damage in the nineteenth century by promoting the notion of the dignity or even the romance of hard graft. "Man was created to work, not to speculate, or feel, or dream," he wrote, adding: "Every idle moment is treason." It is your patriotic duty to work hard—another myth, particularly convenient to the rich, who, as Bertrand Russell said, "preach the dignity of labour, while taking care themselves to remain undignified in this respect." Or as the late, great British writer Jeffrey Bernard put it when I went to interview him: "As if there was something romantic and glamorous about hard work . . . if there was something romantic about it, the Duke of Westminster would be digging his own fucking garden, wouldn't he?"

Indeed, in the early Middle Ages, those who worked—the "laboratores"—were looked down upon by society. At the top were the idle—the clerics and the warriors. Warriors, indeed, according to Tacitus, held it to be lazy and spiritless to get by working what they could get by blood, and in between campaigns they spent their time eating, drinking, sleeping and shagging.

Ignorance, of course, was another weapon in the armoury of the capitalists. It was important to keep the working classes in a state of stupidity so they were unaware of how wickedly they were being exploited. "Use your senses much and your mind little," wrote Carlyle's disciple James Froude. "Think little and read less."

Faced with this formidable attack, it is not surprising that most of us just carried on digging or spinning and kept our heads down. But there was also resistance to this injustice. There were a few renegade writers at the time who could see clearly what was going on. William Blake, of course, was an early critic of the "cogs tyrannic," and later Paul Lafargue, Karl Marx's French son-in-law, published a pamphlet entitled "The Right to be Lazy" (1883), in which he demolished the gospel of work in magnificent, visionary style:

> A strange delusion possesses the working classes of the nations where capitalist civilisation holds its sway. This delusion drags in its train the individual and social woes which for two centuries have tortured sad humanity. This delusion is the love

of work, the furious passion for work, pushed even to the exhaustion of the vital force of the individual and his progeny. Instead of opposing this mental aberration, the priests, the economists and the moralists have cast a sacred halo over work. Blind and finite men, they have wished to be wiser than their God; weak and contemptible men, they have presumed to re-habilitate what their God had cursed . . . Our epoch has been called the century of work. It is in fact the century of pain, misery and corruption.

There was also widespread popular agitation against the new Protestant work ethic at the time among those whose lives it was destroying. The Luddites of 1811 to 1813, routinely carica-tured in our schools as unthinking clot-heads and daft enemies of progress, were in fact breaking the machines because they correctly predicted that they would destroy the old ways of life and strip men and women of their independence. E. P. Thompson lists more acts of revolt: "In 1817 the Pentridge Rising; in 1819, Peterloo; throughout the next decade the prolif-eration of trade union activity, Owenite propaganda, Radical journalism, the Ten Hours Movement, the revolutionary crisis of 1831–2; and, beyond that, the multitude of movements which made up Chartism." But Progress, steam and the factory triumphed. Work and life were rent asunder; the joyful swain became a downtrodden slave.

Looking back at the horrors inflicted on the people in the Victorian Age, it is all too easy to feel grateful for the slight improvements in working conditions that the trade-union move-ment has achieved against heavy odds in the last 100 years. It is also easy for us to marvel at the credulousness of the populace when oppressed with Methodist doctrine. How could they fall for it, we wonder?

But are we so free today? As the academic Juliet Schor points out in *The Overworked American* (1991), things only look good when compared with recent times:

> The claim that capitalism has delivered us from excessive toil can be sustained only if we take as our point of comparison eighteenth- and nineteenth-century Europe and America—a period that witnessed what were probably the longest and most arduous work schedules in the history of mankind.

And there are new enemies of leisure today. Hunger and God have been replaced in the consumer age by possessions and status. The advertising industry leads us to believe that life will be improved by the purchase of a product. The purchase of a product requires money. Money requires hard work. Or debt. We go into debt to chase our desires, and then keep working to pay the debt. It's the modern form of indentured labour. In *Nickel and Dimed*, Barbara Ehrenreich discovers that many of her co-workers in restaurants and cleaning agencies are toiling in two jobs in order to meet the payments on—for example—a $4,000 jeep.

Capitalism has promoted the job as a religion; but so too, tragically, has socialism. The left have been brainwashed with the socialist dream of "full employment." But wouldn't full *unemployment* be better? A world where everyone is free to create their own life, their own work, their own money. In his great essay "The Soul of Man under Socialism" (1891), Oscar Wilde pointed out the absurdity of the idea of full employment: "It is to be regretted that a portion of our community should be practically in slavery, but to propose to solve the problem by enslaving the entire community is childish."

We need to be responsible for ourselves; we must create our own republics. Today we hand over our responsibility to the boss, to the company, to government, and then blame them when everything goes wrong.

Let us be clear also that work, particularly at the bottom end of the scale, is highly dangerous. Worldwide, the mania for consumer goods has created a deadly culture of overwork. A recent UN report stated that work kills two million people per year: that's an amount equivalent to two September 11 disasters every day. Yet I see no "War on Work" being declared by governments around the world. In fact, the story went widely unreported. In the UK it did make it into the *Guardian*, but was granted only a few paragraphs on page 17.

Newspapers aren't much help to those pursuing an idle life. They present themselves as independent, but since they are funded by advertising, they do much to promote the work-and-consume ethic. Newspapers offer a problem and a solution. The problem is presented in the news pages and consists of stories of war, starvation, political corruption, death, famine, scandal, theft, abduction, paedophilia. In short, they promote anxiety. The solution to this anxiety is presented in the magazine sections, and consists of editorial about—and, of course, advertising for—fridges, lighting systems, cars, sex advice, burglar alarms, loans, insurance policies, recipes, rugs, scented candles and various cultural products such as music, film and books. Problem: anxiety. Solution: money. Method: work.

If you want religious justification for your refractory habits, then remember that parts of the Bible, so often quoted by pro-work propagandists, argue against toil. Work is a curse, caused not by God but by the serpent in the Garden of Eden. He led Adam and Eve to fall from the work-free state of paradise by awakening material desire in them, thereby condemning them to toil and pain. If you want nothing, you don't need to work. If you are full of desires, then you will have to work in order to get the money to fulfil those desires. Jesus said, "Consider the lilies of the field, how they grow; they toil not, neither do they spin: And yet I say unto you, That even Solomon in all his glory was not arrayed like one of these" (Matthew 6:28–9). God himself, argues Paul Lafargue in "The Right to be Lazy," set a good example: after working for six days, he rests for all eternity.

At the bottom of it all is fear. Fear paralyses us. Be fearless, quit your job! You have nothing to lose but your anxieties, debts and misery! Or follow the lead of those brave proto-idlers who have elected to work a three-day week, a bona fide social trend. There is an immense psychological benefit to knowing that your days of free time each week outnumber your days of time sold to another. It makes the work more bearable and it leaves four days in which to pursue your own projects. There is certainly a financial knock, but most find that the loss of income is easily compensated for by the extra time.

Time is not money! Work and leisure can join once again! This was the dream of D. H. Lawrence, who, in his poem "A Sane Revolution" (1929), wrote that if self-directed and fun, work need not be a burden. It is time to take control, to bring work and life back into happy harmony.

For do we not still feel trapped? And do we not still wonder sadly, with the nineteenth-century poet Charles Lamb:

Who first invented work—and bound the free
And holy-day rejoicing spirit down
To the ever-haunting importunity
Of business, in the green fields, and the town—
To plough, loom, anvil, spade—and oh! most sad
To that dry drudgery at the desk's dead wood? ("Work," 1819)

10 a.m.

Sleeping In

The happiest part of a man's life is what he
passes lying awake in bed in the morning.
Dr. Johnson (1709–84)

It's 10 a.m. The successful idler, having avoided the guilt produced by 8 a.m., the culturally determined hour of rising, and the guilt produced by 9 a.m., the hour of work, may now be lying in bed, and thinking of perhaps getting up. Don't! The lie-in—by which I mean lying in bed awake—is not a selfish indulgence but an essential tool for any student of the art of living, which is what the idler really is. Lying in bed doing nothing is noble and right, pleasurable and productive.

To the bureaucrat, the man of business, there is nothing more offensive than the idea that potentially productive citizens are prone, inactive, staring at the ceiling, while he is bustling away doing something "useful," like inventing new ways to sell popcorn to the masses or delivering summonses for non-payment of parking fines. Inaction appals him; he cannot understand it; it frightens him.

At 10 a.m. the idler is probably awake, possibly staring at the ceiling, and certainly in no hurry to get vertical. Quiet and stillness reign once more; the workers are now at their desks or in the warehouses and factories; he has managed to resist his own guilt at lying in and is now master of his own time. And what is he to do? Well, nothing. Nothing, save contemplate, think, read.

Let's look at the masters for inspiration. John Lennon is one of the great idlers of the modern age. To me, he embodies the paradox of the productive idler; he lived life according to his own rules, he was given to indolence but this laziness produced great songs. As titles such as "I'm Only Sleeping," "I'm So Tired" and later "Watching the Wheels" demonstrate, Lennon saw no virtue in work for its own sake, and, in fact, praised sloth. Famously, in 1969, in a magnificent bout of heroic idleness, Lennon and Yoko Ono lay in bed for a week, doing absolutely nothing, for world peace. But their act had enormous impact. As art should, it altered the perspective of millions, in the same way that heroes like the late Joe Strummer and now Peter Doherty of the fabulous Libertines have the power to change lives: by opening a new range of possibilities for people, by showing them that authority is not necessarily on the side of truth, good and justice, by demonstrating that it's possible to think for yourself and create your own reality. In this sense, Lennon's songs and stunts admirably fulfilled Wilde's formulation of art's purpose: "[What art] seeks to disturb is monotony of type, slavery of custom, tyranny of habit, and the reduction of man to the level of a machine."

By lying in bed we are elevating ourselves above the level of a machine. Robots do not ponder; they get on with it. As T. E. Lawrence tells us: "Mankind has been no gainer by its drudges."

So much can be accomplished by doing nothing. One of Sherlock Holmes's great secrets was to combine time with tobacco and comfy cushions. Lolling around in his smoking jacket, puffing his pipe, Holmes would sit and ponder for hours on a tricky case. In one superb story, the opium-drenched "The Man with the Twisted Lip," Holmes solves yet another case with ease. An incredulous Mr. Plod character muses: "I wish I knew how you reach your results," to which Holmes replies: "I reached this one by sitting upon five pillows and consuming an ounce of shag."

René Descartes, in the seventeenth century, was similarly addicted to inactivity. Indeed, it was absolutely at the centre of his philosophy. When young and studying with the Jesuits, he was completely unable to get up in the morning. They would throw buckets of cold water over him and he would turn over and go back to sleep. Then, because of his obvious genius, he was granted the special privilege of getting up late. This was his modus operandi, because, of course, when he was lying in bed he was thinking—he was solving mathematical conundrums. It is easy to see how someone so inactive should conclude that the body and the mind are separate entities. Laziness produced Cartesian duality. For him, lying in bed and thinking was the very essence of being human: *Cogito ergo sum*, or in other words, I lie in bed thinking, therefore I am.

For it is while prone that ideas come. "A writer could get more ideas for his articles or his novels in this posture than he could by sitting doggedly before his desk morning and afternoon," writes Lin Yutang in his essay "On Lying in Bed." "For there, free from telephone calls and well-meaning visitors and the common trivialities of everyday life, he sees life through a glass or a beaded screen, as it were, and a halo of poetic fancy is cast around the world of realities and informs it with a magic beauty."

Idleness as a waste of time is a damaging notion put about by its spiritually vacant enemies. The fact that idling can be enormously productive is repressed. Musicians are characterized as slackers; writers as selfish ingrates; artists as dangerous. Robert Louis Stevenson expressed the paradox as follows in "An Apology for Idlers" (1885): "Idleness . . . does not consist in doing nothing, but in doing a great deal not recognized in the dogmatic formularies of the ruling class." Long periods of languor, indolence and staring at the ceiling are needed by any creative person in order to develop ideas.

Walter Benjamin, one of the great literary Euro-slackers of the early twentieth century, was alive to this paradox, and quoted a favourite line from Larousse's dictionary in his giant commonplace book *Arcades*: "Often it is at the time when the artist or poet seems the least occupied in their work, that they are plunged in it the deepest." Lin Yutang tells us that the Chinese scholar Ouyang Hsiu confessed to three "ons" where he did his best writing: "on the pillow, on horseback and on the toilet." But tell your boss that you didn't come in till lunchtime because you were dreaming up some great new ideas for product development and he is unlikely to be very sympathetic.

It is precisely to prevent us from thinking too much that society pressurizes us all to get out of bed. In 1993, I went to interview the late radical philosopher and drugs researcher Terence McKenna. I asked him why society doesn't allow us to be more idle. He replied:

> I think the reason we don't organise society in that way can be summed up in the aphorism, "idle hands are the devil's tool." In other words, institutions fear idle populations because an Idler is a thinker and thinkers are not a welcome addition to most social situations. Thinkers become malcontents, that's almost a substitute word for idle, "malcontent." Essentially, we are all kept very busy . . . under no circumstances are you to quietly inspect the contents of your own mind. Freud called introspection "morbid"—unhealthy, introverted, anti-social, possibly neurotic, potentially pathological.

Introspection could lead to that terrible thing: a vision of the truth, a clear image of the horror of our fractured, dissonant world. The writer Will Self, arguing that long periods of motorway driving can be a method of recapturing lost idling time, puts it like this: "This cultural taboo against thinking . . . exists in England because of the Protestant work ethic which demands that people shouldn't be idle—ergo they shouldn't think."

This prejudice is well established in the Western world. Governments do not like the idle. The idle worry them. They do not manufacture useless objects and they do not consume the useless products of labour. They cannot be monitored. They are *out of control*. They do not want to live like their leaders. They do not want to be helped.

The Nazis were particularly fearful of the lazy. Indeed, on 26 January 1938, that most brutal of bureaucrats Himmler ordered for all idlers—called "work-shy elements"—to be rounded up and sent to work camps:

> Work-shy elements within the meaning of this order are men who are old enough to work and who have recently been certified fit by an official doctor or who will be certified fit and who can be proved to have rejected offers of work on two occasions without just cause or have accepted work only to abandon it again shortly afterwards without adequate reason . . . all protective custody prisoners will be sent to concentration camp Buchenwald near Weimar.

Upon arrival at the concentration camps, idlers had a black triangle sewn on to their clothing (political prisoners had a red triangle, Jehovah's Witnesses a purple, criminals a green and homosexuals a pink). Himmler saw the work-shy as an infection, a germ that threatened to disable the healthy organism of the state and destroy from within the Nazis' vision of a perfect world. They didn't fit.

Similarly, but in the realm of fantasy, the marvellous Hollywood animation *Shrek* shows the despot Lord Farquaad making a ruling that all "fairy-tale creatures" are to be passed to the authorities who will rehouse them in special camps, out of the way of his "perfect world." So we have the spectacle of the three blind mice, Pinocchio, the three pigs all being put in trucks and "relocated." Again, the fairy-tale creatures do not have a place in Farquaad's orderly state. But as we all know, it is the fairy-tale creatures—the misfits, the weirdos, the wanderers, the flakes, the poets, the vagabonds, the idlers—who make life worth living.

In our own time, Mrs. Thatcher was suspicious of the arts

and indeed tried to found a series of colleges which taught only the practical skills. Now most governments are similarly pro-work: France has recently cancelled the 35-hour week; the US gives younger toilers only two weeks' holiday a year; in the UK the chancellor is always announcing ingenious new initiatives to get the unemployed "back to work." I have many friends who are long-term unemployed and are regularly subjected to patronizing "getting you back to work" sessions. A great deal of ingenuity is still being devoted to the problem of the work-shy.

Now, returning to the pleasures of inaction, we may reiterate that one of the great things about lying in bed is that it's so very comfortable. Here is Lin Yutang again: "Take any Chinese redwood furniture and saw off its legs a few inches, and it immediately becomes more comfortable; and if you saw off another few inches, then it becomes still more comfortable. The logical conclusion of this is, of course, that one is most comfortable when lying perfectly flat on a bed. The matter is as simple as that."

In this luxurious posture, what better way to start the day than with a poem? I stumbled across this idea while reading John Keats's letters. Poetry is routinely shunned by sophisticated urbanites who think they simply don't have the time to waste on such indulgences. But a poem can be read in a few minutes and have great effect. The horizontal idler, in bed at 10 a.m., has the time to do this.

"I have an idea," wrote Keats, then just 23 years old, "that a Man might pass a very pleasant life in this manner—let him on any certain day read a certain Page of full Poesy or distilled prose and let him wander with it, and muse upon it, and reflect from it, and bring home to it, and prophesy upon it, and dream upon it . . . How happy such a voyage of conception, what delicious diligent Indolence!"

And what genius of Keats to create such a superb phrase as "delicious diligent indolence," which encapsulates so precisely and elegantly the paradoxical pleasures of productive inactivity. Over the page, Keats goes on to assert the nobility of idling. "Now it is more noble to sit like Jove than to fly like Mercury— let us not therefore go hurrying about and collecting honey-bee like, buzzing here and there impatiently from a knowledge of what is to be arrived at: but let us open our leaves like a flower and be passive and receptive."

How much better life would be if we began the day with a poem rather than the empty prattle of newspapers, with their diet of fear, hate, envy and jealousy. Newspapers are merely a negative diversion from the self, a bit like soap operas. The writer Marcel Theroux said to me on January 9 last year: "I have been in great spirits this year, and I attribute this entirely to the fact that I have not read the *Daily Telegraph* for nine days."

Imagine instead musing on a few lines from Keats's "An Ode to Indolence" (1819). To save you the trouble of looking it up, I'll quote three lines here:

> O, for an age so shelter'd from annoy,
> That I may never know how change the moons,
> Or hear the voice of busy common-sense!

Inaction is noble; action is for losers. Here is how Oscar Wilde attacks the notion of "action" as an ideal, in his essay "The Critic as Artist" (1890):

Action is . . . the refuge of people who have nothing whatsoever to do . . . Its basis is the lack of imagination. It is the last resource of those who know not how to dream . . . Action is limited and relative. Unlimited and absolute is the vision of him who sits at ease and watches, who walks in loneliness and dreams . . .

. . . so completely are people dominated by the tyranny of this dreadful social ideal that they are always coming shamelessly up to one at Private Views and other places that are open to the general public, and saying in a loud stentorian voice, "What are you doing?" whereas "What are you thinking" is the only question that any civilised being should ever be allowed to whisper to another . . . Contemplation is the gravest sin of which any citizen can be guilty, in the opinion of the highest culture it is the proper occupation of man . . . Let me say to you now that to do nothing at all is the most difficult thing in the world, the most difficult and the most intellectual . . . It is to do nothing that the elect exist.

[T]he contemplative life, the life that has for its aim not *doing* but *being*, and not *being* merely, but *becoming*—this is what the critical spirit can give us. The gods live thus . . .

In this passage, Wilde elevates the idler from the status of a regrettable drain on society, a useless, irrational irritation, to something close to a god. Idlers, far from being a burden, are in fact an elite, an elect. They are apostles, visionaries. They see more clearly than the rest; they have refused to be victimized by the customs of others; their eyes are open, they have created time.

Become human; become infinite in reason; become godlike; stay in bed.

11 a.m.

Skiving for Pleasure and Profit

[H]e was generally seen lounging at the College gate, with a
circle of young students around him, whom he was entertaining
with wit, and keeping from their studies, if not spiriting
them up to rebellion against the College discipline.

Bishop Percy remembers Dr. Johnson at Oxford,
from James Boswell's *Life of Samuel Johnson* (1791)

It's 11 a.m. and the idler feels it is time for a break. A little smack-
erel of something, as Pooh Bear had it, a coffee break, a tea break,
a fag break. We even have a word for it: elevenses. Graham Greene,
who was lucky enough to live in the days before the drinking of
alcohol had been pathologized to such an absurd degree, drank
his first cocktail of the day at 11 a.m. Truly, it is the skiver's hour.

It is the time when you will see scores of office workers huddled in doorways, sneaking in a crafty cigarette; schoolboys, ties askew, laughing and smoking in cafés; other boys in arcades; girls chatting on park benches. In the classrooms, someone at the back is staring out of the window, daydreaming. At home, those who called in sick are watching TV or staring at the ceiling. What do these people have in common? They are skivers, and they are rebelling.

Skiving is a direct act of revolt against the arid philosophies of living that we're indoctrinated with at school and at work, the notion of suffering now, pleasure later. Well, this way of thinking is anathema to your idler. He can't wait till tomorrow. He believes that the deferral of pleasure in service of an imaginary future of stability is a bourgeois myth. Therefore he decides to seize the day and takes off. Skiving is an expression of the individual will set against the oppressing machine. Skiving is living in the moment; it is freedom; it is at once a nose thumbed at authority and a pleasure in itself.

The great pleasure of skiving is that you are not working while you are meant to be working. In my own case, this might include pacing around the room, frittering time away on emailing and word counts while I am supposed to be writing. This pleasure was observed and beautifully defined by Jerome K. Jerome in the phrase: "There is no fun in doing nothing when you have nothing to do." Jerome, whose own version of idling consisted of spending inordinate amounts of time over small amounts of work, continued: "Idleness, like kisses, to be sweet must be stolen."

And dawdling, mucking about or playing at sanctioned times, such as weekends, break and holidays is all right, but the real treat is to be derived from not working *while others toil*. Knowing that Jenkins is sitting in double maths while you sit in a café with a cup of tea multiplies the pleasure a thousandfold. There is no fun in joining the frisbee-throwing hordes in the park on Saturday. The idler wants to be throwing frisbees while the hordes are suffering. Frisbee-throwing becomes incalculably more delicious under these conditions.

For a practical defence of skiving, I'd like to cite that great friend to idleness, Robert Louis Stevenson. His essay "An Apology for Idlers," written at 26 when he was a struggling writer, includes a magnficent defence of taking off, in which he argues that we learn more about life and more richly during such an escape than in the classroom:

> If you look back at your own education, I am sure that it will not be the full, vivid, instructive hours of truantry that you regret; you would rather cancel some lack-lustre periods between sleep and waking in the class . . . As a matter of fact, an intelligent person, looking out of his eyes and hearkening in his ears, with a smile on his face all the time, will get more true education than many another in a life of heroic vigils. There is certainly some chill and arid knowledge to be found upon the summits of formal and laborious science; but it is all around you, and for the trouble of looking, that you will acquire the warm and palpitating facts of life. While others are filling their memory with a lumber of words, one-half of which they will forget before the week be out, your truant may learn some really useful art: to play the fiddle, to know a good cigar, or to speak with ease and opportunity to all varieties of men.

How true: the illicit hours I spent as a teenager in coffee shops during the school day, smoking Benson & Hedges and not working, stand out far more colourfully in the mind than any lesson. A modern version of this argument is advanced in the movie *Ferris Bueller's Day Off*. Its hero uses his charm and intelligence to take a day off school while fooling the entire town into thinking that he is ill. But Ferris's day off is not mere indulgence; it is also a journey of self-exploration for him and his friend Cameron, for whose benefit the day off really takes place. It is through the course of the day that Cameron finally finds the strength to stand up to his tyrannical father. Cameron needs to take time out of the daily, grinding routine in order to get some perspective on his problems, to see his father in his true light.

The skiver is stealing back time that has been stolen from him, and this stolen time has an intensity and richness all its own. It is out in the arcades that the idler can learn about life. The amusement arcade, the pier, these pleasure palaces exert a magnetic pull on your teenage runaway. Actually for the true idler, I think pinball, so much more physical and more satisfying than modern computer games, is a more suitable activity. There is nothing so perfect as pinball and a pint at 11 a.m.

Skiving has a long and noble history. In *Some Habits and Customs of the Working Classes*, published in 1867, Thomas Wright reports that the apprentice's first task on joining a workshop is to "keep nix"—or keep a lookout for the boss so his co-workers can skive without fear:

> Keeping nix, consists in keeping a bright look-out for the approach of managers or foremen, so as to be able to give prompt

and timely notice to men who may be skulking, or having a sly read or smoke, or who are engaged on "corporation work"—that is, work of their own.

But there was a time when skiving was practised openly and with pride, as the little-known phenomenon of Saint Monday demonstrates. Saint Monday, as we learn from historians such as E. P. Thompson and Douglas Reid, was a tradition of institutionalized skiving. It is first mentioned in the seventeenth century, persisted through the eighteenth and gradually withered and died in the nineteenth, destroyed by industry. It essentially consisted in an extension of the Sabbath into Monday. Instead of working, shoemakers, silk-stocking makers and weavers preferred to spend Monday knocking back ales at the tavern or watching bare-knuckle fights and cockfights. A contemporary rhyme runs:

> When in due course SAINT MONDAY wakes the day
> Off to a [Gin-shop] straight they haste away
> Perhaps at work they transitory peep
> But vice and lathe are soon consigned to sleep:
> The shop is left untenanted awhile,
> And a cessation is proclaim'd from toil.

The key feature of Saint Monday was that, unlike modern institutions such as "duvet days," where supposedly enlightened companies munificently bestow free time on their employees, Saint Monday was a bottom-up initiative; it was taken by the workers, it was self-constituted, often against the will of the employers.

Saint Monday could exist in part because those who followed the custom had not been infected by the modern-day desire to accumulate possessions. Therefore, they did not see the need to earn cash beyond what subsistence required. As one nineteenth-century observer put it:

> When the framework knitters or makers of silk stockings had a great price for their work, they have been observed seldom to work on Mondays and Tuesdays but to spend most of their time at the ale-house or nine-pins . . . The weavers, 'tis common with them to be drunk on Monday, have their head-ache on Tuesday, and their tools out of order on Wednesday. As for the shoe-makers, they'll rather be hanged than not remember St. Crispin on Monday . . . and it commonly holds as long as they have a penny of money or pennyworth in credit.

Saint Monday died, but its spirit lives on, and one of the strategies available to today's slacking worker is the sickie. The sickie is so well entrenched in the working mindset that the authorities use newspapers to wage a propaganda war against it. Newspapers inspire guilt in the potential skiver by running a perpetual stream of stories telling us just how many millions are "lost to British industry" every year as a result of sick leave taken. The newspapers never write about the incalculable gains to the feelings of dignity or self-worth of the millions who have skived off. The implication is: call in sick, and you let everyone else down! The individual must be sacrificed to the smooth functioning of society!

In one of these guilt-inducing reports, the Confederation of British Industry wailed that in 1998 200 million days were lost to sickness. And if I know the British public, it's a fair guess that a good proportion of those were simply skives. Perhaps significantly, those in the most apparently anti-idle jobs were those who feel the keenest need to grab some time back for themselves. Interestingly, in the sickie stakes, police and prison warders come top, reportedly taking on average 12 days off sick a year. These figures have even led to an official government campaign against the sickie, the latest effort in the centuries-long battle between the skiving worker and the industrious capitalist. The BBC recently reported that the chancellor Gordon Brown has pledged to cut down public-sector absenteeism by a third within five years. Good luck, Gordon!

The revolutionary power of the sickie has been demonstrated in recent years by the satirical anarchist group Decadent Action, who in 1999 created "Phone-In-Sick Day," which now takes place on May Day, traditionally a day for protest and revolt. The idea attracted countless column inches. I asked Iain Aitch, writer and founder of Phone-In-Sick Day, to explain the rationale behind it:

> The idea was to turn the act of phoning in sick from a solitary, guilt-inducing act into something where it felt that you were rightfully taking back your time. It was about restoring the balance in the boss/worker agreement and making people realize who needed who the most. In the end it wasn't even necessary to actually take phone-in-sick day on the day we designated. As long as it planted the seed of rebellion in your mind it had worked. You could then use the time out, whether it was one day or six months, to think about what you really wanted to do.

As if to prove the point, Iain Aitch was mid skive when he came up with this idea, and reveals how staff can often work together to help one another skive:

I was working in a dole office whilst I was dreaming all of this up. The working conditions and staff morale were so low that everyone took a good deal of time off and the six-month sick stretch, which was the maximum you could get away with and still get paid, was seen as a kind of worker's sabbatical by many. It was time to sort your head out, look for a new career and just catch up with doing what you wanted. I spent my six months rediscovering the fact that I could write and deciding that was the way to go. When I was at work I would often only be in the office for six hours a day and would manage to spend three of those playing cards. I became very good at that and was obviously equally good at skiving, as I never once got caught.

One tried-and-tested method of getting the day off is to provide an official-looking note from the doctor. The most masterful sick note I have ever read comes from that classic of idling literature, *Oblomov*, by Ivan Goncharov. This Russian novel, published in 1859, is a portrait of a gentle, aristocratic idler who is simply constitutionally incapable of exertion, has no ambition and sees nothing wrong in this attitude. Towards the beginning of the book, Oblomov finds himself with a job as a clerk in the civil service. But the demands put on him soon become intolerable.

Twice he had been roused at night and made to write "notes," several times he had been fetched by a courier from a visit to friends—always because of those notes. All this frightened him and bored him terribly. "But when am I to live?" he repeated in distress.

After two years of toil, Oblomov decides that he has had enough. To get some time off, he asks his doctor for a sick note. The result is a masterpiece of medical language in service of skiving. Why not copy it out and give it to your own employer?

I, the undersigned, certify and append my seal thereto that the collegiate secretary, Ilya Oblomov, suffers from an enlarged heart and a dilation of its left ventricle (*Hypertrophia cordis cum dilatione ejus ventriculi sinistri*), and also from a chronic pain in the liver (hepatitis), which may endanger the patient's health and life, the attacks being due, it is to be surmised, to his daily going to the office. Therefore, to prevent the repetition and increase of these painful attacks, I find it necessary to forbid Mr. Oblomov to go to the office and insist that he should all together abstain from intellectual pursuits and any sort of activity.

Another form of skiving that deserves a mention is the art of delegation. Such a skive is outlined in *The Adventures of Tom Sawyer* (1876) by Mark Twain (another idle writer who worked in bed). Tom Sawyer is ordered to whitewash a fence by his Aunt Polly, but he succeeds in convincing his chums that fence-painting is not work but fun, and not only does he manage to get the fence painted through no effort of his own but he also extracts payment from his friends for the fun of painting, and returns home with the job done and a bounty of treasures in his pockets, including tadpoles, a kitten, firecrackers, a tin soldier and a brass doorknob.

> Tom said to himself that it was not such a hollow world, after all. He had discovered a great law of human action, without knowing it—namely, that in order to make a man or boy covet a thing, it is only necessary to make the thing difficult to attain. If he had been a great and wise philosopher, like the writer of this book, he would have now comprehended that Work consists of whatever a body is *obliged* to do, and that Play consists of whatever a body is not obliged to do. And this would help him to understand why constructing artificial flowers or performing a tread-mill is work, while rolling ten-pins or climbing Mont Blanc is only amusement. There are wealthy gentlemen in England who drive four-horse passenger-coaches twenty or thirty miles on a daily line, in the summer, because the privilege costs them considerable money; but if they were offered wages for the service, that would turn it into work and then they would resign.

Such are the wily expedients that are developed through hatred of work, and are they not useful skills in life? I personally have never understood people who can't delegate; surely it simply means that someone else is going to do the work, and surely that's better than doing it oneself? Twain's Tom Sawyer has all the makings of an entrepreneur or business leader, using his ingenuity to convince others to do all the hard graft while he sits in his box at the Cheltenham Festival getting gently drunk on a Tuesday afternoon.

In the thus-far unwritten literary history of the skive, though, one story stands out from the rest as perhaps the greatest of them all: Herman Melville's classic, "Bartleby, the Scrivener: A Story of Wall-street," published in 1853. "Bartleby" is the story of a liberal lawyer who takes on a new clerk. At first this clerk, Bartleby, despite being worryingly joyless, appears to be an exemplary employee with all those so-called virtues that a boss rates highly: punctuality, attention to detail, accuracy, application, neatness of dress. Soon, however, the mysterious Bartleby starts to exhibit odd behavioural tics. One morning, his employer asks Bartleby to go over some paperwork with him:

> Imagine my surprise, nay, my consternation, when, without moving from his privacy, Bartleby, in a singularly mild, firm voice, replied, "I would prefer not to."
>
> I sat awhile in perfect silence, rallying my stunned faculties. Immediately it occurred to me that my ears had deceived me, or Bartleby had entirely misunderstood my meaning. I repeated my request in the clearest tone I could assume. But in quite as clear a one came the previous reply, "I would prefer not to."
>
> "Prefer not to," echoed I, rising in high excitement, and crossing the room with a stride. "What do you mean? Are you moonstruck? I want you to help me compare this sheet here—take it," and I thrust it towards him.
>
> "I would prefer not to," said he.

Bartleby is almost Gandhi-like in his protest against work: passive, firm, elegant, dignified. He embodies the essence of refusal. As the story progresses, Bartleby does less and less work. He never leaves the office and sleeps on the sofa, living on ginger nuts. His boss tries to sack him and fails, and finds himself moving offices to be rid of the inscrutable scrivener. The new tenants find Bartleby lurking in the corridors day and night. He is eventually arrested and sent to prison, where he refuses to talk or eat. After a few days, Bartleby commits the ultimate skive: he dies.

Noon

The Hangover

My heart aches, and a drowsy numbness pains
My sense, as though of hemlock I had drunk . . .
John Keats, "Ode to a Nightingale" (1819)

It is at around twelve that a hangover really starts to kick in.
Before noon, one is either generally still drunk from the night
before or surviving on the small amount of energy derived from
a broken sleep. Perhaps this is why mythology talks of the
midday demons, which, says Thierry Paquot in *The Art of the
Siesta*, "can overwhelm certain individuals at midday." Islam says
it is an unholy hour, and Plutarch, too, associates it with super-
stition. Many, many are the days when I have lolled at the office
or other place of work, groaning quietly, unable to concentrate,

unable to work, able only to put my head in my hands, and curse myself for the excesses of the previous night. Woe is me.

The hangover is generally seen as one of the inconveniences of a life of excess, a punishment for pleasure. Descriptions of its pains can often be very funny: one thinks of the self-pitying Withnail in Bruce Robinson's film *Withnail and I*, who moans, the morning after a heavy whisky session: "I feel like a pig shat in my head."

The problem with the hangover, the secret of its deadly power, is that it presents a double agony: the physical and the mental. It attacks both body and soul. Physically we feel full of headache, nauseous, possibly achy; we have that feeling of gently vibrating innards and a headful of noise. But the physical pain is made incalculably worse by the mental anguish, the feelings of guilt, self-loathing, paranoia and the weight of things-to-do that accompany the physical pains. The one feeds off the other, producing an unbearable spiralling of agonies which drains mind, body and spirit. We feel we deserve the pain; that it is our just reward for abandoning those tedious virtues: responsibility and duty. In our self-torturing world view, every pleasure is balanced by equivalent suffering.

There is, however, a way of dealing with the hangover that can make it into a positive experience. Crazy as it sounds, with a little mental ingenuity and a modicum of planning, a hangover can actually be *enjoyed*. It can be a creative force, offering its sufferer an unfamiliar and even pleasurable outlook on the world; if, that is, we allow it to do so.

The first mistake of the traditional hangover cure (eggs, aspirin, Coke, lemon, etc.) is that it makes one think in terms of a cure at all. The hangover cannot be cured; it can only be lived with in different ways. The second mistake is to focus exclusively on softening the physical pain. The mind is actually the most powerful component in a hangover, and it is the mind that we must concentrate on to disarm it. "I think you do not feel so well," wrote Zen philosopher Shunryu Suzuki of the hangover. "Your mind is full of 'weeds.' But if you can cease striving to overcome those weeds, they, too, can enrich your path to enlightenment."

That the hangover is at least to an extent "mind-forg'd" is demonstrated in this anecdote from the late journalist Gavin Hills (which is not to say that the headache, the nausea, the tiredness and inability to concentrate are mere phantasms):

> On a recent Sunday morn, I rose with my usual tirade against the injustice of existence. My body ached, my stomach retched, the head it did hurt. I blamed drugs, I blamed alcohol, I blamed the whole sorry affair of the previous evening. Only in this denial did it come to me: I'd actually spent the previous night at home, in the utmost sobriety, watching *Match of the Day* and retiring to bed early.

Gavin's expectation of morning misery and hung-over feelings was so powerful that he actually *induced* the familiar physical symptoms. He was so ready to slip into self-loathing mode that he went into a mental hangover which brought on a physical hangover before he realized that his mind was playing tricks on him.

So my question is: if the mind can create a hangover, could the mind not remove one, too? Could we use the mind—the will—to accept the hangover and therefore remove its power to disturb us?

If we somehow manage to avoid both guilt and work during the hangover, then it can be altered from a positive to a negative experience. I experimented with this notion recently when on a trip to London for a few days. I needed to go into my office to sort out some paperwork and make a few calls, but this task did not need to take place at any particular time. Instead of fighting what was turning into a particularly bad hangover after two nights of drinking, I persuaded my mind to accept it, and then ended up floating through the day in quite an enjoyable fashion. The snow, the buses, the cold, the other people on the underground, the unanswered emails on the office computer, the bills to pay, the little problems that litter our days: normally, hung-over, these inconveniences would have been unbearable. But, perhaps as a result of asking very little of myself, I moved slowly and enjoyably and even got a few things done (and I had a very pleasant lunch, during which, if I can digress to a little anecdote, my friend Mark Manning, my companion in debauch from two nights previously, popped by. "Well, no hangover from last night!" he said, proudly. "Mark," I pointed out, "it wasn't last night we went out. It was the night before." "Oh. Really?" he said. Manning had simply skipped the hangover day, presumably by sleeping, which is another way of dealing with it).

Crucially, I had by an act of will refused to submit to the comfort of self-admonishment and guilt. As a result, the physical discomfort of the hangover was easy to deal with. On the third night, I went to bed early and rose after nine hours' sleep feeling fine. I even caught the early train back to the country.

I first realized that there might be a new way to deal with the hangover when the American writer Josh Glenn contributed a piece on the subject to the *Idler*. He argued that the hung-over state can lead to a fascinating sharpening of the senses:

> The hungover person is abnormally aware of sights, sounds (everything seems TOO LOUD!), tastes, odours, and textures which normally would go unremarked. That's a good thing, not a bad thing. The hungover eye, for instance, because it is neither obstructed by the blinkers of our everyday biases, nor deceived by intoxicated hallucinations, is magnetically attracted to seemingly ordinary objects which take on an incredible, luminous significance: Anyone who has ever experienced the "stares" when hungover knows exactly what I mean.

Josh takes this argument yet further. He claims that the hangover can even act as a portal to a visionary state:

> Although the sudden awareness of the sacred in the mundane is what most religious traditions refer to as nirvana, or some type of grace, we too often shrug off these moments in our haste to get rid of our hangovers. (I suspect, actually, that the hungover eye which is somehow between the appraising eye of the teetotaler and the foggy eye of the drunkard may be the model for Hinduism's "third eye" of enlightenment.) Thus it is that the moment of the hangover can propel us into a "middle state" of perceptivity quite unlike anything we're ever likely to experience outside of a monastery.

I wonder if Blake was hung-over when he saw the universe in a grain of sand?

Of course, it's not that easy to tune in to the spiritual benefits of feeling like shit. To be sure, the benefits of a hangover are completely obliterated if one is forced to go into the office or do any sort of unpleasant work. I have found that the way to deal with a hangover is to abandon oneself completely to it, not to try and function like a normal person. We need to embrace the apparent "uselessness" of the state, to resist the pressure to normalize oneself. The hangover should be embraced as a day off, time out from reality, a chance to live in the moment. Ideally, the hangover should be spent at home, with endless cups of tea, friends who are in the same state as you, a daft film like *Zoolander* (we watched it on New Year's Day and I cannot remember anything so hilarious). My friend Nora recently came to stay armed with three of David Attenborough's *Secret Life of Mammals* videos as the ideal hangover accompaniment. And she was right: watching comical penguins lolloping around in the Antarctic wastes was indeed most enjoyable in our flaccid post-party condition.

A yet more radical theory of the hangover comes from the notorious hell-raising duo English actor Keith Allen and artist Damien Hirst. In their case, their hangovers may have been particularly severe since their drinking sessions could go on for days. But they evolved a theory that the comedown was the "best bit" of the whole partying process: "Hangovers are a way of telling you that you haven't gone far enough," Keith told me. "We used to keep drinking until we fell asleep. We'd write poems about the previous 36 hours, remember bits of what had happened and laugh about them. It's a question of planning. You need to get your work out of the way and to have a day or two clear after the drinking."

For Damien Hirst (who has, by the way, now given up drinking and smoking completely), the key was to suffer the comedown in the company of your fellow debauchees:

> When it was wearing off and getting really ugly and horrible, and you feel like shit and you want to commit suicide and you hate yourself, we'd sit together and go, "This is the best bit." And force ourselves through it and fight it out. It used to be great . . . it's brilliant to have other people there when you're doing that . . . I'd rather be awful with my mates than be fucking awful on my own in bed.

In my own case, I know that being hung-over can be a time of loose, giggly laughter and fun if you can simply sit through it with pots of tea and a group of friends. The problems of the hangover stem partly from the fact that generally we are trying to behave as if we didn't have one; we are working in the office, we are in meetings, we are doing things and we are doing them alone. Avoid any useful activity, then. Embrace the useless. Plan for the hangover: don't fight it.

As with all aspects of idleness, we should resist the pressure to reject the elements of our lives which do not fit into the productive, rational, busy paradigm that society and our own selves impose upon us. Learning how to live can involve learning how to love the hangover. This trick is for the advanced student of idleness, to be sure, but try it and see how your life improves.

1 p.m.
The Death of Lunch

I have a vague notion that once upon a time, not so long ago, lunch was a meal to be enjoyed. The midday meal was an occasion to be deliberated over, shared with friends and colleagues, savoured, taken over two or three hours. It was a time for gossip, laughter, booze. It was a dreamy oasis of pleasure which took the edge off the dreary afternoon and was to be looked forward to during the busy morning. It might even involve a stroll around town, a taxi-ride, a trip to a gallery. Sometimes lunch would go on all afternoon and into the evening, and leave behind it a delightful trail of cancelled appointments and drudgery postponed. "Lunch," wrote the great journalist Keith Waterhouse in his *The Thoery and Practice of Lunch* (1986), "is free will."

But what does lunch mean now, to the modern worker in the twenty-first-century West? Sadly, lunch has been reduced to a merely practical affair. The tradition of the leisurely lunch has taken a beating from the new work ethic. Hence the rise of the sandwich as the most efficient means of satisfying hunger with the minimum of fuss, and hence the huge success in the UK of "quality" sandwich suppliers Pret A Manger, who, with their French name, perky staff and piped jazz music, pretend to be "passionate about food," but are in reality more interested in stuffing the office worker efficiently in order for him or her to return to their desk more quickly. Their real passion, of course, is profit, and to create cash they have appealed to the culture of the time-starved worker. And in any case, any pretensions towards being passionate about food were surely revealed to be pure bunkum when the chain was bought up by those renowned lovers of quality McDonald's.

We might lay the blame, indeed, at the feet of the busy, restless, striving Americans. Right back in 1882, Nietzsche noted that lunch was under threat from the new work ethic in the US. "The breathless haste with which they work," he wrote in *The Gay Science*, "is already beginning to infect the old Europe . . . One thinks with a watch in one's hand, even as one eats one's midday meal while reading the latest news of the stock-market; one lives as if one 'might miss out on something.'" The death of lunch was an event more calamitous to some of us than the death of God.

Observing 1930s New York, Lin Yutang also complained that the speed of life was destroying the pleasure of eating. "The tempo of modern life is such that we are giving less and less time and thought to the matter of cooking and feeding . . . it is a pretty crazy life when one eats to work and does not work in order to eat."

This attitude to food, that it is a mere enabler of work, was carried forward by the fascists. Lunch, they believed, was useful if it increased production. Pleasure was not a consideration. The following passage is taken from an Italian factory-management manual from 1940:

> It cannot be a matter of indifference to the industrialist that his own employees should be more or less able to feed themselves appropriately while at the factory. As well as considerations of a humanitarian nature, he should recognize that the function of food is to give the worker's body an injection of energy which will allow him to replenish that consumed by physical and mental effort, and to achieve and maintain as high a point as possible in the production curve, which as we know descends quickly when the worker has exhausted his reserves of energy.

The sacrifice of food to work reaches its apotheosis in the 1980s. In Oliver Stone's movie *Wall Street*, thrusting broker Gordon Gekko utters the immortal line: "Lunch? You gotta be kidding. Lunch is for wimps." Lunch meant wasting an hour which could be better spent working. Sociability and pleasure were off the menu. Lunch had been sacrificed to the great gods of work, progress and "beating the other guy." No one has the time to eat at leisure, it seems. It's a common sight to see people snaffling down a burger or sandwich between stops on the underground. This kind of eating has something almost guilty and furtive about it. It's not eating, it's lonely refuelling. The same thing has happened to breakfast. Handy little bits of solid cereal called "breakfast bars" advertise themselves with the slogan "Good Food on the Go." So much more efficient that way.

Today the workers' canteens have been privatized, and in the cities we eat alone, in McDonald's, Burger King, KFC and the aforementioned Pret A Manger. These are the places which today fulfil the fascist definition of the function of food, "to give the worker's body an injection of energy." It's a miserable sight, the rows of lone toilers sitting in the windows of these outlets, munching joylessly, reading the paper or staring blankly on to the street outside. The French philosopher Jean Baudrillard, in *America* (1986), comments on his sadness at the sight of another strange modern phenomenon—joggers—and then writes: "The only comparable distress is that of a man eating alone in the heart of the city."

In the UK and in the United States, idlers have witnessed with horror the rise of the Starbucks-style coffee shop, which is where many of us grab a lunchtime sandwich these days. The coffee shops of the twenty-first century have little or nothing in common with the coffee shops of the eighteenth century, which were loafing centres par excellence, serving vast bowls of alcoholic punch and existing to facilitate convivial exchanges. The modern Costas and Starbucks have as their secret mission purely useful goals: give you strong coffee and some bread to help you survive the day in a state of high anxiety and fear. They give off the unpleasant aroma of efficiency.

Hitting British shores in 1996, the first wave of coffee shops was led by the Seattle Coffee Company. At first, the notion seemed tempting. Squashy sofas, good coffee, soft lighting, yummy munchies. Admittedly, it was our own fault: the British café had never really got it right, what with its scorched instant coffee, cold toast, surly service, neon strip lighting, orange tables bolted to the floor, grime and charmlessness. So there was a gap in the market, no doubt. I remember being quite enthusiastic about them when writing an article in the *Face* magazine explaining the difference between a skinny latte and a double choco-mocha. The new coffee shops had a West Coast chic about them; they faintly reminded one of a Beatnik San Francisco establishment; they *looked* like loafing zones, somewhere you could hang out, smoke and feel like a French intellectual. Could they be a gift to the non-employed?

But the cosy and entrepreneurial Seattle Coffee Company was wiped out when the vast Starbucks outfit bought all 65 of them in 1998, and these days every high street has its Costa, Starbucks, Aroma or Nero. Far from being loafing zones, these places are simply pit stops for working machines, petrol stations for human beings. As the writer Iain Sinclair puts it: "[T]he whole culture has speeded up so that people just queue to get takeaways. And it's the death of cafés. Who's going to spend days hanging out at cafés? It's gone."

And what's the result of all this coffee-drinking? We're all wired. The UK is beginning to resemble the USA where drinking alcohol has been replaced by drinking coffee. So instead of being half cut all afternoon as in the days of the three-martini lunch, businessmen are wound up on caffeine, perspiring, worrying, rushing, shouting at junior staff and developing ulcers. I'm certain that we will soon discover the appalling effect of this coffee frenzy on the nation's physical and mental health. Truly, the coffee culture is inimical to the idler.

But not so long ago, in London and in New York City—those two poles of the work ethic—the leisurely lunch thrived.

"New York is the greatest city in the world for lunch . . . That's the gregarious time," wrote the humorist William Emerson, Jr., in 1975 in *Newsweek*. These lunches were seriously booze-soaked, too; the president Gerald Ford in a 1978 speech said, "The three-martini lunch is the epitome of American efficiency. Where else can you get an earful, a bellyful and a snootful at the same time?" And why has such wit and light humour disappeared from presidential discourse?

Now if you've ever had three martinis you'll know that the effect is powerful. They are so strong that you practically inhale them. They make only the briefest contact with the stomach before entering the head. (We'll return to the subject in our First Drink of the Day chapter.) Three over lunch must have led to the sight of some delightfully tipsy, not to mention big-haired and kipper-tied, statesmen and businessmen reeling into taxis on Park Avenue at 4 p.m., before going back to the wood-panelled office to loosen their tie, put their feet on the desk and give the staff the rest of the day off.

The 1970s was also a golden era for lunch in London. The journalist and writer Keith Waterhouse was a master of the art of lunch, and even wrote a wonderful book about it, *The Theory and Practice of Lunch*, published in 1986 when lunch had not quite degenerated into a mere stomach-filling exercise. In it, Waterhouse provided a lengthy definition of what lunch meant to him and, crucially, its pure use-factor was not among his criteria: "It is not a meal partaken of, however congenial the company, with the principal object of nourishment . . . It is not when either party is on a diet, on the wagon or in a hurry." Lunch, said Waterhouse, "is a midday meal taken at leisure by, ideally, two people . . . it is essential that lunch companions are drawn together by some motivation beyond the pangs of hunger or the needs of commerce. A little light business may be touched, but the occasion is firmly social."

Happily, the culture of the long business lunch thrives in some European countries. A couple of years ago I was in France on business to meet a firm of distillers. They were manufacturing a new brand of absinthe that my company had named and branded. About eight of us enjoyed a three-course meal, with snails, wine and absolutely no business discussed whatsoever. Just a lot of laughter. As the lunch went on and on, I started to get fidgety. Surely we should get back to their office, and conclude our business? After all, we had to catch the Eurostar. But on voicing my anxieties, my desire to work was roundly dismissed by the French distillers. They laughed, arguing that there was no hurry, that things would happen all in good time, and they justified themselves with the following paradox: *Travailler moins, produire plus*. The less you work, the more you produce. They were right of course: the half hour which we had left to do our work was plenty. If we had allowed ourselves an hour and a half, then that is how long the job would have taken. Work expands to fit the time provided.

Anyway, this superb aphorism stuck in my mind. I might add that the whole incident was rather embarrassing for me, in that the editor of the *Idler* had been out-idled by some provincial businessmen.

But mutter *"travailler moins, produire plus"* when you stumble back to the office at 3:30 and your boss upbraids you for slacking and you are unlikely to get much sympathy.

There is hope for Brits, and it comes in the form of the International Movement for the Defense of and the Right to Pleasure, more commonly known as Slow Food. Founded in 1986 by a group of left-wing Italians who were appalled by the cultural ascendancy of fast food, Slow Food's plan is to bring pleasure, quality, variety and humanity back to the production and eating of food. They do this by running events and tastings, and producing books and a superb magazine. From humble beginnings it has now spread all over Europe, with nearly 100,000 members. It has even recently opened an office in the US, birthplace of fast food. Their logo is the snail, and founder Carlo Petrini sees the movement as a "fully fledged cultural revolution," and I agree.

As the Slow Food manifesto demonstrates, their philosophy reaches well beyond food, and can be seen as a protest against the dehumanizing mechanization of life:

Our century, which began and has developed under the insignia of industrial civilization, first invented the machine and then took it as its life model.

We are enslaved by speed and have all succumbed to the same insidious virus: Fast Life, which disrupts our habits, pervades the privacy of our homes and forces us to eat Fast Foods.

To be worthy of the name, Homo Sapiens should rid himself of speed before it reduces him to a species in danger of extinction.

A firm defense of quiet material pleasure is the only way to oppose the universal folly of Fast Life.

May suitable doses of guaranteed sensual pleasure and slow, long-lasting enjoyment preserve us from the contagion of the multitude who mistake frenzy for efficiency.

Our defense should begin at the table with Slow Food. Let us rediscover the flavors and savors of regional cooking and banish the degrading effects of Fast Food.

In the name of productivity, Fast Life has changed our way of being and threatens our environment and our landscapes. So Slow Food is now the only truly progressive answer.

That is what real culture is all about: developing taste rather than demeaning it. And what better way to set about this than an international exchange of experiences, knowledge, projects?

Slow Food guarantees a better future.

The British and the Americans are ripe for a Slow Food invasion. Long enough have we put up with food made by robots. The huge success of Eric Schlosser's book *Fast Food Nation* (2001), which describes the inhuman processes by which modern hamburger, chicken and French fry products are manufactured, and by the way revealing some of the appalling conditions and low wages suffered by the unskilled labour force which produces this stuff, is surely a positive sign. Perhaps we are waking up.

We need more lunches like the following, described in *An Angler at Large*, written by William Caine in 1911, when the pace of life was a little slower. He describes the pleasures of a picnic lunch taken on the riverbank:

One eats with no sense of time lost. One's enjoyment of food— a very proper enjoyment—is not marred by any anxiety about the river. One lingers over the cigarette that follows and the cigarette that follows it. One does not hurry. There are no fish anywhere at all. One dismisses fish from one's mind and takes one's pleasure in mastication, like a wise man.

We need to claim lunch back. It is our natural right. It has been stolen from us by our rulers. The fear that keeps you chained to your desk, staring at your screen, does not serve your spirit. Lunch is a time to forget about being sensible, practical, efficient. A proper lunch should be spiritually as well as physically nourishing. Cosy, convivial, a treat; lunch is for loafers.

2 p.m.

On Being Ill

Illness is an obstacle for the body, but not necessarily for the will.
Epictetus (*c.* AD 50–*c.* 138), *The Golden Sayings of Epictetus*

That being ill can be a delightful way to recapture lost idling time is a fact well known to all young children. In schooldays, the independent child soon learns that if he is ill, then he can lie in bed all day, avoid work and be looked after. What a different world from the everyday one of punishments, recriminations and duties. Suddenly everyone is very nice to you. You can read comics and watch TV. You can very decisively NOT be at school. It is a time to embrace the "exquisite languor of surrender," as the writer Peter Bradshaw put it in his 1994 *Idler* article "The Joy of Sicks."

Being ill—nothing life-threatening, of course—should be welcomed as a pleasure in adult life, too, as a holiday from responsibility and burden. Indeed, it may be one of the few legitimate ways left to be idle. "Calling in sick," Bradshaw added, "is the only way adult professionals are allowed to experience inactivity: they are deprived of any other circumstances in which to cultivate the arts of enforced solitude and leisure."

When ill, you can avoid all those irksome tasks which make living such hard work. You don't even have to get dressed, for one thing. You can pad around the house in your dressing gown like Sherlock Holmes, Noël Coward or our friend, that hero of laziness, Oblomov. "The dressing gown had a number of invaluable qualities in Oblomov's eyes: it was soft and pliable; it did not get in his way; it obeyed the least movement of his body, like a docile slave."

When ill, you are the master. You do what you like. You can wander over to the record player and put on your old Clash albums. Stare out of the window. Laugh inwardly at the sufferings of your co-workers. You can surrender to delirious netherworlds as you fall in and out of sleep. You can even imagine yourself to be a latter-day romantic poet, pale, consumptive, surrounded by beautiful adoring young girls.

Looking a little deeper at the benefits of being ill, we may argue that the physical pain can lead to positive character development, that bodily suffering can improve the mind. "That which does not kill me makes me stronger," said Nietzsche.

The intellectual benefits of being ill are demonstrated and reflected upon at length by Marcel Proust. Famously chronically ill and frequently bed-bound, in his prone state he had plenty of time to theorize on why being ill was beneficial to mental health:

"Infirmity alone makes us notice and learn, and enables us to analyse processes which we would otherwise know nothing about. A man who falls straight into bed every night, and ceases to live until the moment when he wakes and rises, will surely never dream of making, not necessarily great discoveries, but even minor observations about sleep."

Proust was accused by contemporaries of being a hypochondriac, which may have been true. But how else would he have found the time to write the hundreds of thousands of words which make up *À la Recherche du temps perdu*? And how else would we find the time to read it, were we not sometimes ill? If Proust had been a healthy upstanding member of society, then he may well have suffered a successful career in the upper reaches of the civil service, and the world of letters would have been a good deal poorer.

There is quite a lot of philosophizing about illness by writers, perhaps because they are a sickly bunch. Albert Camus, for example, with typical Gallic morbidity, describes illness as "a remedy against death, because it prepares us for death, creating an apprenticeship whose first step is self-pity. Illness supports man in the great attempt to shirk the fact that he will surely die."

This is not a view that is useful to society, if one sees society as an efficient organism. You would never see a newspaper report which read, "spiritual insights and moments of true joy gained by slumbering wage slave while confined to bed."

But in the far-off days before painkillers and Lemsip, illness and trauma were not to be swept under the carpet and ignored. They were to be respected, listened to and given time to work themselves out. When Samuel Pepys had an immensely painful operation to remove a kidney stone, he did not rush back into the office 36 hours later. No. He had the right to a full 40 days' recovery period during which time he was not allowed to do anything.

Imagine that! Forty days to lie in bed and think! Enlightened employers should also recognize that a few days off can help return the worker to the office with less of his old resentment and more good ideas for the company. After all, aren't modern companies always saying how much they value creativity and innovation? How much they need ideas? Perhaps the truth is rather sadder—that they actually value steadfastness, application and your bum being on your revolving seat for as many hours in the day as you can stand. Or as the song "The Company Way," from the 1960s musical satire on office politics *How to Succeed in Business without Really Trying*, puts it:

> Suppose a man of genius makes suggestions
> Watch that genius get suggested to resign

"Convalescing" is a word one doesn't hear much these days. It's as if we have banished the notion that time is a healer, and replaced it with a battery of procedures and products designed to skip convalescence altogether. The idea of convalescence was to extend the period of being ill beyond the time of the actual illness or trauma, and allow time to get one's strength back up again. So when the flu has gone, you then need another few days to convalesce. The whole concept is a friend to the idler. We should bring the word back and dignify inactivity with a kind of purpose. "What are you doing at the moment?" "Very busy, actually, I'm convalescing." I suppose convalescing is equivalent to digestion, it means allowing the body a period of rest to recover after the energy it has just expended in being ill or eating.

What happened, I wonder, to the doctors of the turn of the century, who used to recommend long periods of inactivity on the South Coast for minor ailments? These days doctors just sell you pills, but there used to be a wonderful medical prescription known as the "rest cure"—in other words, the only way we can cure this is for you to do as little as possible for as long as possible. When the sickly velvet-coated dandy Robert Louis Stevenson fell ill in 1873, aged 23, the diagnosis was "nervous exhaustion with a threatening of phthisis" and the prescription was a winter on the Riviera "in complete freedom from anxiety or worry." (Stevenson wrote a lovely essay about the pleasures of this trip called "Ordered South" [1874].)

In "On Being Idle," Jerome K. Jerome recalls one particular bout of sickness: "I was very ill, and was ordered to Buxton for a month, with strict instructions to do nothing whatever all the while that I was there. 'Rest is what you require,' said the doctor, 'perfect rest.'"

He goes on to imagine the delights to come in a superb description of the pleasures of being ill:

> I pictured to myself a glorious time—a four weeks' *dolce far niente* with a dash of illness in it. Not too much illness, but just illness enough—just sufficient to give it the flavour of suffering, and make it poetical. I should get up late, sip chocolate, and have my breakfast in slippers and a dressing gown. I should lie out in the garden in a hammock, and read sentimental novels with a melancholy ending, until the book would fall from my listless

hand, and I should recline there, dreamily gazing into the deep blue of the firmament, watching the fleecy clouds, floating like white-sailed ships, across its depths, and listening to the joyous songs of the birds, and the low rustling of the trees. Or, when I became too weak to go out of doors, I should sit, propped up with pillows, at the open window of the ground floor front, and look wasted and interesting, so that all the pretty girls would sigh as they passed by.

The fact that Jerome goes on to say that he did not actually enjoy his month's retreat, for the reason that he enjoys doing nothing only when he has lots of work to do, should not let us stray from our conviction that being ill should be returned to its proper place in the idling agenda.

We know from historians such as Roy Porter and Jenny Uglow that in the eighteenth century, time and opium were pretty much the universal prescriptions. Erasmus Darwin, the celebrated doctor, poet, liberal Renaissance man and grandfather of Charles, often spoke of "time" as his secret ingredient.

Once upon a time, it seems, we knew how to be ill. Now we have lost the art. Everyone, everywhere disapproves of being ill. Being ill is just not useful. The newspapers create a climate of guilt around it because of the time it takes away from useful, productive work. As we saw in our chapter on skiving, headlines reading "days lost to British industry due to sickness" are a regular sight. The stories make one feel that when ill you are somehow letting the side down, losing the nation money. Being ill is unpatriotic and terribly inconvenient to the work culture. It results in days off and expense for employers. It makes us feel guilty. Society today simply does not allow us to be ill or, at least, it would prefer us to be uncomplaining automatons. Suffering is swept under the carpet, denied, ignored, made war upon.

When we are struck down with illness, we should be thinking not, "Oh no, my boss will get annoyed," but, "Oh great, I can lie in bed, watch old movies, stare at the ceiling, read books—in short, do all those things that I am always complaining that I don't have the time to do." We can't take laudanum any more but I understand that Collis Browne's cough mixture has a similar effect.

The great programme, indeed, of modern medicine is the total eradication of illness. Are you ill? Take a pill. That is the solution of the medical orthodoxy. Drugs companies make vast profits out of magic beans which promise to deliver us from torment and return us to the desk. Advertising agencies create ads which suggest we take medicine in order not to lose our job. First it was lunch; now we are told that being ill is for wimps.

Our attitudes to illness have grown dramatically less idler-friendly in recent years. To demonstrate this, we need only look at the recent history of Lemsip's marketing. When I was a child, a mug of Lemsip mixed with honey was one of the pleasures of lying in bed with a heavy cold or with flu. It went with being wrapped in a dressing gown and watching *Crown Court*. It was all part of the fun. Your mother might bring you a steaming cup of the soothing nectar in bed. You would sip it, cough weakly and luxuriate in its fumes. It had some positive effect on the physical symptoms of the illness, to be sure, but it was also a pleasure in itself. Lemsip was part of the delicious and much-needed slow-down that illness can bring into our life.

Not any more. Lemsip has reinvented itself as a "hard-working medicine." It has changed from a friend of the idler to his worst enemy. Why? "Because Life Doesn't Stop," as one of their horrifyingly go-getting slogans has it. The implication is that rather than enjoying your illness and waiting a few days till it has gone away, you should manfully repress the symptoms and carry on as normal, competing, working, consuming.

Lemsip even suggest that taking their medicine will somehow elevate the ordinary man into something more noble. "New Lemsip products for hard-working heroes" their website proclaims. We must soldier on and do our bit. No time to be ill. No time for bed. Go, go, go.

Most appalling of all was their recent ad line "Stop Snivelling and Get Back to Work." I recognize that there is a pun here, but the voice is still that of a stern authoritarian boss figure, deliberately inducing feelings of guilt. Other ads preyed on workers' insecurities by showing that the man who took Lemsip and struggled into the office while suffering from flu was less likely to lose his job than the wimp who took a day or two off. What they are saying is: "Getting a cold could result in you losing your job, your home, your mortgage—everything you hold dear. Take Lemsip and you'll be all right. You may not be happy, but at least you'll be safe."

In its latest product innovation, Lemsip has gone even further towards becoming a strictly pleasure-free remedy. Now it is no longer even something you sip. It has invented a new range of pills called Lemsip Max Strength Direct, which you can take "without the need for water." It is, they claim, "the first truly convenient cold and flu remedy." In other words, you can snaffle a couple of these while getting dressed or as you run for the bus. You no longer have to waste precious time suffering the dreadful inconvenience of boiling a kettle, pouring the water on the powder and then slowly sipping it. Lemsip without the tedious sipping. And without the lem, most probably. Merely an effective tool for helping the busy toiler work at "max strength."

This culture of working while ill is endemic in the US, too. In *Nickel and Dimed*, Barbara Ehrenreich describes an advert for the painkiller Aleve in which "the cute blue-collar guy asks: If you quit working after four hours, what would your boss say? And the not-so-cute blue-collar guy, who's lugging a metal beam on his back, answers: He'd fire me, that's what." Ehrenreich says that her co-workers at the maids service would rather dose themselves up on painkillers than run the risk of losing their job. This culture is promoted by one cleaning-firm boss, "Ted":

Ted doesn't have much sympathy for illness . . . one of our morning meetings was on the subject of "working through it." Somebody, and he wasn't going to name names, he told us, was out with a migraine. "Now if I get a migraine I just pop two Excedrins and get on with my life. That's what you have to do—work through it."

But even if the symptoms are repressed by a painkiller, the illness is still there. It will take longer to go away if ignored. And isn't there more chance of spreading the illness around co-workers and co-commuters if you struggle in to the office or factory while ill? The Lemsip campaign and others like it have a lot to answer for.

So: I have knocked down one ideal. Can I erect another in its place? It seems to me that the mission to banish illness from our bodies and from our lives for ever is a futile one. It's a fascist-style programme—the idea that any element potentially damaging to the efficient functioning of the body must be destroyed. As is the case with many other aspects of the idle life, the sane solution to illness is not to attempt to destroy it but to evolve strategies for dealing with it. Suffering is part of life; it is how one deals with suffering that counts. Then the illness can become a pleasure as much as a trial. First we need to overcome our guilt at being ill, then we need to take time off work as necessary. We need to welcome the illness in, cosset it, make friends with it, ask it to stay, be sad to see it leave.

To help us in this mission we need more idler-friendly doctors. Instead of prescribing drugs and trying to blitz illness in the shortest possible period of time, they would order their patients to take long periods off work. Three days would be the minimum; but they could prescribe a rest cure of anything up to two months. We need to educate our doctors ourselves. Refuse antibiotics, refuse paracetamol. Tell them that all you need is a few days' recovery period, and you would like a note to give to your boss. Doctors, join us! I call on you! You are servants of the work ethic! We need you to inject much-needed time into our lives! This way, your period off work has been sanctioned by a higher authority. It's hard to be idle on your own.

Appealing to authority to help us, though, is a temporary fix for apprentice idlers making their first steps down the road to freedom. The final battle must be with our own sense of guilt about taking time off. We need to take responsibility for our own illnesses, rather than being grateful that an "expert" has helped us out. Faced with a boss like "Ted," though, this is not an easy task. But you must be bold. You must have the confidence to say, "I am ill, I'm not coming in for a few days." Remember that "soldiering on" is a slave's way of thinking. If you take a positive lead and simply refuse to "work through it," others will follow. Remove the shame from being ill. Take care of yourself. Legislation and unions have failed us. We're on our own. The answer? Sleep through it.

3 p.m.
The Nap

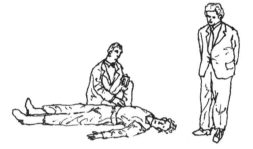

Mahomet was taking his afternoon nap in his Paradise.
An houri had rolled a cloud under his head, and he was
snoring serenely near the fountain of Salsabil.

Ernest L'Epine, *The Legend of Croquemitaine* (1863)

I count it as an absolute certainty that in paradise, everyone
naps. A nap is a perfect pleasure and it's useful, too. It splits the
day into two halves, making each half more manageable and
enjoyable. How much easier it is to work in the morning if we
know we have a nap to look forward to after lunch; and how
much more pleasant the late afternoon and evening become
after a little sleep. If you know there is a nap to come later in
the day, then you can banish for ever that terrible sense of doom

one feels at 9 a.m. with eight hours of straight toil ahead.

Not only that, but the nap can offer a glimpse into a twilight nether world where gods play and dreams happen. Here is the French academic Thierry Paquot, in his essential book *The Art of the Siesta*:

> Your body, which was weighing you down just a moment before, now seems progressively lighter, invisible, non-existent. Happiness—or a form of happiness—overwhelms you. Let yourself be, let yourself go and, with surprise, surrender yourself. To what? A new master? Or mistress? Little conspirator . . . are you trying to hide an illicit liaison? Yes, an assignation in broad daylight—disapproved of by productive morality—with the night, with Hypnos . . .

Yes: our inalienable right to nap has been taken from us by the agents of industry. This is all wrong. "The Siesta," Paquot goes on to argue, "is a high point of living—yes, an act of living!— that should be defined, popularized and practised with both joy and solemnity." We're particularly unlucky, I think, in the USA and northern Europe. In countries where the dogma of work and industry has not taken such a firm, unforgiving grip on the nation's psyche, the nap is a hallowed part of the day. Many are the times when the aspiring idler of self-lacerating northern Europe (whose ancestors founded the United States) has cast a jealous glance at the more laid-back Mediterranean countries and their custom of the siesta. In Spain, for example, the nap is built into the working day. Workers will go home at lunchtime, eat, doze and then return to the office or factory for a quick session of work before going out into the night.

This way of dividing the day has the welcome corollary of bringing more fun to the evening, which starts later and goes on later than in northern Europe. Why are evenings more fun? Because if you know that you are able to make up for sleep loss with your daytime nap, then the pressure to go to bed early is somewhat relieved. How many great nights out have been ruined by you or a friend rising regretfully from the table and saying, "I really ought to get back. I've got an early start."

The more relaxed work rhythms of the South, where work is split into two chunks by a long nap or down time, used to be common in England before they were completely destroyed by the idler's great enemy, the Industrial Revolution. In his essay on Saint Monday (see Skiving chapter), Dr. Douglas Reid quotes a contemporary description of the work patterns of the independent Birmingham weavers in the late seventeenth century:

> They lived like the inhabitants of Spain, or after the custom of the Orientals. Three or four o'clock in the morning found them at work. At noon they rested; many enjoyed their siesta; others spent their time in the workshops eating and drinking, these places being often turned into taprooms and the apprentices into potboys; others again enjoyed themselves at marbles or in the skittle alley. Three or four hours were thus devoted to "play" and then came work again . . .

Wherever people are given the option to nap, a nap is taken. It is only when the nap is not allowed that we do not take it. In his book *Sleep Thieves* (1996), an eloquent argument for more sleep all round, the popular academic Stanley Coren reports an experiment in which members of a research group were left to sleep as and when they pleased. After a week or so, most of the subjects were taking naps of between one and two hours per day. Coren goes on to argue that people who are not sleep-deprived are half as likely to succumb to infections as those suffering what he calls "sleep debt."

There is little doubt, therefore, that a nap is a natural part of our daily cycle, or "circadian rhythms" (derived from the Latin *circa*, "approximately," and *diem*, "day"). All our cycles are different. Yet, from schooldays on, the nap is frowned on as ineffective use of time, and we are encouraged to believe in centralized timetabling. This anti-nappery results in dedicated nappers, those who choose not to resist their body's demands for a break, resorting to subterfuge to get their forty winks. I personally used to find it almost impossible to sit through double maths on a Tuesday afternoon without falling asleep, which I would do with my chin cradled by my hand, my elbow resting on the table. In this posture I could happily doze off, until such time as the teacher would notice and dramatically slam my desk with his hand to wake me up. I suppose he found my torpor insulting to his teaching methods; I maintain that it wasn't his fault. If the school had factored in nap time to the day, then I wouldn't have had to take it during lessons. The same happened to me when I worked in offices. Chin again cradled by my hand, elbows on the desk, face shielded by the computer, it would have taken close study by a supervisor to realize that my eyes were closed and I was floating on a cloud somewhere.

I have heard of another technique for covert dozing, from a lowly office worker who had perfected the art of napping in the lavatory cubicle. He sat across the seat, leant his head back on the toilet roll holder, the toilet roll making a comfy pillow, and jammed his feet up against the opposite wall. In this position, he said, he could doze happily for fifteen or twenty minutes.

It is a terrible state of affairs when we have become ashamed of napping. Shouldn't all offices provide day beds for their workers? The day bed is one of the few positive legacies of the Victorian age. Its very name is a delicious concept, even naughty: a bed for the day! When I worked in an office full time, and we were installing furniture, I suggested to the bosses that instead of spending £200 on one of those characterless bright-green cuboid sofas from the catalogue, they should give me £200 and I would go to the market and bring back a lovely Victorian day bed, which we could sit on for meetings and lie on for naps. Perhaps you will not be surprised to hear that I lost that particular battle, and we therefore had to rearrange the green cubes when we fancied a doze.

In China recently, the widespread custom of *hsiuhsi*, or afternoon nap, has taken a bashing from Western-style work schedules. "Our businessmen are being told by people in your country that sleeping in the afternoon is a sign of laziness," a traveller recently heard. "We are not lazy and do not wish to appear that way, so most business people have given up *hsiuhsi*."

Now that I work from home, I have fulfilled my dream, and a nice squashy day bed (price: £100) sits across the room from my desk. One of the great pleasures of writing this book is that it justifies all the idle pleasures I have indulged in all my life but which hitherto have been surrounded by at least a little guilt, and sometimes a lot. Now I can indulge them fearlessly, and yesterday, for example, I enjoyed the most glorious post-lunch snooze from two to four. When I woke, I happily went to my desk and put in an hour or two on a tedious administrative task which I had been putting off for weeks. I'm certain that on a napless day I would have been less productive and enjoyed myself less as well.

For Paquot, the siesta represents freedom and self-mastery. It sets itself up in direct opposition to the work-discipline that was introduced in the eighteenth century. To nap is to take some time back for ourselves:

> This break in the straight path of waged employment indicates a surprise, a detour, a sidetrack . . . The siesta is a sidetrack leading away from all activity that is distinct, obligatory, habitual and mechanical . . . the siesta is a means for us to reclaim our own time, outside the clockmakers' control. The siesta is our liberator.

But, sadly, our manly struggle to conform to the slave-like work rhythms of present-day custom has led to the nap being replaced by that costly and damaging drink, coffee. As paracetamol is to the cold, so coffee is to the nap: a way of riding it out, a sort of competition with one's own body, a civil war. When we feel tired after lunch, the socially acceptable solution is to dose up on coffee and ride out the tiredness, rather than simply take a nap. The coffee may produce a temporary perking of the senses, but irritability will follow, not to mention a sleep debt later in the day. You cannot win the battle against sleep. Don't fight, surrender!

The nap also has a deserved reputation for its spiritual benefits. The founders of great world religions were dedicated nappers, and indeed, it was during their roadside dozes that their visions often came. The nap is a sort of easy version of meditation. Jesus was an idler. Buddha was definitely an idler.

Naps can even be life-saving. I recall a story of an Indian devotee of the meditation practice Raja Yoga who was caught up in the Bhopal disaster. She was in the meditation centre quite close to the chemical plant when the explosion happened. There was panic in the streets and many of those running from the gas cloud died. Something led her instead to take a shower, and then go to bed, pulling the blankets over her head. She survived unharmed when thousands were injured and died. Simply by doing nothing she saved her life. Never has the truth of the axiom "When you can't figure out what to do, it's time for a nap" (Mason Cooley) been more decisively proved.

I might add that the battle against the nap is odd even when seen from a practical perspective. Even the strictest of work-ethic-promoting utilitarians seem agreed on the positive power of the nap. Indeed, the unpleasant phrase "power nap" has lately entered the language and describes a brief doze that will return the worker to the office with his competitive edge yet more finely honed. I've discovered lately that even certain renowned enemies of idleness were themselves great nappers. Winston Churchill, who abhorred laziness in other people, himself took a nap every afternoon. He defended his afternoon doze in practical terms as an absolute necessity:

> You must sleep sometime between lunch and dinner, and no halfway measures. Take off your clothes and get into bed. That's what I always do. Don't think you will be doing less work because you sleep during the day. That's a foolish notion held by people who have no imagination. You will be able to accomplish more.

You get two days in one—well, at least one and a half, I'm sure. When the war started, I had to sleep during the day because that was the only way I could cope with my responsibilities.

Take off your clothes and get into bed in your office, however, and you are likely to be reprimanded for public nudity and laziness. Employers would rather you put in four hours of sitting and accomplishing nothing than an hour's nap, clothed or otherwise, followed by three hours of productive toil.

Another dedicated enemy of idleness was Thomas Edison, the dastardly work-ethic promoter who invented the light bulb in order that people could work all through the night. He enabled that terrible thing—shift work—to come into being. After Edison, the machines never rested. In his own propaganda, Edison claimed only to need three or four hours of sleep a night, but, as Stanley Coren reports, he napped a lot. A Croatian electrical engineer called Nikola Tesla who worked with him claimed of Edison: "Although he needs only four sleep hours a night, he needs two three-hour naps each day." Coren also tells the story of when Henry Ford (another enemy of idleness) came to visit Edison one afternoon and was surprised to discover that the renowned enemy of sleep was himself dozing. When he questioned an assistant on this apparent hypocrisy, the assistant insisted: "He doesn't sleep very much at all, he just naps a lot."

In the more carefree work culture of 1950s America, businessmen were even advised through official channels that they should sleep and drink alcohol. This health-giving treatment had the attractive name "nap and nip": "Every businessman over 50 should have a daily nap and nip—a short nap after lunch and a relaxing highball before dinner," advised one Dr. Sara Murray

Jordan, gastroenterologist, in a *Reader's Digest* of 1958. (You'll read more about the positive power of the cocktail in a later chapter.)

The closest description I have ever read of a near-contemporary paradise shows its inhabitants as constantly napping. It comes from Robert Dean Frisbie's 1929 book *The Book of Puka-puka*. Frisbie was a middle-class American in his twenties (let's imagine Dustin Hoffman in *The Graduate*) who escaped the pressures of his ambitious parents and set up a little shop on the South Seas island of Puka-puka. He settled there and married a native girl. Here is how Frisbie's friend describes the indolent island culture:

> The people see no reason at all for getting up in the morning, and most of 'em don't: they sleep all day, but at night they wake up, and you'll see them fishing by torchlight off the reef—eating, dancing, love-making on shore. Trading skippers—the few that know Puka-puka—hate the island because they can't get the people to work loading their ships.

In Paradise, we sleep all day. We have learned an important lesson: don't fight the nap. The only downside is that many people have a tendency to wake from their nap in a grumpy mood. This I put down to a deep-seated guilt against the inactivity we have just been indulging in, which is expressed as self-hatred. And in any case, there is a simple remedy for this grumpiness, and it's to take tea, which is the subject of our next chapter.

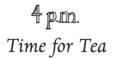

4 p.m.

Time for Tea

One drinks tea to forget the world's noise; it is not for those
who eat rich food and dress in silk pyjamas.

T'ien Yiheng, *c.* 1570

The calming ritual of tea is another of those idle pleasures that
have been sacrificed to productivity and profit in recent years.
Whoever first conceived the idea of taking it at four o'clock was
a genius. This is because 4 p.m. marks the point in the day at
which one's energies are turning. The long, listless, flat hours
between two and four, when it is impossible to do much and
when the sensible idler has taken to his bed, have come to a
close, and our brains are once again stirring. It's time not to do,
but to think about doing.

Tea should be a time for gentle chat and reflection, a cigarette, a little mental workout. It should last for at least half an hour. I remember tea being a wonderful part of the day when I had a holiday job as a removal man. Removal man, by the way, is not a bad job for an idler, because it offers "paroxysms of diligence" followed by long rest periods. We would work and sweat and toil for an hour or two, then take a break. I enjoyed this rhythm much more than the endless tedium of office-based admin jobs. There was a lot of driving, which was fun, long lunch breaks and, of course, the tea break. The tea break was absolutely sacrosanct, and it was taken properly. There was none of this grabbing a quick cuppa (oh vulgar word) while staring at your screen.

I also remember very clearly that it was during the tea break that the removal men's conversation would take on a rather more visionary aspect. Morning conversation would centre around farting jokes, sex stories and generally taking the piss out of each other and innocent bystanders. At tea time, however, the men, reclining in the back of the truck with the shutter door open, looking out on to the street, would enter a more languid state. They would describe beautiful places they had been to on holiday, talk fondly of children or wives, or discuss their dreams of a better quality of life.

In a strange way, this sort of tea break has a lot in common with the tea ritual of China and Japan, which was intimately bound up with the seeking of enlightenment. Like many life-improving inventions, tea was discovered during a moment of pure inactivity. According to legend, in 2737 BC the Chinese herbalist Shen Nong was sitting under a tree, staring into space, when a leaf from a wild tea bush floated down into a cup of boiled water that was sitting in front of him, creating the first ever cup of tea.

There then seems to be a gap of about 2000 years in the history of tea before it appears in government tax records of 400 BC. Around this time, Zen Buddhist monks in Japan took to tea like Catholics to red wine. The monks, it is said, drank tea to help with meditation. It sharpened the intellect and helped them to stay up for hours. Looked at another way, then, tea was used as a tool to help one do absolutely nothing for as long as possible. In other words, it helped you to be idle. After all, what is meditation but total inactivity? Tea became almost a religion in itself, becoming known as The Way of Tea.

Buddhism certainly seems to me the most human of all religions, the most life-giving and fun, for the paradoxical reason that it embraces suffering. There seems to be none of the guilt or sense of indebtedness that ruins Christianity for most of us. As well as using tea for meditation, the Chinese were also keen on the ritual aspects of the beverage: its preparation, the serving, the decorum and politeness around sharing tea. Indeed, Confucius suggested that by behaving correctly in social situations, one promotes the smooth functioning of society in a way that pleases heaven. So it appears that tea sought to combine the collective and the individual. It was a meeting place between the inner and the outer worlds. Its purpose was to harmonize.

Now, in England during medieval times and in the sixteenth, seventeenth and early eighteenth centuries there was a different social harmonizer: beer. Beer was brewed at home and drunk morning, noon and night. A good wife would ensure a steady supply; good employers attracted labourers with the quality of their ale. It was the national drink for a chaotic and strong-willed country of ruddy-faced boozers. We may not have been particularly refined, but we knew how to have a good time. Thanks, however, to new trade routes, tea began to filter in to English culture in the late seventeenth century. It was at first fashionable at court, probably because it was expensive and rare. But its popularity began to spread.

One early apologist for tea was Dr. Johnson. There was none of the oriental refinement in the way he drank it, and the custom of tea at four or five o'clock had not yet been invented. Dr. Johnson's attitude to tea seems to have had more in common with an inner-city crackhead than a Zen Buddhist. Here is how Johnson describes his habit:

> [I am] a hardened and shameless tea-drinker, who has for many years diluted his meals with only the infusion of this fascinating plant; whose kettle has scarcely time to cool; who with tea amuses the evening, with tea solaces the midnight, and with tea welcomes the morning.

Johnson became renowned for the sheer quantity he drank and the graceless speed at which he drank it. One evening, his friend the painter Joshua Reynolds observed that Johnson had drunk eleven cupfuls. Riled, Johnson answered: "Sir, I did not count your glasses of wine, why should you number my cups of tea?" He then softened and asked for a twelfth, in order to bring his tally up to a round dozen.

A contemporary called John Hawkins described Johnson's tea habits in a tone of amused horror: ". . . he was a lover of tea to an excess hardly credible; whenever it appeared, he was almost raving, and by his impatience to be served, his incessant calls for those ingredients which make that liquor palatable, and the haste with which he swallowed it down, he seldom failed to make that a fatigue to everyone else, which was intended as a general refreshment."

Meanwhile, as the Industrial Revolution gathered pace, tea became more and more popular and began to replace beer as Britain's national drink. One reason for this development may have been that the new work rhythms of the factories did not suit all-day boozing. People grew tired and had to be perked up. In *Cottage Economy* (1821), his practical guidebook for the aspiring smallholder, reformer William Cobbett was unimpressed by this new custom:

> The drink which has come to supply the place of beer has, in general, been tea. It is notorious that tea has no useful strength in it; that it contains nothing nutritious; that it, besides being good for nothing, has badness in it, because it is well known to produce want of sleep in many cases, and in all cases, to shake and weaken the nerves. It is, in fact, a weaker kind of laudanum, which enlivens for the moment and deadens afterwards. At any rate it communicates no strength to the body; it does not in any degree assist in affording what labour demands. It is, then, of no use.

Tea was urban; beer was rural. Tea was for wimps; beer was for men. Cobbett then goes on to prove how the habit is chronically expensive compared with beer-brewing, concluding:

> I view the tea drinking as a destroyer of health, an enfeebler of the frame, an engenderer of effeminacy and laziness, a

debaucher of youth, and a maker of misery for old age . . .
[from tea-drinking] succeeds a softness, an effeminacy, a seeking
for the fire-side, a lurking in the bed, and, in short, all the char-
acteristics of idleness, for which, in this case, real want of
strength furnishes an apology.

The strange thing is that these are precisely the arguments that
were used against alcohol-drinking by the Temperance campaign-
ers of the time.

But it is precisely tea's quality as a sort of nothing that makes
it so attractive to the man or woman of reflective bent. It injects
idleness into the working day. It provides a stop, a moment of
calm. In 1821, the same year that Cobbett published *Cottage
Economy*, the great writer and seeker of the fireside Thomas De
Quincey, in his classic drug memoir, *Confessions of an English
Opium Eater*, defended tea as follows:

From the latter weeks of October to Christmas Eve . . . is the
period during which happiness is in season, which, in my judgment, enters the room with the tea-tray; for tea, though ridiculed
by those who are naturally of coarse nerves, or are become so
from wine-drinking, and are not susceptible of influence from
so refined a stimulant, will always be the favourite beverage of
the intellectual . . .

De Quincey drank tea all night, and although it could be argued
that his enjoyment of it was somewhat amplified by the fact
that he was out of his mind on opium during those hours, I
think the point is clear.

It was a little later that tea as a formal social ritual took hold, around 1840. In a sort of parody of the harmonious Chinese tea ceremony, the English created a tea ceremony that, though well timed, was characterized by social obligation, status display, reserve, awkwardness and stiff formality. I think of William in the Richmal Crompton stories and the absolute agony he must have gone through when having tea with great-aunts. In fact, I can still remember the awkwardness of tea with my elderly relations, when 45 minutes seemed to stretch into several days of total ego death.

Another positive corollary of tea was the urban Tea Room. Young secretaries and clerks would go to eat pastries and talk and dance. They continued to be popular beyond the end of the nineteenth century, and also provided venues for "tango teas" during the 1920s. The Tea Rooms were also popular because they were the first socially acceptable places where ladies could hang out without male escorts.

Afternoon tea as a social event lives on in parts of rural France. Only recently I attended a *thé dansant* at a village hall one Sunday afternoon in a small town in the north. The hall was brightly lit and rows of trestle tables had been set up. A little band with a Casio organ played classic dance tunes on the stage. Tea and cakes were served, as well as beer for the men. The audience was made up of local farmers and their wives, mainly in their fifties. It would be easy to snigger at the lack of sophistication but in fact there was a great spirit and lots of laughter and dancing.

We should all help to reintroduce tea as a daily ritual, to make it sacrosanct. But how should we take tea? How should we enjoy it? I think we've largely got it wrong at the moment, unless you're lucky enough to be a removal man. Tea should not come out of machines, it should not be served in plastic cups with the tea bag still swimming around in it and slurped down while staring at a computer screen. So let us turn to the Chinese to find inspiration for the reinstatement of the tea ritual. This sixteenth-century poem describes the various ideal conditions for the enjoyment of tea:

When one's heart and hands are idle.
Tired after reading poetry.
When one's thoughts are disturbed.
Listening to songs and ditties.
When a song is completed.
Shut up at one's home on a holiday.
Playing the ch'in and looking over paintings.
Engaged in conversation deep at night.
Before a bright window and a clean desk.
With charming friends and slender concubines.
Returning from a visit with friends.
When the day is clear and the breeze is mild.
On a day of light showers.
In a painted boat near a small wooden bridge.
In a forest with tall bamboos.
In a pavilion overlooking lotus flowers on a summer day.
Having lighted incense in a small studio.
After a feast is over and the guests are gone.
When children are at school.
In a quiet, secluded temple.
Near famous springs and quaint rocks.

So reads "Proper Moments for Drinking Tea" by Hsü Ts'eshu. I particularly like the idea of tea with slender concubines but I'm not sure whether most Western wives and girlfriends would tolerate it. But the other suggestions are not beyond the bounds of possibility. Further Chinese guidance comes from Lin Yutang:

> There is something in the nature of tea that leads us into a world of quiet contemplation of life. It would be as disastrous to drink tea with babies crying around, or with loud-voiced women or politics-talking men, as to pick tea on a rainy or cloudy day . . . Tea is then symbolic of earthly purity, requiring the most fastidious cleanliness in its preparation, from picking, frying and preserving to its final infusion and drinking, easily upset or spoiled by the slightest contamination of oily hands or oily cups. Consequently, its enjoyment is appropriate in an atmosphere where all ostentation or suggestion of luxury is banished from one's eyes and one's thoughts . . . the preparation and drinking of tea is always a performance of loving pleasure, importance and distinction. In fact, the preparation is half the fun of the drinking, as cracking melon-seeds between one's teeth is half the pleasure of eating them.

It was with the idea of a celebration and a rebirth of tea-taking that we introduced a tea column into the *Idler* magazine, and appointed the legendary fisherman Chris Yates (of whom more in the Fishing chapter) as our Tea Correspondent. Yates's first piece, an attack on the tea bag, revealed him as a natural ancestor of the Chinese tea writers:

> Tea must be taken slowly, yet modern society—with its alarm clocks, exercise bikes and its rush to work—has created the tea bag, which is an abuse of nature, and the quick cuppa, which is

a cardinal sin . . . tea-making, like tea-drinking, must be a leisurely, contemplative affair, the mind calming as the loose leaves are given ample time to swirl, separate and glow in your teapot, the spirit rising as you pour the golden fluid.

It is extraordinary how few people use loose-leaf tea and how much they are missing out. Tea bags are supposed to be more convenient and quicker, but being the essence of "tea in a hurry" run completely contrary to the real spirit of tea. It is actually far more convenient, not to mention more elegant and pleasurable, to keep half a pound of loose tea in a caddy near the kettle than one of those vast and ugly boxes of tea bags. Loose-leaf tea is also easy to throw away—no soggy tea bags spattering brown juice on the sides of the sink.

Let us now look at two of tea's enemies: the first is, paradoxically, the Tea Council, which promotes tea as merely health-giving and useful. It has a horribly colourful and buzzy website which includes such vulgar images as a naked woman reclining in a cup of tea, and there is little suggestion of tea's provenance as an aid to enlightenment and social harmony. The website even displays tables of figures designed to demonstrate tea's nutritional value. But it becomes very clear after a moment's inspection of these that the only serious nutrients in tea come from the milk that we Brits habitually serve with it.

Tea's other enemy, of course, is coffee. Rather as tea supplanted beer during the Industrial Revolution in the UK, the last ten years have seen coffee replace alcohol in the US, and the US-style coffee culture has now hit Europe. The quantities are vast; the manner of drinking rushed. Whereas the traditional continental manner of taking coffee is to have a small cup in a café, we are now all to be seen carrying around vast paper flagons of latte. We buy coffee "to go"; drink it on the hoof, in the car, on the train, in meetings, even, and saddest of all, while walking along the street. We have been invaded and polluted by joyless coffee.

Coffee is for winners, go-getters, tea-ignorers, lunch-cancellers, early-risers, guilt-ridden strivers, money obsessives and status-driven spiritually empty lunatics. It is an enervating force. We should resist it and embrace tea, the ancient drink of poets, philosophers and meditators.

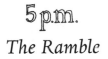

5 p.m.

The Ramble

It's a shame that the noble word "pedestrian" has come to be used in a pejorative sense. "Terribly pedestrian" is how we dismiss a piece of creative work if we want to convey the idea that it is humdrum, ordinary, unspectacular. It's as if the humble ramble has become tedious and boring in comparison with flashier, faster modes of transport like trains, planes and automobiles. But in the pedestrian, the wanderer, the rambler, the *flâneur*, can be found the soul of the idler. The pedestrian is the highest and most mighty of beings; he walks for pleasure, he observes but does not interfere, he is not in a hurry, he is happy in the company of his own mind, he wanders detached, wise and merry, godlike. He is free.

Most of those, however, who stride along the streets of our big cities are not enjoying their stroll. They are merely using their legs to get from A to B. There is no component of fun in their walk; it simply has to be done. Their walking has a purpose in mind: to move from the underground station to the office, from bus stop to factory, sandwich shop to bank. The journey itself is unimportant, a waste of time. The goal is the important thing. Caught up in this sort of walking, we find it hard to abandon ourselves to the moment. We pace with purpose, head down, staring at the pavement. Through our mind runs a stream of anxieties: things to do, things not done, commitments broken. If anyone saw us they would get the vibe: busy, important, things to do, places to go.

I find it terribly easy to slip into this sort of forlorn pacing, which is the norm in cities. Walking for pleasure tends to be something we reserve for weekends and holidays. However, with a little effort of will it is not so hard to get into a reflective walking-mindset even amid the bustle and turmoil of the working day.

The greatest example of the attitude I am describing is the French *flâneur*. *Flâneur* literally means stroller or idler, and, in the nineteenth century, came to describe an elegant kind of gentlemanly moocher, who ambled purposelessly through the Parisian arcades, watching, waiting, hanging around. His hero was Baudelaire, as an anti-bourgeois who had somehow freed himself from wage slavery and was at liberty to wander the streets with no particular place to go.

The twentieth-century philosopher and radical political thinker Walter Benjamin was particularly captivated by the idea of the *flâneur*. He produced a giant piece of work called the *Arcades*, which is a compendium of thousands of short reflections and aphorisms, some his own, some quoted from others. It is a classic piece of *flânerie*; the reader can easily picture Benjamin, notebook in one hand, pipe in the other, taking notes on his observations, ready to type them out when back at home. It is in this work, for example, that Benjamin imparts the following gem:

> In 1839 it was considered elegant to take a tortoise out walking. This gives us an idea of the tempo of the *flânerie* in the arcades.

A tortoise on a lead! How wonderful. And so much more calming than the hyperactive, sniffing, yapping, snorting, pissing, dashing dog. (Why do people have dogs? I do not understand them.)

Like idleness itself, there is a paradoxical purpose to *flânerie*: slow walking may seem like a waste of time to your man of business, but to the creative spirit it is a fertile activity, for it is when walking that the *flâneur* thinks and generates ideas. Benjamin gives many examples of these. No less a figure than Beethoven, Benjamin tells us, via a quote from dictionary-writer Pierre Larousse, wrote music in his head while out and about:

> In the first years of this century, a man was seen walking each and every day—regardless of the weather, be it sunshine or snow—around the ramparts of the city of Vienna. This man was Beethoven, who, in the midst of his wanderings, would work out his magnificent symphonies in his head before putting them down on paper. For him, the world no longer existed; in vain would people greet him respectfully as he passed. He saw nothing; his mind was elsewhere.

Victor Hugo was another great wanderer: "The morning, for him, was consecrated to sedentary labours, the afternoon to labours of wandering. He adored the upper levels of omnibuses—those 'travelling balconies' as he called them—from which he could study at his leisure the various aspects of the gigantic city. He claimed that the deafening brouhaha of Paris produced in him the same effect as the sea," wrote his biographer Edouard Drumont in 1900.

We can all probably think of our own examples. I have just thought of the great do-nothing Jim Morrison, who loved to listen to the cars going by his window in LA. Of course, there's John Lennon, who loved to watch the wheels go round and round when living in New York in the 1970s. And I understand that the filmmaker Russ Meyer, *auteur* of such greats as *Supervixens!* and *Beyond the Valley of the Ultra-Vixens*, works out his scripts and plots on a two-hour post-lunch walk.

City wandering was not just a nineteenth-century pursuit: the visionary poet of the city William Blake often walked through pre-industrial London as a boy. His biographer Peter Ackroyd reports that he experienced spectacular visions on these rambles: he saw a tree filled with angels at Peckham Rye; the prophet Ezekiel under a tree in the fields; and angels among the haymakers. Reporting such apparitions to his parents would earn him a sound hiding for being a liar. Blake demonstrated, in *Jerusalem* (1804), that the city can be as stimulating as the countryside as a feeder of the imagination:

> The fields from Islington to Marybone,
> To Primrose Hill and Saint Johns Wood,
> Were builded over with pillars of gold;
> And there Jerusalem's pillars stood.

There is the solitary walk, but there is also the walk in company. *Idler* contributors Mark Manning and John Nicholson could well describe themselves as *flâneurs*: they spend their days and nights strolling the streets of London. As a consequence, a walk, which would otherwise be a routine exercise, becomes in their company a fascinating journey. Just the walk, for example, from my office in Clerkenwell through Holborn to Covent Garden can be filled with adventure by Manning. Avoiding the main streets, he takes you past the museum of the Royal College of Surgeons with its misshapen foetuses in jars, the Sir John Soane's Museum where Hogarth's *Rake's Progress* is on display, the Old Curiosity Shop, the statues on Holborn Viaduct representing icons of Commerce and Agriculture; he will take you through the law courts at Lincoln's Inn, past the lawyers' flash cars. London comes alive with history; you see things that you have never seen before; your eyes are opened.

There are one or two others raising the standard of the moocher. The cantankerous British journalist Jonathan Meades sees himself as a modern *flâneur*. "Our cities are full of people hurrying," he complained recently in an article in the London *Times*. "Their narrow pavements are not made for promenades at snail's pace; they are for getting from A to B rather than civic recreation. Walking for its own sake may be further discouraged by the climate and, equally, by the work 'ethic.' This week I put in several hours' sterling loitering interspersed with energy-saving bouts of *farniente* supinity. Observant sloth is its own reward. Just hanging around and seeing what happens . . . Time, in the form of a few minutes spent lounging about doing nothing in particular, is . . . a healer."

In Mediterranean countries, of course, there is none of the

anti-snailery Meades describes. In Italy, there is the custom of the *passeggiata*, the stroll. Indeed, one of the first things that strikes the visitor to Italy is the slow pace of walking. On Sunday mornings, after Mass, you will see whole families, arm in arm, walking at a tortoise's pace down the cobbled streets, talking about food, wine, family and philosophy.

"The *passeggiata* is also taken before dinner," said my Italian friend Cristina when I asked her to describe the custom. "There are set routes, usually going up and down *il corso*, the high street, in the village or town. It's when the whole village comes together. For young people it's the equivalent of going to the pub; it's when you see your friends and meet guys."

In London in the 1970s, it was the punks who briefly re-invented the promenade or *passeggiata*. They would spend the whole day walking up and down the King's Road, sitting on benches, looking in shop windows, hanging out, displaying their eccentric clothes. The punks were the last *flâneurs*.

And by conspicuously wandering in this way, for its own sake, without purpose, you become a figure of suspicion in fast-moving cities like London. "Move on, move on," policemen will say to loiterers. In the accusation "loitering with intent" is captured the authorities' inherent distrust of a loafer; I mean, how could they possibly know that the loiterer has some evil intent in mind? Are they mind-readers? It is assumed that someone who is doing nothing is necessarily planning mischief, when in fact what could be more harmless than going for a walk?

But the act of ambling is an act of revolt. It is a statement against bourgeois values, against goal-centred living, busy-ness, bustle, toil and trouble. For the creative spirit, the act of walking harmonizes work and play. For Benjamin, "[T]he idleness of the *flâneur* is a demonstration against the division of labour."

Walking well is a mental state as much as a physical one. How to walk? One of Benjamin's quotes in *Arcades* stresses the importance of keeping your eyes open. "To walk out of your front door as if you've just arrived from a foreign country; to discover the world in which you already live; to begin the day as if you've just gotten off the boat from Singapore and have never seen your own doormat or the people on the landing . . . it is this that reveals the humanity before you, unknown until now."

The great period for *flânerie* in London was of course the eighteenth century. It was then that the whole notion of the gentlemanly observer was at its zenith. Indeed, just look at the titles of the magazines and newspapers that sprang up in that literary century: the *Spectator*, the *Observer*, the *Tatler*, the *Wanderer*, the *Rambler*, the *Adventurer*. The art of wandering the city and reporting with a wry journalistic detachment, in the manner of Addison and Steele, and Johnson and others, was born in these years. The eighteenth-century city wanderer was more worldly and less depressed than his Parisian counterpart a century later, but perhaps that's because society had not yet been ravaged by the Industrial Revolution. There are a number of wannabe Dr. Johnsons contributing to papers like the *Spectator* today, but the tone is hard to get right; in recent years, perhaps only the late Soho sloucher Jeffrey Bernard's "Low Life" column came near to genuine *flânerie*. He somehow achieved a sort of world-weary insouciance that led to observations—on the death of cosiness, the wit of market traders, the futility of "self-help"—that others would be too busy to make.

In the late eighteenth and early nineteenth centuries, the era of romantic poetry, countryside walking became the thing. The nature poets Wordsworth and Coleridge were great walkers. They ambled all over the coast of North Devon and Somerset in the years immediately following the French Revolution, and later wandered in the Lake District. Walking for them was a crucial part of the creative act; it was when they thought, dreamed and also gathered images. Rural rambles were central to their new poetic philosophy, expounded in *Lyrical Ballads* (1798), of getting back to nature and simplicity. Says Coleridge in his *Biographia Literaria* (1817):

> My walks were almost daily on top Quantock, and among its sloping combes. With my pencil and memorandum book in my hand, I was making studies, as the artists call them, and often moulding my thoughts into verse, with the objects and imagery immediately before my senses.

Indeed, it was on a walk along the North Devon coast, just a few miles from where I sit this moment, that Coleridge stopped off at the now famous Ash Farm, took opium and conceived and possibly wrote "Kubla Khan."

In rather the same way as urban wanderings can be seen as seditious, these poets' rambles were viewed with suspicion by the authorities of the time, who assumed that the pair, who were known for their radical views, were up to no good, were, indeed, "loitering with intent." A spy sent by the Home Office to monitor their activities saw the two poets taking notes on the riverbank and assumed that they were plotting to bring firearms from Bristol for a planned insurrection. The government agent, whom Coleridge nicknamed "Spy Nozy" in *Bio-*

graphia Literaria, described the pair as "a mischievous gang of disaffected Englishmen" and a "sett of violent Democrats."

No chapter on walking could be complete without a nod to the private detective, who started to appear in the nineteenth century. He is an attractive character precisely because he is essentially an idler, as Walter Benjamin wrote in *Arcades*:

> Performed in the figure of the *flâneur* is that of the detective. The *flâneur* required a social legitimation of his habitus. It suited him very well to see the indolence presented as a plausible front, behind which, in reality, hides the riveted attention of an observer who will not let the unsuspecting malefactor out of his sight.

The truth of Benjamin's observation is embodied in that great literary loafer Sherlock Holmes, who, we conjecture, became a detective *because* he loved to loaf in his fictional world; to watch, to think, to walk. Like the poet, the detective does his work by walking and by sitting. He is not a victim of society; instead he watches it, he stands outside it, he enjoys it, he smiles at its foibles. And thus it is that Holmes can allow himself what seems to us, time-starved as we are, the enormous luxury of long city walks; in "The Resident Patient," he says to Watson: "What do you say to a ramble through London?" And off they go for a three-hour walk. Three hours! When was the last time you wandered round the city for three hours in congenial company, or alone? No time! Too busy! Things to do!

And who has time and leisure today in our cities? Perhaps only the homeless do. And is it not possible that some of the homeless people we pity are actually *flâneurs* in their souls? Let's not over-romanticize this, but, even today, there is a misconception about tramps. Governments and well-meaning social reformers who write columns in liberal newspapers believe that the homeless, the tramps, the vagabonds and their ilk merely need to be helped to rejoin society. They need a leg up, the theory goes, to get off the street and into productive work. This is their most fervent desire, apparently. A job would solve their problems. It does not occur to this type of interferer that maybe, just maybe, the homeless, the tramp, the vagabond has rejected those very values. They do not want a job. They do not want to become middle class, freighted with debt, worry and a boss. They do not want to keep fixed hours and spend their surplus income in department stores and theme parks. The tramp in the song "D. W. Washburn," recorded by the Monkees, says he has no job, just a bottle of wine, and that he feels fine. He doesn't want to be bothered by the do-gooders.

Yet even tramps are not too low to be exploited by the capitalist economy. George Orwell in *Down and Out in Paris and London* (1933) pointed to the swindles perpetrated on tramps in the 1930s, and revealed how, in William Cobbett's phrase, those who should be feeding the poor actually feed off the poor. In return for their freedom, tramps had to put up with being preached at by the Salvation Army and endure the most dreadful sleeping conditions.

The vagabond has traditionally been attacked by law-makers. I found this nugget in the current GCSE history syllabus for UK schoolkids: "In 1598 Parliament accepted a distinction between 'sturdy beggars' who could work but refused to and the 'impotent poor' who were too old, young, disabled or ill. Each parish, under the supervision of the JPs, was made to accept responsibility for its own poor, who were forbidden to wander about. Those unable to work were given money ('poor relief') from a poor rate levied on all inhabitants of the parish. But able-bodied vagabonds were to be 'stripped naked from the middle upwards and shall be openly whipped until his or her body be bloody.' They were then to be sent back to the parish of their birth and made to work in a 'house of correction.'"

This attitude to vagabondage was enthusiastically taken up by Nazi Germany in the mid 1930s. A list of "anti-social elements," issued by the Bavarian Political Police in August 1936, included beggars, vagabonds, gypsies and vagrants. Such freedom-seekers could, if necessary, be taken into "protective custody" (i.e. concentration camps) where they would be forcibly taught the values of hard work and discipline. "Arbeit Macht Frei" ran the legend above the gates of Auschwitz, "Work Makes Us Free."

While writing in praise of the tramp's life, I must quote this song from Izaak Walton's *The Compleat Angler*, a masterpiece of idler literature published in 1653. In this book, the happiness of the angler is thought to be exceeded only by the happiness of the beggar, the man of the road, in the summertime. Like the angler, he is poor but free:

> Bright shines the Sun, play beggars, play,
> Here's scraps enough to serve to day.
> What noise of viols is so sweet
> As when our merry clappers ring?
> What mirth doth want when beggars meet?
> A beggar's life is for a King:
> Eat, drink and play, sleep when we list,
> Go where we will, so stocks be mist.

The beggar's life is idealized as one of freedom: from work, from desire, from consumer slavery. There is a truth to this, and it's a shame that today we see homeless people as simply victims who need to be helped. This may well be the case with many; but it is also possible that others have actually chosen to live this way. They would rather be homeless, poor and free than mortgaged, employed and enslaved.

Indeed, in much of the East tramps are venerated rather than pitied. The Chinese have a deep love of the vagabond. According to Lin Yutang, the scamp, the mischievous scoundrel, the free wanderer is an ideal in Chinese society. He recounts the story of Mingliaotse, written by T'u Lung at the end of the sixteenth century. Mingliaotse was a government official who decided one day to give it all up and become a Taoist tramp, a gentleman of the road seeking nourishment in wandering: "I am going to emancipate my heart and release my spirit and travel in the Country of the Nonchalant." He finds solace in his travels, everyone he meets is enchanted by his wit, and he writes poetry distinctly Wordsworthian in character:

> I tread along the sandy bank,
> Where clouds are golden, water clear;
> The startled fairy hounds go barking
> Into the peach grove; disappear.

In Buddhism the beggar, the tramp, the vagabond is not a subject for reform or liberal hand-wringing, but, on the contrary, he represents an ideal of living, of pure living in the moment, of wandering without destination, of freedom from worldly care.

In Hindu culture, too, we find the figure of the Sadhu, a middle-aged man who, having performed his worldly responsibilities in the form of service to employer and family, decides that he will wander off with a begging bowl. He abandons all possessions ("Imagine!") and takes to the road. He is a holy figure, admired.

The great American loafing poet Walt Whitman once wrote:

> How I do love a loafer! Of all human beings, none equals your genuine, inbred, unvarying loafer. Now when I say loafer, I mean loafer; not a fellow who is lazy by fits and starts—who today will work his twelve or fourteen hours, and tomorrow doze and idle. I stand up for no such half-way business. Give me your calm, steady, philosophick son of indolence . . . he belongs to that ancient and honourable fraternity, whom I venerate above all your upstarts, your dandies, and your political oracles.

"Ancient and honourable," that's the key. Try it. Start small: be a *flâneur* in your lunch hour. Mooch. Dawdle. Float. There is a highly pleasurable feeling of superiority over others and of being in control of one's own destiny when one simply slows down the pace, and allows oneself to drift. To walk in this way is to refuse to become a victim of the city, but instead helps one to grasp it and enjoy it. You are a saint, not a sinner!

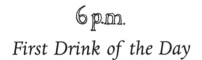

6 p.m.

First Drink of the Day

Is that the time?
Everyone

The cocktail symbolises a well-being of the spirit, so dream
all those dreams that are nearest to your heart. They can
come true and at no other time will their fulfillment
seem so near. For this is the Cocktail Hour.
CAD, The Lounge Artiste's Guidebook

Every evening at six o'clock, the homes of England resound
with the phrase, often spoken in mock-pompous tones by the
master of the house, "Well, the sun's over the yardarm, I think
we might allow ourselves a little drinky." And out comes the

gin and tonic and a collective lifting of the spirits. In really stylish homes, the cocktail shaker will emerge, closely followed by an invigorating margarita. In our house, we make do with beer.

Sensible people advise against drinking on an empty stomach, but to my mind it is the best sort of drinking. There is a sublime magic to that first drink of the evening. The cocktail, beer or wine goes straight to the nervous system, unblocked by food. There is really nothing to beat it. It marks the end of the working day, when you put worldly cares to one side and embrace good cheer and company. It is when the soul opens and we are seized by the need to chat. We are liberated. After spending the day either living in the past (regrets, reports) or in the future (anxieties, Powerpoint presentations), the first drink of the day brings us into the present moment: we become Buddhists.

That first drink also has a physically restorative effect. I find I can spend all day complaining about being tired, listless, lacking in energy, desperate for sleep. Then at six, in the pub or at home, with a pint of foaming nut-brown ale before me instead of a computer screen, I will suddenly perk up. Energy will rush back into my body. I am alive.

And with one drink, the wage slaves of the day are transformed into thinking, feeling, laughing, independent human beings. We are our own masters once more. You can see it in our faces: just walk round a city at 6 p.m. and look in through the windows of the pubs and bars—you will see smiling people, full of animated chatter. They may be complaining about the boss or their lot in general, but for a little while, and before they return to the realities of home, they are in a delightful suspended reality, where everyone is a little king or queen.

Often, we want to stretch out this moment. We stay in the pub drinking, afraid to go out into the street and back home. This results in hubby calling wife to apologize for being late; or wife calling hubby on the mobile telephone to enquire as to his whereabouts (or vice versa). This phenomenon goes right back to medieval days, when hubby would tarry on his way home from the market, drinking away the money he had just made, as Robert Burns describes it in the opening lines of "Tam O'Shanter" (1790):

> When chapman billies leave the street,
> And drouthy neibors neibors meet,
> As market-days are wearing late,
> An' folk begin to tak the gate;
> While we sit bousing at the nappy,
> An' getting fou and unco happy,
> We think na on the lang Scots miles,
> The mosses, waters, slaps, and styles,
> That lie between us and our hame,
> Where sits our sulky sullen dame,
> Gathering her brows like gathering storm,
> Nursing her wrath to keep it warm.

The drink does something to time, too. The hours we have just spent in office, shop or factory have dragged on, they have been interminable. We thought six o'clock would never arrive. My mother tells a story about her Fleet Street days as a journalist in the 1970s. Most of her colleagues were heavy boozers, and this was in the dark ages when pubs were closed from three till 5:30 p.m. She says that, somewhere around five, her colleague

Jack would start glancing up at the clock, and every two minutes would wail: "Will the pubs never open?"

But once in the bar or pub, the time simply flies by. "Is that the time?" you will hear people say. "I promised to be home by eight." We have promised ourselves to leave the pub at 7:30 p.m.; suddenly it is nine, and the dinner is in the oven.

Six o'clock is the perfect time for conversation, as we have had enough alcohol to inject our brains with a bright-eyed rush of energy, but not so much that we have descended into drawling, shouting, swearing and aggression. It's when the ideas flow and we revel in the pure pleasure of company. It's actually a perfect time for an ideas meeting.

This phenomenon of the "livener" was noted by the great painter and friend of Dr. Johnson Sir Joshua Reynolds, who said: "I am in very good spirits, when I get up in the morning. By dinner-time I am exhausted; wine puts me in the same state as when I got up; and I am sure that moderate drinking makes people talk better."

Johnson disagreed with him on this point; he thought that alcohol merely gave the illusion to oneself that one was talking better, no more. For him, to drink was to forget. "I have then often wished for it, and often taken it . . . [t]o get rid of myself, to send myself away. Wine gives great pleasure; and every pleasure is of itself a good. It is a good, unless counterbalanced by evil. A man may have a strong reason not to drink wine; and that may be greater than the pleasure. Wine makes a man better pleased with himself. I do not say that it makes him more pleasing to others."

It was in the late nineteenth century in Paris that the six o'clock feeling became so widespread as to earn its own name,

L'Heure Verte, the Green Hour. It was so called after the colour of the absinthe that was drunk at that time. Perhaps L'Heure Verte could not have existed before, as never before had so many people kept such similar hours. For one of the effects of the Industrial Revolution was a standardization, or urbanization, of working time. With this came the never-before witnessed phenomenon of vast multitudes of weary people pouring from the factories and offices and rushing to the bars and cafés.

Absinthe is a very strong, green spirit. It can be 60 to 70 per cent in strength. The French grew an absinthe habit of epic proportions (in 1874, they drank 700,000 litres of absinthe a year; in 1910, that figure had risen to 36 million litres). In Paris, in the late nineteenth century, simply *tout le monde* was sitting outside cafés sipping at the powerful spirit. "Absinthe lights up the sooty soul," wrote the decadent poet Charles Cros.

We learn from contemporary accounts that the Green Hour actually lasted at least two hours, or even all night, although I'm sure it felt like only one. "The sickly odour of absinthe lies heavily on the air," wrote a contemporary observer, H. P. Hugh. "The 'absinthe hour' of the Boulevards begins vaguely at half past five, and ends just as vaguely at half past seven." It was the idling glamour of absinthe that led me and a group of friends to begin importing it into the UK in 1999, promoting it with the slogan "Tonight We're Gonna Party Like It's 1899."

The beaux arts illustrator Henri Toulouse-Lautrec was a well-known absintheur; he even had a specially made walking stick which contained a generous supply of the Green Fairy. "At the end of the day," related the painter Gustave Moreau,

"Henri would hobble from the atelier down the curved Rue Lepic . . . he liked to go in the twilight to *étouffer un perroquet* [literally: choke a parrot—a Montmartre expression meaning to down a glass of green absinthe, commonly known as a *perroquet*]."

Toulouse-Lautrec was doubtless among those who made every effort to elongate the green hour. ". . . on the hill [the Montmartre district of Paris] it never ends. Not that it is the home of the drunkard in any way; but the deadly opal drink lasts longer than anything else, and it is the aim of Montmartre to stop as long as possible . . . and watch the world go by. To spend an hour in a really typical haunt of the Bohemians is a liberal education. There is none of the reckless gaiety of the Latin Quarter, but at the same time there is a grim delight in chaffing at death and bankruptcy." Green hours turned into green days and green nights.

Ernest Hemingway was an absinthe fan. I always liked his diary entry: "Got tight last night on absinthe. Did knife tricks." In his *For Whom the Bell Tolls* (1940), the exiled hero describes how one glass of the green stuff could conjure up fond memories of early-evening boulevard drinking:

One cup of it took the place of the evening papers, of all the old evenings in cafés, of all the chestnut trees that would be in bloom now in this month, of the great slow horses of the outer boulevards, of book shops, of kiosks, and of galleries, of the Parc Montsouris, of the Stade Buffalo, and of the Butte Chaumont, of the Guaranty Trust Company and the Île de la Cité, of Foyet's old hotel, and of being able to read and relax in the evening; of all the things he had enjoyed and forgotten and that came back to him when he tasted that opaque, bitter, tongue-numbing, brain-warming, stomach-warming, idea-changing liquid alchemy.

The English decadent poet Ernest Dowson was an absinthe fan, too. Always impecunious, his financial priorities will be familiar to anyone who has spent their twenties in the pursuit of oblivion; he wrote in a letter to a friend: "I tighten my belt in order to allow myself a sufficiency of cigarettes and absinthe." Dowson died in 1900 at the age of 32.

Absinthe was also the drink of such characters as Alfred Jarry, the crazed author of political satire *Ubu Roi* (1896), who was in the habit of dying his hair green, brandishing a revolver and had a mortal fear of water. Other acolytes included Oscar Wilde, Paul Verlaine and Degas: an elegant trio of wasters whose artistic legacy lives today. For them, absinthe-drinking was intimately bound up with a new concept of art as a force for freedom and an attack on bourgeois morals.

As is well known, there were terrific downsides to absinthe abuse. It was seen as the crack cocaine of its day. And its fans were sensitive to its paradox: absinthe kills you, but it makes you live. The very thing that seems to make life worth living is also slowly destroying your health.

Absinthe was banned in 1914 following a moral panic but over the following decades the custom of the Green Hour evolved into the cocktail hour (and its vulgar kid brother, the so-called Happy Hour).

In *The Book of Tiki: The Cult of Polynesian Pop in Fifties America* (2000), anthropologist Sven A. Kirsten reveals how, in the mid twentieth century, first California and then the whole of America began to adopt the primitive styles of Polynesia and Hawaii, of the Easter Islands and the South Seas islands, as symbolic of an earthly paradise, free of work and responsibility, an antidote to the civilized Western world. By the 1950s, America was entering a new period of material prosperity, but the work-ethic-loving Americans needed to be told how to enjoy the fruits of their labour. The answer came in Tiki. Tiki was about rum cocktails and exotic holidays and brought with it its own music—Exotica—and a host of appealing iconography.

"By the late 1950s it was definitely *de rigueur* to have a striking tribal art piece to break the monotony of your living room decor," writes Kirsten. And at the heart of this culture was the cocktail, more specifically the rum cocktail, served in a lavish Tiki cup or a bowl to be shared by couples who had removed their work clothes and put on flowery Hawaiian shirts. The most famous of these was the Zombie, and here is a 1960 recipe to get you in the mood:

> 1 oz dark Jamaican rum
> 2 oz gold Barbados rum
> 1 oz white Puerto Rican rum
> 1 oz apricot brandy
> ¾ oz papaya nectar
> ¾ oz unsweetened pineapple juice
> juice of one large lime
> teaspoon finely granulated sugar

Fine poetry indeed. Kirsten also reproduces the following inscription from a Hawaiian bar which gave its customers special certificates:

Beachcombers of the South Seas welcome to their indolent, care-free ranks

Your Name Here

who has lived beneath the Southern Cross on a Pacific island of Eden—Tahiti; who has languorously lolled on sparkling beaches, breathed the intoxicating scent of frangipani, and been lulled by the soft caress of South Sea zephyrs; who has made an art out of indulging in the luxury of relaxation and enjoyment of life. Attest. J. Combard, General Manager on Oct 1, 1960.

The next logical step was to bring a piece of this holiday idyll back home, and Tiki was a way of creating a paradise in your own backyard. Easy-listening music by the likes of Martin Denny was played, and front rooms were converted into cocktail lounges. Picasso, funnily enough, pops up as a key figure in the world of Tiki. He was a fan of primitive art and came up with the line, much loved by Tiki fanatics: "Ah, good taste! What a dreadful thing! Taste is the enemy of creativeness."

The early *Playboy* magazines of the 1960s embraced this cocktail culture fantasy. The cocktail was associated with Hawaiian shirts, pipes, pleasure and free-and-easy sexuality. *Playboy*s of the time teem with images of boss Hugh Hefner enjoying himself with a cocktail in one hand, a bevy of beauties around him and a pipe clamped in his grinning jaws. It might have been a fantasy, but it was a great fantasy, and must have done much to ease the heavy work burdens which were beginning to become a reality in post-war America.

I imagine the efficient martini was the *Playboy* first drink of the day, rather than the rum fantasy of the Tiki world. Just as the newly industrialized Paris of the late nineteenth century needed absinthe to relax, New York and other US cities in the fifties and sixties needed the martini. The triangular martini glass, with its single olive, became a symbol of the age. "[W]hen that first martini hits the liver like a silver bullet," wrote a contemporary wag, "there is a sigh of contentment that can be heard in Dubuque." The world of the martini belongs to a lost era of elegance, It is *The Sweet Smell of Success*, *Grand Hotel*, Holly Golightly, Cary Grant, Frank Sinatra.

I myself have calmed down somewhat, and find myself in the strange position of having forsaken cocktails for real ale. Worse, I have just ordered a home-brew kit. This is all part of my experiment to live as in a pre-industrial age. The cocktail is really a corollary of the hard-work culture: extreme toil needs an extreme drink to counteract the misery. In a life where work and play are more closely mingled, the true idle life, then a gentler brew is perhaps all that is required. I suppose if we were really happy, there would be no need to drink at all, but a life without booze seems to me to be a pretty miserable prospect.

7p.m.

On Fishing

With my silken line and delicate hook
I wander in a myriad of ripples
And find freedom

Li Yu, "Fisherman's Song,"
c. tenth century

In the wall of Winchester Cathedral is a stained-glass window. It depicts a man sitting in the shade of a tree. He wears a black stovepipe hat and knee-length boots, and has shoulder-length white hair. His right hand supports his chin and his left hand cradles a book. At his feet sit a wicker basket, a net and a rod. Behind him, in the background, a river winds twice into the distance. Trees border it; a hill rises behind its banks. At the foot of this idyllic portrait of riverbank loafing there is an inscription that reads: "Study to be quiet."

The man in this languid posture is Sir Izaak Walton, the seventeenth-century author of *The Compleat Angler, or, the Contemplative Man's Recreation*, first published in 1653. *The Compleat Angler* is a how-to fishing manual, but it is also a work of philosophy, a defence of angling as a noble calling, a celebration of tranquillity and the *vita contemplativa*. One of the best-selling books the world has ever seen, supposedly second only to the Bible, it was recommended by the poet, dramatist and clerk at the East India Company Charles Lamb to his friend Coleridge in the following glowing terms:

> It breathes the very spirit of innocence, purity and simplicity of heart. It would sweeten a man's temper at any time to read it; it would Christianise every angry, discordant passion; pray make yourself acquainted with it.

Lamb was absolutely right; even today, to read *The Compleat Angler* is to enter a delicious world of peace and calm. But to put the emphasis on its Christian nature makes it sound more pious than it actually is. In fact Walton's world is also filled with lusty pleasures. There are rosy-cheeked milkmaids singing ballads in the woods, visits to the alehouse (where he appears to spend as much time as by the river), trout cooked slowly in white wine. But it does not merely offer escapism or an amusing insight into pre-industrial living: its truths and its wisdom stay with you. It is a nourishing read rather than just a distraction.

What *The Compleat Angler* proves is something I had long suspected: that fishing is a superb way of doing nothing. It legitimizes idleness. Although I am not much of an angler myself, and have only been fishing a handful of times, it has always seemed clear to me that fishing is the idler's sport *par excellence*. True, there is a purpose in mind (catching a fish) and true, angling involves all manner of hooks, lines and baits, and there is a certain amount of activity required in getting to the place where one is to fish. But the real meat of fishing, what lies at its heart, is surely perfect stillness and inactivity. It is about being quiet, immobile; it is about waiting. It is about being and nothingness. It is for philosophers and poets. In fact, it *is* philosophy and poetry.

The Compleat Angler is written in the form of a dialogue between a fisher (*pescator*) and a traveller (*viator*). Through the book, *pescator* takes *viator* fishing and teaches him his watery philosophy. Each evening, the pair return to the alehouse and after eating that day's catch, they sing a song in praise of the country life, or of fishing. Here is an example for us all to learn and bellow to our fellow commuters in the morning:

> Oh, the brave Fishers life,
> It is the best of any,
> 'Tis full of pleasure, void of strife,
> And 'tis belov'd of many:
> Other joyes
> are but toyes,
> only this
> lawful is,
> for our skil
> breeds no ill,
> but content and pleasure.

For Walton, angling is a great harmonizer. It elegantly brings together two seemingly opposing attitudes: doing and not doing. Walton alludes to the ancient debate, first argued in classical times, "whether *Contemplation* or *Action* be the chiefest thing wherin the happiness of a man doth most consist in this world?" Well, argues Walton: "[B]oth these meet together, and do most properly belong to the most honest, ingenious, harmless Art of Angling." One might argue that there is a lot more contemplation than action, but fishing does have an end in mind, and more so in the seventeenth century, when one was actually allowed to keep and eat the fish one caught. Nowadays, the fish get thrown back in the river. In 1653 there were, of course, more fish to go round: the population of Britain then was six million, a tenth of what it is now.

It is also a fact that, at around the time of the publication of *The Compleat Angler*, roughly 90 per cent of the population lived in small villages or towns and worked in agriculture or crafts. But Walton could see that the rural way of life was beginning to be threatened by a new urban work ethic, promoted by the go-getting Puritans, and he saw angling as a statement against the new materialism. Defending angling against the "serious grave men" who "scoff" at it, Walton writes:

[T]here be many men that are by others taken to be serious grave men, which we contemn and pitie; men of sowre complexions; money-getting-men, that spend all their time first in getting, and next in anxious care to keep it; men that are condemn'd to be rich, and alwayes discontented, or busie. For these poor-rich-men, wee Anglers pitie them . . .

Any idler with his eyes open will be familiar with the "sowre complexions" of those busy men who seek riches, and who would haughtily "scoff" at anglers, or, as the modern parlance has it, "take the piss." I should think that fishing becomes all the more enjoyable when one sees it as a revolutionary act, a protest against the consumer culture. Here is another angling rhyme from Walton:

> Man's life is but vain;
> For 'tis subject to pain,
> And sorrow, and short as a bubble;
> 'Tis a hodge podge of business
> And money, and care,
> And care, and money and trouble.
> But we'll take no care
> When the weather proves fair
> Nor will we vex now, though it rain;
> We'll banish all sorrow
> And sing till to morrow,
> And Angle and Angle again.

This may not be the most elegant piece of verse ever committed to paper, but it has its own charms, I think, and certainly gets the point across. In a world of toil, trouble and money worries, angling provides a welcome oasis of serenity. And if this was true in 1653, when the consumer culture was a mere bring-and-buy sale compared to the vast global shopping mall it has since become, think how much truer it is today. And the great thing is that even now there is so much countryside left to enjoy, so many tranquil spots. It is nonsense to complain that the countryside has been destroyed by urbanization; there are still millions of acres of unspoilt riverbanks, fields and woods out there for the finding. It's even possible that they are less populated than they were four hundred years ago, since most of the rural population have gradually migrated to the towns.

Central to the restful power of angling, says Walton, is that it brings man into close proximity with water. Rivers are the ideal spot for tranquil reflection; Walton cites the children of Israel who chose the banks of the Babylon to sit down and remember Zion. "Both Rivers, and the inhabitants of the watery Element," he maintains, "were created for wise men to contemplate, and fools to pass by without consideration."

So it is that the idler has through history been drawn to water and to rivers. The children's classic *The Wind in the Willows* (1908) by Kenneth Grahame (who also wrote *The Golden Age* [1895] and *Dream Days* [1898] about his idyllic country childhood) opens with Mole deciding to abandon his duties and responsibilities and go out and enjoy the day:

> Spring was moving in the air above and in the earth below and around him, penetrating even his dark and lowly little house with its spirit of divine discontent and longing. It was small wonder, then, that he suddenly flung down his brush on the floor, said "Bother!" and "O blow!" and also "Hang spring-cleaning!" and bolted out of the house without even waiting to put on his coat.

So begins Mole's day, and so begins his transformation from a put-upon little slave creature to a liver of life, thanks to the teachings of Rat. "This day was only the first of many similar ones for the emancipated Mole, each of them longer and full of interest as the ripening summer moved onward. He learnt to swim and to row, and entered into the joy of running water . . ."

The spiritual descendant of Sir Izaak Walton is a man called Chris Yates, and I have him to thank for sending me on this enjoyable journey into the soul of fishing. I first encountered Yates when we ran an interview with him in the *Idler*. Celebrated in fishing circles for catching a record-breaking carp, Yates is also a true eccentric who has never allowed work or other people's expectations to get in the way of the life he wants to lead: the angler's life.

Yates chose his Wiltshire home for its proximity to the fish-packed Avon and has published numerous books, all written in bed or on the riverbank. He also edits *Waterlog* magazine, a publication for soul fishers. One autumn day, Yates took me fishing in an attempt to reveal its pleasures and mysteries. He was *pescator* and I was *viator*. The first great thing was that, in the six hours from lunch to dusk, we caught no fish. "It's nice to catch a fish," the master explained, "but it's not really the point."

What is the point? Well, what the angler is trying to achieve—although if you try too hard you're missing the point—is to be. Yates talks of merging with the water, abandoning oneself to the contemplation of the mysterious world beneath the surface of the water. "It's like a veil," he says. "You want to lift it, make contact with that other dimension. Water can hypnotize and tranquillize, inspire and galvanize like no other medium."

Ted Hughes captures this sense of total immersion beautifully in his poem "Go Fishing" (1983), in which he writes of joining the water, letting the mind melt into the earth and forgetting language.

When fishing for long periods, then, the intellect vanishes; rationality and even language are abandoned. One starts to flow, to float. And we think of John Lennon in "Tomorrow Never Knows," the well-known Beatles fishing song, where he counsels floating downstream and turning off your mind.

Angling is a form of meditation, an out-of-body, out-of-mind experience. But sooner or later the angler must return to the world. As Hughes puts it, the world comes back like a white hospital, urgent, anxious, busy, ill, sterile, filled with death, rationality pitted hopelessly against suffering. The image of the white hospital is a brilliant one for the world and our attempts to control it.

The angler's privilege, of course, especially today when most of us live in cities and towns, is to escape the urban brouhaha and get down with nature, and therein lies one of the real appeals. In the 1911 classic *An Angler at Large*, William Caine describes a day when he catches no fish but has encounters with many other creatures. "Fishing I had had none, but with a swift, a duck's egg, a waterhen, and a rat to my credit, I could not complain that I had lacked sport."

Fishing is democratic. Anyone can do it, and anyone can be transformed by it into a poet or philosopher. The best-selling angling book of the fifties was an illustrated manual called *Mr. Crabtree Goes Fishing* (1950), written and drawn by Bernard Venables. Originally serialized in the *Daily Mirror*, it followed in essence the form of *The Compleat Angler*, being a dialogue between a master, the kindly, paternal, pipe-smoking Mr. Crabtree, and a novice, Mr. Crabtree's eager son, Robert. And like *The Compleat Angler*, the passages of practical instruction are interspersed with reflective interludes. Through fishing, Venables promoted the joys of doing nothing in beautiful surroundings to ordinary working people: "In Bedfordshire, in Huntingdonshire, in Suffolk and Rutland you may go with your rod and forget time. Nothing will seem real but this drowsy solitude in which you are lost . . . For to me, though there comes all the action of hooking and playing, there is a trance-like idling about it all. The morning has such a fragile loveliness that it seems far removed from ordinary reality."

For Venables, carp fishing is the idlest of all, as it involves very long periods of inactivity broken by a paroxysm of excitement when the fish bites: "He who fishes for carp must be ready to do so with the greatest devotion. He must be ready to wait long hours of tense inactivity. But when a climax does come to the vigil, it may be so tempestuous that many a fisherman is not equal to it." This way of working—long periods of doing nothing followed by a sudden frenetic burst of activity—is just how an idler likes it. Anything but the tedium of regular and sustained application. This methodology goes back to Dr. Johnson's characterization of the idler's work patterns: "The Idler, though sluggish, is yet alive, and may be stimulated to vigour and activity . . . the diligence of an idler is rapid and impetuous." I suppose it's no surprise, then, that Chris Yates is a carp fisherman. No surprise, either, that Dr. Johnson was a fan of the work of Izaak Walton.

Why 7 p.m.? Well, the reason I have put fishing at this time is because dusk is one of the best times to catch fish: it is when they are coming out of their hiding places underwater to seek out food. "It is the time when everything comes alive," says

Yates. "It's when the big fish come out." Or as William Caine puts it in *An Angler at Large*: "As the light fades, sport is brisk."

Dusk is also a time of peculiar magic: I remember on my fishing trip with Yates that it was at dusk that I really started to "cease" as Ted Hughes put it, when I merged with the water and stopped thinking. The light fades, other anglers are going home, water and not-water become one. Outlines lose their distinctness, trees become a mass of shadow, the moon may start to appear. Here is Caine on the dusk hour: "An hour passed, a delicious hour in which the sun, creeping unwillingly to bed after his riot among the clouds, threw out longer and longer shadows under the trees, flushed the green downs with rose, performed miracles—for me." I like that final "for me," for I remember clearly the sense that at this time, standing on the riverbank, you really are extremely lucky, and that there is a lot to enjoy in life if you make the effort to go out there and drink it in.

Reflecting again on the stained glass window in Winchester Cathedral, I'm struck by how the phrase "Study to be Quiet" expresses the paradox of idling, which is that you have to work at being idle. "Being Quiet"—to those accustomed to noise, bustle, turmoil, work—does not necessarily come easily. You have to study for it, practise, think, reflect, ponder. And ponder daily if one is not to get caught up in a whirlwind of duties and obligations, of "have tos" rather than "want tos." The journey towards idleness is the journey of a lifetime. The great thing is that we know how the journey will end, and that is in total idleness, which is death.

8 p.m.
Smoking

Je ne veux pas travailler
Je ne veux pas déjeuner
Je veux seulement oublier
Et puis je fume
From "Sympathique" by the Pink Martinis
(with apologies to Apollinaire)

When I first started smoking, at the age of 14, I felt as if I had undergone a kind of rebirth or reawakening. Discovering tobacco was like finding a secret portal, a gateway into a sophisticated garden of worldly pleasures and independent living. Smoking felt good, it looked cool and it expressed one's urge to rebel against authority, to create one's own path through life rather than meekly following the pre-approved paths of parents and teachers. To smoke was to be free. I had also found a friend, a very good friend. Possibly a friend for life. To give up would be to suffer a bereavement, made doubly worse by the fact that for the rest of my life I would have to endure the sight of others enjoying the company of that lost friend.

But we also know—how could we possibly avoid the fact, so efficient are the healthists—that smoking is bad, and so begins the lifelong struggle between saying "yes" and saying "no." At 14, I resolved to give up when I was 18. At 18, I resolved to give up at 21. At 21, I felt sure I would actively want to give up by the time I reached 30. Now in my mid thirties, I feel certain that by 40 I will have rid myself of this vice. However, for now, I smoke. In fact I am smoking at this very moment, and when I have finished this sentence, I will read it while blowing smoke at the computer screen.

The inner battle that smoking presents—to give up or not to give up—is mirrored by the civic battle that has been played out ever since tobacco was brought back from the Americas to England by Sir Walter Raleigh in the sixteenth century. Just a few decades after Raleigh got us hooked on the soothing weed, the moralists started saying "no." In 1604, King James I, self-appointed Keeper of the Public Morals, the kind of man who relished torturing witches, published his diatribe against smoking, "A Counterblaste to Tobacco," a rare example of good writing coming from the pen of a moralist. Motivated partly by his personal hatred of the libertine ways and cool easy charm of Sir Walter, his "Counterblaste" is a spirited rant that introduces all the great arguments against smoking that are still employed by its detractors today: it's bad for you, it stinks, your wife hates it, it's selfish, uncivilized and encourages laziness.

For one thing, King James was incensed that we genteel Britons should have lowered ourselves so far as to mimic the habits of the uncouth savage. To James I, smoking was a primitive custom: "what honour or policie can moove us to imitate the barbarous and beastly maners of the wilde, godlesse, and slavish Indians, especially in so vile and stinking a custome? . . . Why doe we not as well imitate them in walking naked as they doe? in preferring glasses, feathers, and such toyes, to golde and precious stones, as they doe? yea why do we not denie God and adore the Devill, as they doe?" He saw tobacco as a revolt against so-called civilized values: property, money-worship and deference to a Christian God.

Another argument King James makes against smoking is one I remember being attacked with by teenage non-smokers: that we only smoke because we think it's cool. "[W]e cannot be content unless we imitate every thing that our fellowes doe," writes James, which is rather like our parents saying: "And if Johnny jumped off a bridge, would you jump off a bridge as well?"

To smoke, James I says, is to be irresponsible, it is to abandon one's duty to "King and Commonwealth." It is, moreover, corrupting to women: "the husband shall not bee ashamed, to reduce thereby his delicate, wholesome and cleane complexioned wife, to that extremitie, that either shee must also corrupt her sweete breath therewith, or else resolve to live in a perpetuall stinking torment." The essay ends with the damning conclusion: "A custome lothsome to the eye, hatefull to the Nose, harmefull to the braine, dangerous to the Lungs, and in the blacke stinking fume thereof, neerest resembling the horrible Stigian smoke of the pit that is bottomelesse."

Needless to say, King James's "Counterblaste" had absolutely no effect whatsoever on the smoking habits of his people, and a year after its publication he tried a more direct attack: tax. Importers were required to cough up (sorry) six shillings and eight pence for every pound of tobacco they brought to the country. This double salvo—combining anti-smoking propaganda with punitive tax on the smoker—is a method still in use today by Western governments. In the UK, all tobacco advertising has been banned and we pay £3.50 per pack to the treasury in tax. The public health warnings that adorn packets of cigarettes grow more terrifying and dominating every year. After toying around with gentle suggestions such as "Tobacco Seriously Damages Health" or "Smoking While Pregnant May Harm Your Baby," discreetly placed on the pack, they now require tobacco companies to print the unambiguous legend "SMOKING KILLS" in giant letters, and in a font designed to look as ugly as possible. Will these measures have much effect? One doubts it. In fact, it would be difficult to think of a more effective inducement to smoke to the reckless 14-year-old, who is going to live for ever.

Why did smoking catch on in such a big way, and why at this particular point in history? For the Francophile academic Richard Klein, author of *Cigarettes are Sublime* (1993), there is a simple answer: tobacco was needed to calm us down because the passing of the medieval age, with its religious certainties, was making us anxious. "The introduction of tobacco into Europe in the sixteenth century corresponded with the arrival of the Age of Anxiety, the beginning of modern consciousness that accompanied the invention and universalization of printed books, the discovery of the New World, the development of rational, scientific methods, and the concurrent loss of medieval theological reassurances." Which is another way of saying: God felt so sorry for man he gave us tobacco.

The Victorian writer J. M. Barrie, author of the Peter Pan books, takes a more positive view, arguing that the dawn of the Elizabethan age was a sort of year zero for smokers. He wrote a hymn to tobacco called *My Lady Nicotine* (1890), a smoking biography, where he argued that tobacco woke us up and helped us become great, noble and wise:

> The Elizabethan age might be better named the beginning of the smoking era. No unprejudiced person who has given thought to the subject can question the propriety of dividing our history into two periods—the pre-smoking and the smoking. When Raleigh, in honor of whom England should have changed its name, introduced tobacco into this country, the glorious Elizabethan age began. I am aware that those hateful persons called Original Researchers now maintain that Raleigh was not the man; but to them I turn a deaf ear. I know, I feel, that with the introduction of tobacco England woke up from a long sleep. Suddenly a new zest had been given to life. The glory of existence became a thing to speak of. Men who had hitherto only concerned themselves with the narrow things of home put a pipe into their mouths and became philosophers. Poets and dramatists smoked until all ignoble ideas were driven from them, and into their place rushed such high thoughts as the world had not known before. Petty jealousies no longer had hold of statesmen, who smoked, and agreed to work together for the public weal. Soldiers and sailors felt, when engaged with a foreign foe, that they were fighting for their pipes. The whole country was

stirred by the ambition to live up to tobacco. Every one, in short, had now a lofty ideal constantly before him.

The connection between lofty ideals and smoking is, I would argue, the same as the connection between lofty ideals and doing nothing. Smoking is idleness, and it is hard to be lofty when you're toiling and busy. Like angling, smoking transforms the common man into something more heroic, more complete; it makes a master of a serf. "The pipe," wrote William Makepeace Thackeray, "draws wisdom from the lips of the philosopher, and shuts up the mouths of the foolish; it generates a style of conversation contemplative, thoughtful, benevolent, and unaffected."

My favourite oriental philosopher, Lin Yutang, was a fan of smoking. In fact, he was heroically irresponsible in this regard, and tells us that he "started a magazine called the *Analects Fortnightly*, in which I consistently tried to disprove the myth of the harmfulness of smoking." Yutang is in agreement with Thackeray on the philosophical benefits of smoking. Smoking, he wrote in 1938, brings about "complete spiritual well-being, that condition of keen, imaginative perception, and full, vibrant, creative energy—a condition necessary to our perfect enjoyment of a friend's conversation by the fireside, or to the creating of real warmth in the reading of an ancient book, or to that bringing forth of a perfect cadence of words and thought from the mind that we know as authorship."

Smoking has often been linked to laziness. King James warned the heavy smoker that "all his members shall become feeble, his spirits dull, and in the end, as a drowsie lazy belly-god, he shall evanish in a Lethargie." But we "drowsie lazy-belly gods" see this injection of "Lethargie" as a good thing. In *Cigarettes are*

Sublime, Richard Klein argues this point in almost poetic terms: "The moment of taking a cigarette allows one to open a parenthesis in the time of ordinary experience, a space and a time of heightened attention that give rise to a feeling of transcendence, evoked through the ritual of fire, smoke, cinder connecting hand, lungs, breath and mouth. It procures a little rush of infinity that alters perspectives, however slightly, and permits, albeit briefly, an ecstatic standing outside of oneself." Phew! So that's what we're doing when we have a fag break, when we ecstatically stand outside the office door.

Like fishing, smoking harmonizes activity and inactivity. When smoking, you are not doing nothing, you are smoking. You are both busy and still. This paradox is eloquently expressed by Oscar Wilde in *The Importance of Being Earnest* (1899):

LADY BRACKNELL: . . . Do you smoke?

JACK: Well, yes, I must admit I smoke.

LADY BRACKNELL: I am glad to hear it. A man should always have an occupation of some kind.

Smoking and idleness go hand in hand partly because it's almost impossible to do physical work (although very possible to think) while smoking. "The smoker of cigarettes must always, at each instant, have two hands free and lips also; he can therefore be neither someone ambitious, nor a worker, nor, with very few exceptions, a poet or an artist; every task is forbidden him, even the ineffable pleasure of screwing." So wrote Théodore de Banville, the French critic and friend to smokers Baudelaire and Manet, in 1890.

The French are much given to contemplation of abstracts, so

it comes as no surprise that they are particularly good at smoking. Every schoolboy with pretensions towards being an intellectual treasures in his mind the famous photograph of Albert Camus looking distinctly Bogartesque with his collars turned up, a cigarette between his lips and an expression of amused detachment on his face. And his fellow existentialist Jean-Paul Sartre, when asked in the 1940s by a magazine to name the most important things in his life, answered: "I don't know. Everything. Living. Smoking." We might even say that smoking actually brings together being and nothingness: it is while smoking that you can actually *be* for a moment, but smoking is also a nothing, it has no practical use. It was a Frenchman, too, who came up with the phrase *"la cigarette: faire vivre tout en tuant"*: smoking makes you feel alive while killing you.

In France, the iconography of smoking is intimately bound up with ideas of freedom and abandon. In France, you have Le Zouave cigarette papers which depict the Algerian soldier; you have gypsy images on Gauloises, a sort of Bizet's Carmen type, a dangerous woman. With the exception of Camel, British and American cigarette packets don't feature pictures at all. They rely on typography. (And have you also noticed that the cheaper the cigarette, the grander the name? Camel are expensive, Mayfair and Superkings are cheap.)

Smoking as an expression of the will to freedom is noted also by Virginia Nicholson in her study of the radical British writers and artists of the early part of the twentieth century, *Among the Bohemians* (2002):

> [T]obacco smoking had long been regarded by male Bohemians as an activity of primary significance, almost a poetic initiation.

Like the smoking of marijuana in a later epoch, it was celebrated by Théophile Gautier's romantic contemporaries in verse and fiction. Arthur Ransome placed talking, drinking and smoking together as the three indispensable pleasures of life—to be enjoyed in the company of "half a dozen fellows."

It was only natural, then, that smoking should also be taken up by the feisty females of the era, on the threshold of feminism:

But females were not content to be left out of such pleasures, and soon Ransome's male havens were invaded by advanced women brandishing cheroots. [Contemporary novelist] Ethel Mannin recalled how flagrant such behaviour seemed in those early years: 'The year would have been 1916 or 1917, not later. The girl, whose name I remember as Monica, gave me a De Reszke Turkish cigarette from a small packet, and there we two young girls viciously sat, with our pot of tea and our toasted scones, smoking, and in public . . ."

This craving for independence was also exploited in the 1920s by the manufacturers of Lucky Strike, who cleverly branded their cigarettes as "torches of freedom" in a successful effort to attract female smokers. The idea was repeated in the emancipated 1960s by Virginia Slims, with their "You've Come a Long Way, Baby" tagline. Doubtless the Bohemian ladies of leisure enjoyed the aura of devil-may-care loucheness that smoking conferred on them. And back in the nineteenth century, Baudelaire had observed in his "Les Salons de 1848" the same attitude in prostitutes of the Paris bordellos: "Prostrate they display themselves in desperate attitudes of boredom, in bar-

room indolence, with masculine cynicism, smoking cigarettes
to kill time with the resignation of oriental fatalism."

Smoking is shocking, stinky, useless, harmful to the health;
no wonder its use is opposed by those unfortunates, epitomized
by New York's Mayor Bloomberg, who feel weighed down by a
sense of civic responsibility (my New York friend Tom says that
there are so many people smoking in the street that you have
to go *inside* for a breath of fresh air). And for Lin Yutang, this
itself is another advantage of smoking. It annoys the great and
the good, the rational, the correct, the proper, the sensible:

> Much as I like reasonable persons, I hate completely rational
> beings. For that reason, I am always scared and ill at ease when
> I enter a house in which there are no ash trays. The room is apt
> to be too clean and orderly, the cushions are apt to be in their
> right places, and the people are apt to be correct and unemo-
> tional. And immediately I am put on my best behavior, which
> means the same thing as the most uncomfortable behavior.

Smoking actually does what great satire is supposed to do: it
comforts the afflicted and afflicts the comfortable. The good hate
it—liberal commentators still wonder why poor people waste
their meagre resources on smoking, without realizing that it
actually makes life worth living. The oppressed love it. George
Orwell, writing of the physical hardships of being *Down and Out
in Paris and London*, said: "It was tobacco that made everything
tolerable." And in *Nickel and Dimed*, Barbara Ehrenreich reports
that smoking gives a fleeting sense of autonomy to waitresses
at grim restaurants: "[W]ork is what you do for others; smoking
is what you do for yourself. I don't know why the antismoking

crusaders have never grasped the element of defiant self-nurturance that makes the habit so endearing to its victims—as if, in the American workplace, the only thing people have to call their own is the tumors they are nourishing and the spare moments they devote to feeding them."

And now to an important question: how to smoke? Should true idlers roll their own? Smoke ready-made cigarettes? Or perhaps cigars? Or even the pipe? Let us look to the poets for an answer.

> Sublime tobacco! which from East to West
> Cheers the tar's labour or the Turkman's rest;
> Which on the Moslem's ottoman divides
> His hours, and rivals opium and his brides;
> Magnificent in Stamboul, but less grand,
> Though not less loved, in Wapping or the Strand;
> Divine in hookas, glorious in a pipe,
> When tipp'd with amber, mellow, rich, and ripe;
> Like other charmers, wooing the caress
> More dazzlingly when daring in full dress;
> Yet thy true lovers more admire by far
> Thy naked beauties—Give me a cigar!

Thus spake Lord Byron (in *The Island*, 1823), who clearly favoured the audaciously naked cigar to the demure and clothed pipe. But the problem with cigars nowadays is that they tend to be seen as status symbols rather than instruments of pleasure. A cigar signifies rich, smug capitalist rather than poet/philosopher/monk. As Walt Whitman remarked, a cigar "generally has a smoky fire at one end and a conceited spark at the other."

For my part, I am a convert to rollies. This is a habit that I am teased for by smokers of ready-mades, who say I should smoke a "proper" cigarette, and save myself the hassle of rolling one up. There they are, pre-rolled, easy. But for me, the act of rolling is part of the pleasure. While rolling, you cannot work, and so the rollie extends the pleasure of smoking. They also last longer, and go out more frequently. What's more, they provide a more satisfying smoke (low-tar brands are hypocritical: either smoke, or don't). The final glory of the rollie is that buying tobacco is so much cheaper than buying cigarettes.

Before the 1960s, it was the pipe that was beloved of literary men and reflective types. Its use has all but died out now, but at the turn of the century, it appears that everyone was smoking one. In J. M. Barrie's *My Lady Nicotine* and throughout the works of Jerome K. Jerome, the writers and their buddies were seldom without a pipe. On my desk sits a copy of *Pipe and Pouch: The Smoker's Own Book of Poetry*, published in 1894, which contains 134 poems in praise of smoking.

> O blessed pipe,
> That now I clutch within my gripe,
> What joy is in thy smooth, round bowl,
> As black as coal.

Well, I never claimed it was *good* poetry.

I must say I would recommend the pipe to the student of idleness. If you can withstand the ridicule and admonishments of loved ones, then taking up the pipe can be a way of flying back to a lost age of gentlemanly reflection. Pipes require time and leisure. I occasionally smoke one. My girlfriend, Victoria, hates it. When I asked her why—perhaps she did not like the smell?—she replied: "No. It's the attitude." I suppose she can't stand to see me idle. She has said I am allowed to smoke it as long as she never has to see me doing it and as long as I don't send any photographs of me smoking it into the public domain. This is a great shame, as I would have liked to have been smoking a pipe in my author photograph. I think the pipe would have communicated a love of ease and contemplation. But I suppose I ought not to threaten domestic harmony—a topic, as it happens, which crops up frequently in the *Pipe and Pouch* anthology. Many of the poets fret over that old smoker's conundrum: cigar or wife—and generally opt for the cigar, as Rudyard Kipling did:

> A million surplus Maggies are willing to bear the yoke;
> And a woman is only a woman, but a good cigar is a Smoke.

Another good thing about smoking a pipe is that one does not have to give up smoking cigarettes. Indeed, Mallarmé was of the view "cigarettes for summer, pipe for winter." I suppose the ideal would be to have the whole lot in one's household: a pipe and the whole panoply of pipy products; a carton of cigarettes; an ounce of rolling tobacco and lots of Rizla papers, and a stash of fine cigars for special occasions. I understand that in Victorian times an item known as a "smoking table" was a common feature in middle-class houses. It offered all manner of drawers and shelves for storing the various paraphernalia required by the dedicated smoker. We know, of course, about smoking jackets: those dressing-gown-for-the-day garments which supposedly had the practical purpose of absorbing the smell of smoke, in order that one could retire to one's lady's chamber without offending her delicate nose. The fez, it is said, was designed with the same purpose in mind. Truly, a golden age has passed.

Will the moralists win? Anti-tobacconists are the puritans, controllers, dam-builders, people who interfere and, against nature, try to redirect man's impulses in a direction contrary to the wishes of nature, of God, we might even say. Smokers, they go with the flow. But they may die early.

One of the problems with smoking, it is argued, is the inconvenience it causes to non-smokers. In Victorian days, when we made allowances for smokers rather than banishing them into the cold, houses had special smoking rooms, where any smokers in the company could retire and pursue their vice without molesting others. Smoking rooms should be brought back to the home and the office. They should be comfortable, club-like; they should offer books and newspapers, a place to ponder, reflect and digest.

We should buy fezzes and smoking jackets. We should roll our own. In short: we should celebrate our smoking, and remove the guilt surrounding it. I think we might paradoxically find that if we did so, we would smoke less. Freedom would bring responsibility.

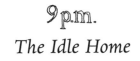 9 p.m.

The Idle Home

Without stirring abroad
One can know the whole world;
Without looking out of the window
One can see the way of heaven.
Lao Tzu, *Tao Te Ching* (*c.* fourth century BC)

And at the doors and windows seem to call,
As heav'n and earth they would together mell;
Yet the least entrance find they none at all;
Whence sweeter grows our rest secure in massy hall.
James Thomson, *The Castle of Indolence* (1748)

"Staying in is the new going out" was a joke I made at a meeting once. I was working at the *Guardian* newspaper on special projects, and we had developed a homes-and-interiors supplement called "Space." The task was to fire up the advertising department with enthusiasm about this new section, and I sought to do this by virtue of what I considered to be this terribly witty line.

Though daft and glib, there remains some truth in the comment. Going out all the time can be oppressive. It's hard work. Trying to keep up with the latest bar, club, movie, gallery, show or band is a full-time occupation, and one always feels as if there is something better going on somewhere else. One goes to a trendy bar and feels *au courant* for a few minutes, until one learns that in the depths of this trendy bar is a VIP room; perhaps that is where the real action is, you think. Get into one of these VIP rooms, and you'll find that the really cool people have just gone up to a private hotel room. Get to the private hotel room, and you find you are talking to the hanger-on rather than the star. Talk to the star, and discover they are boring. It's all really too much psychic effort. So the declaration that you are going to "stay in" is a little victory for the soul, I believe. It means that, for a night at least, you have put aside the world and its seductions. You have said to yourself, "I don't care." You are going to create your own little paradise of duvets, televisions and pizzas, your own castle of indolence.

On a simple level, of course, staying in is the idler's dream, because of the low physical effort involved. It avoids the tedious and costly business of getting ready, leaving the house, travelling somewhere else, attending the function and then enduring the still more tedious and costly business of getting home again at the end of it all. The entertainment is often undertaken out of duty, and is not of one's own choosing. Planned schemes of merriment, as Dr. Johnson rightly pointed out, rarely turn into the best evenings, which are usually the unplanned ones, when you have abandoned yourself to fate and chance and chaos.

Beyond the obvious attractions of staying at home, there are also social and spiritual benefits to this particular piece of in-action. First and foremost, staying at home represents an attack on the "go" culture that surrounds us. Walking through any city during the day, one can hardly fail to notice the number of billboards and shop titles that exhort us to *go*. Go go go! MTV and other satellite channels batter us with images of skydivers, bungee jumpers, skateboarders, snowboarders, jet-skiers, surfers, mountain bikers, off-roaders, and their message is clear: Get out there, dude! Awesome! Don't just sit at home! Do something! Do anything! Don't stop. Don't think. Go for it! Just do it!

The idler surveys this dismal mishmash of lifestyle options and decides: just don't do it. Just don't. Don't go—stop. Instead of *going* he decides to *stay* and simply be. The idler has a soul which requires contemplation, and instead of diverting activity holidays and theme nights out he has a vague dream of sitting in a shack on a hillside in China, a wispy beard on his chin and a wise and merry smile on his lips, reflecting on the beauty of nature and the folly of man. Indeed, many of our wisest thinkers have counselled staying in.

The lines at the opening of this chapter are from the classic of Chinese philosophy, the *Tao Te Ching*. Written around the fourth century BC, its authorship is uncertain but many scholars attribute the sayings it contains to a writer called Lao Tzu. The *Tao Te Ching* is the principal text in the Chinese vein of thought known as Taoism. Full of paradox, its central tenet is *wu wei*, or the philosophy of inaction. Those wild old chuckling Chinese loved the image of the river, which takes the course of least resistance on its path from mountain to sea, and in doing so creates unique and beautiful curves. *Wu wei* is about going with the flow in one's everyday life, it is about surrendering one's destiny to fate and gently floating downstream with detachment, wonder and wisdom. I suppose that the aphorism "good things come to those who wait" would be one way of putting it. The Taoists believe that there is an unseen force directing events, and the wisest course is to give in to that force and surrender our Canute-like vanity:

Do that which consists in taking no action, and order will prevail

Being busy, bothering, doing things: all are a waste of effort, like trying to row upstream. They amount to a lot of huffing and puffing and very little movement. Politically, Taoism preaches a similar wisdom. People make too much effort, it says. Politicians should stop interfering and let the people get on with it:

It is because those in authority are too fond of action
That the people are difficult to govern

My own theory is that the world is divided into two types: the idle and the anti-idle. The anti-idle I hereby christen "botherers." Botherers are people who simply cannot help interfering in other people's lives. They lack imagination, believe in hard work, exploitation and hypocrisy, and make perfect politicians, bureaucrats and fat cats. They want to make something happen, but they don't really care what it is. They impose their beliefs on others by force of law, coercion and newspapers, and justify their actions by saying that they have created jobs, or cut costs, or increased spending or made profits for their shareholders. "Something must be done!" is their motto. And they do things, like building skyscrapers, call-centres, dams and motorways, but they also love to interfere with the plans of others—denying planning permission to increase the window size of an old barn by an inch, for example. What is worse is that the botherers, not content with *doing things* themselves, are constantly trying to force us poor idlers to do things as well. The baldest example of this can be seen in the recent history of the UK government's attempts to force the happily unemployed into meaningless and demeaning full-time employment. "The modern state," wrote C. S. Lewis in 1958, "exists not to protect our rights but to do us good or make us good—anyway, to do something to us or to make us do something." Rather than finding people "things to do," wouldn't a more sensible approach be to help us enjoy doing nothing? In newspapers, the botherers provide reams of unsolicited advice to poor people.

The terrible thing is that the people who do things, the botherers, make such a mess of it. The great French philosopher and mathematician Blaise Pascal, who is most celebrated for his modestly titled *Pensées—Thoughts*—but who also invented public transport, reflected on this theme. *Pensées* (1670) was intended as a defence of Christianity as the only true religion, and as such it jars with modern pluralist sensibilities. However, there is so much quality thought in it that it's well worth a look. Here is how Pascal sees society's botherers:

> Sometimes, when I set to thinking about the various activities of men, the dangers and troubles which they face at Court, or in war, giving rise to so many quarrels and passions, daring and

often wicked enterprises and so on, I have often said that the sole cause of man's unhappiness is that he does not know how to stay quietly in his room. A man wealthy enough for life's needs would never leave his home to go to sea or besiege some fortress if he knew how to stay at home and enjoy it. Men would never spend so much on a commission in the army if they could bear living in town all their lives, and they only seek after the company and diversion of gambling because they do not enjoy staying at home.

Hitler, Stalin, Mao, Amin, Mussolini: before all else, they were simply petty-minded bureaucrats writ frighteningly large. They took advantage of the anxiety of their people to present a promise of total efficiency which the people, in their weakness, were both comforted and deceived by. "Most of the world's troubles seem to come from people who are too busy," wrote Evelyn Waugh. "If only politicians and scientists were lazier, how much happier we would all be."

Those who take time off, who step back to look at the world, the lazy ones, the ones who can't be bothered, the writers, poets and musicians, these people do much to make life worth living in terms of producing a culture, but they tend not to get involved in the running of things, the management of the infrastructure, hospital bureaucracy, the education system, the local councils, the tax inspectorate. And this is because they find all that sort of thing so unutterably dull. Instead of trying to change the way other people live, they focus on transforming their own lives. Were it not for the celibacy, teetotalism and general lack of fun, I would have said that monks have a good life. They have retreated from the world and devoted themselves to prayer and study. Indeed, it is the reflective and time-rich monks, free from the demands of making money and keeping up with the fashions, all of which is terribly hard work, who created much of the world's great art and writing in the Middle Ages.

At home, you can be wild and free. G. K. Chesterton, in *What's Wrong with the World*, attacked the notion that domesticity is somehow constricting. He argued the opposite: "[T]he home is the only place of liberty. Nay, it is the only place of anarchy. It is the only spot on the earth where a man can alter arrangements suddenly, make an experiment or indulge in a whim . . . A man can wear a dressing gown and slippers in his house; while I am sure that this would not be permitted at the Savoy . . ."

The greatest piece of staying-in literature ever composed is *À Rebours* by J. K. Huysmans, published in 1884. Huysmans was a decadent *fin de siècle* writer with a bourgeois day job—he worked as a clerk at the Ministry of Interior for thirty years. But at night he allowed his literary imagination to roam free and created some of the most fascinating works of the period. *À Rebours*, which translates as *Against Nature*, is a study of a wealthy dandy called Des Esseintes. Having exhausted the pleasures of town and failed to find the meaning of life in weird sex and late nights, he decides to retreat to a hillside mansion and create his own artificial reality, a peculiar paradise of colour, smell and beauty, controlled by ingenious mechanical devices. He is motivated by an idleness of the body and a snobbishness of the mind. He doesn't want to exert himself; he doesn't want to consort with his fellow human beings, whom he regards as irredeemably vulgar. Bothering itself, to Des Esseintes, is vulgar. With inner resources and books, there is no need to move about, to "go":

Travel, indeed, struck him as a waste of time, since he believed that the imagination could provide a more-than-adequate substitute for the vulgar reality of actual experience . . . no doubt for instance, that anyone can go on long voyages of exploration sitting by the fire, helping his sluggish or refractory mind, if the need arises, by dipping into some book describing travels in distant lands.

Des Esseintes can't bear the empty materialism of the world and the perceived philistinism of his fellow human beings:

> He could detect such inveterate stupidity, such hatred of his own ideas, such contempt for literature and art and everything he held dear, implanted and rooted in these mean mercenary minds, exclusively preoccupied with thoughts of swindling and money-grubbing and accessible only to that ignoble distinction of mediocre intellects, politics, that he would go home in a fury and shut himself up with his books.

Husymans's intention was to write about a character who "has discovered in artificiality a specific for the disgust inspired by the worries of life and American manners of his time. I imagined him winging his way to the land of dreams, seeking refuge in extravagant illusions, living alone and apart, far from the present-day world, in an atmosphere suggestive of more cordial epochs and less odious surroundings."

So, free of all the bothering go-getters, Husymans sets about creating his indoor wonderland. Helped by a couple of bemused servants, he uses his considerable wealth and imagination to build an absurdly extravagant reality. His first act is to sleep during the day and come alive at night:

What he wanted was colours which would appear stronger and clearer in artificial light. He did not particularly care if they looked crude or insipid in daylight, for he lived most of his life at night, holding that night afforded greater intimacy and isolation and that the mind was truly roused and stimulated only by awareness of the dark; moreover he derived a peculiar pleasure from being in a well-lighted room when all the surrounding houses were wrapped in sleep and darkness, a sort of enjoyment in which vanity may have played some small part, a very special feeling of satisfaction familiar to those who sometimes work late at night and draw aside the curtains to find that all around them the world is dark, silent and dead.

Perhaps the best known of Des Esseintes's innovations is the golden tortoise. He has a fancy that it would be amusing to have an ornament in his sitting room which actually moved around, so orders a tortoise to be plated with gold and encrusted with jewels. Another caprice is an invention he calls the "mouth organ," a complex machine that delivers drops of various different liqueurs from an array of stops, the idea being to mix them up on the palate and create a symphony of flavour. He also orders the most fragile, delicate and overbred hothouse flowers to festoon his house. There is a nice vein of dark humour that undercuts the earnest descriptions of Des Esseintes's experiments: the tortoise, he notices one evening, has died, and after a lengthy description of the "mouth organ," Des Esseintes finds that he can't be bothered to go through the whole palaver and simply helps himself to a shot of whisky before sitting down. Needless to say, the flowers all die, too.

Eventually, Des Esseintes is defeated by the botherers. His

style of living makes him ill, and he is told by various doctors that he must move back to Paris and get out there, have fun and talk to people. Otherwise, "insanity quickly followed by tuberculosis" will be his fate. Des Esseintes gives in to their advice with bad grace: "Had he not outlawed himself from society? Had he heard of anybody else who was trying to organize a life like this, a life of dreamy contemplation? Did he know a single individual who was capable of appreciating the delicacy of an idea, or whose soul was sensitive enough to understand Mallarmé and love Verlaine?"

Des Esseintes's project may have been a failure, but that doesn't mean we shouldn't take inspiration from his heroic attempt to elevate his soul via interior furnishings. The problem today is that the vogue for interiors has become such an industry, such a popular hobby, that it has fallen prey to the same anxieties as any other part of life, viz: am I cool, am I rich? We use our clothes and our home decoration to display our coolness and our wealth. Coolness has been elevated to such a high status that it exerts the same power over us that the virtues of "good taste" or "refinement" or "cleanliness" once did. "It's so cool!" we might say of a friend's bachelor pad, in the same way that one hundred years ago, we might have said approvingly, "It's very clean."

The interiors magazines and TV programmes which depict impossibly idyllic lives all have their part to play in this conspiracy to make us feel small. "Get the look" is the line that magazines use, when they run a list of products similar to the ones we have seen in the celebrity sitting room. This is all pure fantasy: the home is not idyllic, the object will not help us "get the look," and still less will it bring any lasting contentment beyond the initial thrill of the purchase, to say nothing of the huge amount of work involved in getting the look. Moreover, the objects are listed in the hope that the manufacturers will buy advertising in the magazine thus increasing the magazine's profits, and they prey on our insecurities to make us buy things. They make us feel bad: in *The Simpsons*, Marge reads a magazine called *Better Homes* which has the tagline "Than Yours." The aim of the interior, to my mind, should be to help us *escape* from the world outside, not to bring it into our own homes, rather in the same way that the idler escapes from the outside world by retreating into his or her own mental interior world. Where do you think? In your head; in your bed.

This alternative interiors ideal is to be found in Chinese writing and also in the lifestyles of the Bohemians, the freewheeling, pro-smoking Bloomsbury set, whom we have encountered already. The Chinese-Bohemian ideal concerns simplicity and harmony with nature. This has the advantage of making an individual interior affordable, too. "We shall build our houses . . . so simple and elemental in character that they will fit in the nooks of the hills . . . without disturbing the harmony of the landscape or the songs of birds," was the dream of the pre-Bohemian writer Edward Carpenter in 1889.

In a novel by the now-forgotten Ethel Mannin, the hero looks around his unassuming pad with pleasure: "He likes this bare room with its tall window and pale walls and bookshelves and the divan with the hand-woven blue and yellow striped linen cover, and the weathered oak chair with the rush seat, and the blue-paint table and the rush-mat . . . It somehow reduced the business of living to the simplicities."

Simple also means less work and less shopping. The aesthete Cecil Beaton made a similar plea for people to escape fashion and embrace their own individual style when it came to decorating:

> Only the individual taste, in the end, can truly create style or fashion, since it is not concerned with following in the wake of others. Hence, whatever an individual taste may choose, be it a stepladder or a wicker basket, it must always be based on deep personal choice, a spiritual need that truly assesses and gives value to that particular ladder or basket. The beauty of these things is somehow transmitted through the personality of the one who chooses. It is in our selection, after all, that we betray our deepest selves, and the individualist can make us see the objects of his choice with new eyes, with his eyes.

Or as Quentin Crisp told the *NME* in 1981:

> Fashion is never having to decide who you are. Style is deciding who you are and being able to perpetuate it.

If you want to create a comfortable pad, make it personal. A flash, showy-offy place filled with the latest things will only make others feel uncomfortable. "Slavish adherence to the dictates of fashion is a degenerate's method of bolstering flagging self-esteem," wrote the editors of the *Chap* magazine recently. It's also essential for an idler not to commit that terrible bourgeois sin of "trying too hard." Your ideal should not be an ordeal. This is how Beaton describes the house of Dorelia John, wife of painter Augustus John:

> No intention to decorate the house ever existed . . . The colours have gratuitously grown side by side. Nothing is hidden; there

is an honesty of life which is apparent in every detail—the vast dresser with its blue and white cups, the jars of pickled onions, the skeins of wool, the window sills lined with potted geraniums and cacti, while close to the windowpanes tits swing on a coconut shell hung from a tree. The Modigliani bust stands with a cactus pot on its head. In the corner of the entrance hall, boxes of apples and croquet mallets are spontaneously thrown together, constituting a picture of life that is full of sentiment and completely lacking in pretension.

The Chinese writer Li Liwen, in his book *The Art of Living* (we need more books with such titles: living is an art, not something that you fit in around your job), argued that when it came to building houses, wealth was no substitute for imagination:

> Luxury and expensiveness are the things most to be avoided in architecture. This is so because not only the common people, but also the princes and high officials, should cherish the virtue of simplicity. For the important thing in a living house is not splendour, but refinement; not elaborate decorativeness, but novelty and elegance. People like to show off their rich splendour not because they love it, but because they are lacking in originality, and, besides trying to show off, they are at a total loss to invent something else. That is why they have to put up with mere splendour.

"Mere splendour" is the way of the botherer. I'm sure we have all visited houses where huge efforts have been made to keep up with the pressures of fashion. There are pricy artworks dotted around, the sofas are minimal, and yet there is a stifling atmosphere that makes you want to leave five minutes after you have arrived. I personally, perhaps surprisingly, don't like mess. This is partly because I am a messy person by nature, and therefore overreact to messiness in other people, but also because, as an idler, mess ends up stealing time from you. One lets things descend into chaos because one can't be bothered to clean up, but then wastes hours trying to find socks or the right knife because everything is everywhere. Paradoxically, to be truly idle, you also have to be efficient.

Hugh Hefner has perhaps done more than anyone recently to promote the idea of staying in. In the 1960s, his *Playboy* magazine ran superb features which included the floor-layouts of fantasy bachelor pads. The bed would be the focus, naturally, would have an in-built stereo, TV and cocktail cabinet, was probably circular and would certainly have had a leopard skin thrown over it. The *Playboy* fantasy is a superbly attractive one for most men: sexual liberation, freedom from emotional attachment, plenty of booze and luxury.

Similarly, I once had a brief passion for the classic American throne of comfort, the La-Z-Boy recliner. I loved their total naffness, their sacrifice of style to comfort, their huge size and complex mechanics, the way they can turn from armchair to lounger to bed, all the while enfolding you in a squashy embrace. They are a kind of Everyman's *À Rebours*, a giant hulking piece of manmade machinery designed for total relaxation. At £1,000 each, though, I've never had the spare cash to invest in one and have had to settle for a humble armchair and footstool.

The *Playboy* ideal likewise remained a fantasy for me, but I do still wonder: if you manage to achieve it—let's say you are the son of a dictator—then what? Where does it end? Will you, like Scarface, drown in a mountain of cocaine while your citadel is attacked from all sides?

However, the *Playboy* fantasy pad has been a great source of stimulation for that laudable modern trend, the retro pad. Living in the past is an effective way of retreating from the vulgarity of the present. I have noticed this trait in artists. My friend John Moore, a musician, once a member of the very noisy band The Jesus and Mary Chain, now likes having the middlebrow radio station Classic FM playing at home. "We like to pretend that the modern age doesn't exist and we are living in the 1920s," he says. Deference to a former age is not necessarily mere nostalgia and escapism; it can also be a conscious rejection of the values of consumerism and the feeling of being victimized by the constant search for "the latest thing." Any former era will do; for me it is the eighteenth century. I have another friend whose house is a shrine to the 1960s: orange plastic chairs, posters of The Monkees, a jukebox and stacks of 45s, all bought second-hand. Advice for idlers: shop at markets, car-boot sales, thrift stores, auctions and on eBay. You will spend less, create more and live more richly than the city broker who blows three grand on a leather sofa.

We should all admire those who hold out for a better way of life and manage to achieve it on small funds. The great retreaters of contemporary times have been CRASS, the anarchist punk group whose fiercely political, anti-capitalist art, music and writing so enlivened the otherwise depressing early eighties. Their influence was huge and helped to inspire a generation of dissatisfied youth to wear nothing but black and spray anarchy signs in bus shelters. But they also practised what they preached, establishing a hippyish, open-house commune in the Essex countryside on the edge of London, where they grew their own vegetables, made art and loafed about. I went up to visit one day and found a little paradise: a garden full of sheds, workshops and flowers, a vegetable patch, an interior that was somewhere between Barbara Hepworth and New Age traveller. Living on a very low income, founder Penny Rimbaud, who was up on the roof laying felt when I arrived, reaffirmed my belief that lack of funds need not be a barrier to creating one's own patch of paradise. Indeed, it started me thinking that true idleness lies in total responsibility, and that freedom comes from total independence. That's why I've just bought the *Reader's Digest Complete DIY Manual*.

Indeed, I have been inspired to create a pub in my own home. For me, the pleasures of staying in revolve around drinking and talking. So I took the unprepossessing scullery in our rented Devon farmhouse and installed a dartboard and two old dining-room chairs, which cost £7 each in a local bric-a-brac place. I've also added a print of dogs playing pool, fairy lights, a piece of driftwood, a shove-ha'penny board, beer mats, Hogarth prints, an old scythe which I found on a rubbish tip and postcards of Cornish men eating giant pasties. All these items were either found lying around or were donated by friends. The pub is called The Green Man and my friend Pete Loveday has painted the sign. Through the battered casement windows you can see the sun set over the sea, and without stirring abroad I can know the whole world.

10 p.m.
The Pub

O thou, my Muse! guid auld Scotch Drink!
Whether thro' wimplin' worms thou jink,
Or, richly brown, ream owre the brink,
In glorious faem,
Inspire me, till I lisp and wink,
To sing thy name!

Robert Burns, "Scotch Drink," 1786

The pub, the tavern, the alehouse, the inn, the pothouse, the taproom—this is where we send away the trials of workaday life, send them packing with beer and chat. Or even just with beer. I remember that before I had children I used to feel sorry for those lone males you sometimes see in pubs. At odd times of the day, 4 p.m. perhaps, they would be there, sitting alone with a pint and a paper, or just a pint. Then one day, soon after the birth of our second child, I was out doing the Christmas shopping. I was alone; the deal was that Victoria would look after the kids while I got some essential jobs done. It was 3 p.m. As I walked up to the high street, I passed a pub. "Hmmm," I thought. "That looks nice. And how much more enjoyable the shopping would be after a pint." So I popped in, sat on my own and enjoyed the luxury of drinking in peaceful solitude for twenty minutes. It was then that I looked at myself and realized I had turned into exactly the type of sad bloke that I used to pity: the solitary male boozer. And it was then that I understood what all those men were doing. It's not exactly that they were getting away from the wife; more that these solitary pub interludes were a way of creating a bit of time for themselves, time for reflection and peace, time away from work and home. Idle time, free time. Going to the pub is a way of stopping.

"As soon as I enter the door of a tavern, I experience oblivion of care, and a freedom from solicitude," wrote Dr. Johnson. "When I am seated, I find the master courteous, and the servants obsequious to my call; anxious to know and ready to supply my wants . . . I dogmatize and am contradicted, and in this conflict of opinions and sentiments I find delight . . . there is nothing which has yet been contrived by man, by which so much happiness is produced as by a good tavern or inn." And these pleasures are important. As another pub lover, G. K. Chesterton, put it, in *What's Wrong with the World*: "I remember that a roomful of Socialists literally laughed when I told them there were no two nobler words in poetry than Public House."

The pub makes a little master of every man. During the day, you might be downtrodden and abused by your employer, or co-workers, or family. But in the pub, your self-confidence is restored. You are omnipotent, omniscient, you have become a powerful figure. You have opinions, you have answers. The pub is where we discuss our dreams and sorrows, our visions and plans. In the pub, we all become experts. We put the world to rights. My friend Nick Lezard talks of the Beer Degree: holding one of these allows you to talk on any subject at great length with total authority. The pub is where we have ideas. In fact, I'm sure I first conceived the idea of the *Idler* in a pub. It was certainly in the pub that I used to meet the friends with whom I later started an absinthe-importing company. Absinthe was a pub conversation that actually happened. In the pub, we plot revolution, hatch schemes, trade scams. The pub is a safe house for outlaws. Pubs offer freedom of discourse and even of commerce: away from the watchful gaze of the authorities, thieves trade stolen goods, informal bargains are struck, drugs bought and sold and a black-market, tax-free, cash-only economy is sustained.

The pub's informal inception arose out of a medieval custom whereby individual householders would open their doors to weary travellers and offer beer, bacon and a bed for the night. We know from Izaak Walton's *The Compleat Angler* that a good seventeenth-century alehouse brewed its own beer, would cook your fish for you, offered sheets smelling of lavender and, more often than not, provided a comely maiden singing lusty folk songs. Since then the essence of the pub has been in its public nature; it is democratic, anyone can go, it is the common man's members" club. In *The Making of the English Working Class*, E. P.

Thompson demonstrates how the eighteenth- and nineteenth-century pub became the focus for political meetings and gatherings of radical elements, as described in the *Leeds Mercury* newspaper in 1802:

> [They] meet nightly in taverns and public-houses. Almost every street in a large town has a little senate of this description; and the privileges of sitting in council over the affairs of the nation, and a pot of porter, has long been claimed by free Britons, and acknowledged by all administrations.

As the Industrial Revolution changed the working habits of the people and attempted, in effect, to enslave them, the pub was where meetings of dissatisfied workers would take place. Thompson notes that underground societies were forced to move from pub to pub:

> One debating society originated in the "Green Dragon" in Cripplegate in 1795 and moved successively to Finsbury Square, Fetter Lane, the "Scouts Arms" in Little Britain, thence to two public houses in Moorfields, and finally, in 1798, to Hoxton "beyond the limits of the city-officers."

The carousing, the free-and-easy attitudes, the large collections of people, the potential for radical debate—in short, the volatile mixture of hedonism and rebellion has always been a source of worry to our rulers, who prefer order and sobriety and would like everyone to be tucked up in bed, preferably before midnight. Thompson writes of "the natural tendency of authority to regard taverns, fairs, any large congregation of people, as a nuisance—sources of idleness, brawls, sedition or contagion." He quotes a disapproving comment about the common people made in 1757 by a member of the gentry who complains of "their open scoffings at all discipline, religious as well as civil; their contempt of all order, frequent menace to all justice, and extreme promptitude to tumultuous risings from the slightest motives."

Freedom and fun, says Thompson, were not rated as human virtues by the newly powerful Methodists, who were "in a state of civil war with the alehouse and denizens of Satan's strongholds." Indeed, the late nineteenth century saw the rise of the Temperance Movement. To modern eyes, this campaign to sober up the workers and in so doing prevent "tumultuous risings" seems comically hopeless, but the Temperance Movement was a powerful influence at the time, even if most of those who signed the pledge while suffering from a hangover on a Sunday did fall off the wagon on Tuesday. The Temperance Movement can be seen as yet another attempt to stamp out laziness, another weapon in the struggle to create a disciplined workforce for the factories; you can't work while drunk, and hangovers get in the way of efficient toil, too.

Visiting the pub and drinking beer became a form of protest against the new emerging work ethic, and it is fascinating to note the number of ales which still to this day carry seditious names. The Rebellion Brewery in Marlow produces Mutiny and Smuggler; the Freedom Brewery makes Liberty Ale. We have Luddite, The Leveller, Kett's Rebellion and Cornish Rebellion, as well as beers named after great revolutionaries such as Sam Adams, Tom Paine and John Hampden. It's a shame, really, that what we British call "real ale" evokes an image of folk-loving beardies getting drunk in provincial marquees, as there is a depth and tradition to ale-drinking that is missing from this image and sadly lacking in that young pretender, lager.

This independent pub culture was attacked not only by the Methodists but also by the centralizing tendencies of the Industrial Revolution. In the nineteenth century, the "free" alehouse was often taken over by one of the growing monopolies of brewers who created the concept of tied houses. Pubs were closing. Indeed, William Cobbett in *Rural Rides* (1830) laments the lack of public houses in the Cotswolds:

> I asked two men, who were threshing in a barn, how long it was since their public-house was put down, or dropped? They told me about sixteen years. One of these men, who was about fifty years of age, could remember three public-houses . . .

Tax on the sale of beer was also introduced, thereby criminalizing informal pubs and halting much home brewing. For Cobbett, the widespread closure of pubs was a clear sign of the misery and decay caused by industrialization. Pubs once acted as the focus of the community, providing a free front room where people whose own homes were perhaps too modest to do much entertaining could discourse freely, drink deeply and carouse. One gets a real sense that the Industrial Revolution was taking the fun out of life.

The great depicter of the eighteenth century William Hogarth saw a similar decline in the beery pub; in his case he was horrified by the gin boom of the mid eighteenth century, which he watched erode the culture of Merrie England. In 1751, Hogarth produced a set of two prints to make his point. *Gin Lane* is a scene of the utmost depravity. Most of us have probably seen this print—and if we have, we will never forget the image of the emaciated gin-soaked mum letting her poor baby fall over the railings. In *Gin Lane*, the only booming business is the pawnbroker's. *Beer Street*, however, presents a very different picture. Bawdy, sensual pleasures go hand in hand with literacy. The print shows several portly gents; one has a pipe in one hand and a tankard of foaming beer in the other. The other has a tankard of foaming beer in one hand and the breast of his mistress in the other. Two fisherwomen are reading self-improving tracts and the pawnbroker's has closed down. Beneath the print are the following lines, written by Hogarth's friend the Christ's Hospital classics teacher James Townley:

> Beer, happy Produce of our Isle
> Can sinewy Strength impart,
> And wearied with Fatigue and Toil
> Can chear each manly Heart.
>
> Labour and Art upheld by Thee
> Successfully advance,
> We quaff thy balmy Juice with Glee
> And Water leave to France.
>
> Genius of Health, thy grateful Taste
> Rivals the Cup of Jove,
> And warms each English generous Breast
> With Liberty and Love.

Thirty years later, Robert Burns was moved to compose "Scotch Drink," a poem in praise of beer and its central role in binding the community:

Thou art the life o' public haunts;
But thee, what were our fairs and rants?
Ev'n godly meetings o' the saunts,
By thee inspir'd,
When, gaping, they besiege the tents,
Are doubly fir'd.

William Cobbett, too, was a great fan of beer. He saw the essentials of a happy life as "the three Bs: Bread, beer and bacon." Beer, he said, "puts the sweat back in": after a hard day out in the fields, beer replenished the sweat lost through toil. Inspired by Cobbett, I have lately been drinking two, three or four pints of ale each night and eating bacon for breakfast every morning, and, I can report, it works. Never felt better. And it's a habit that need cost only £12.50 a week, which is the price of a case of beer and a pound of bacon.

Pub culture, already eroded by big breweries and morally indignant Methodists and capitalists, was now further undermined by new laws from Parliament limiting the freedom of publicans to serve alcohol at times of their own choosing. Since the late nineteenth century, under the cover of concern about rising levels of drunkenness, governments have sought to control our drinking habits. The first attempt to do this came in a piece of legislation known as the Intoxicating Liquor (Licensing) Bill of 1872. It introduced restrictions on opening hours, introduced the concept of drunkenness as a criminal offence, and was opposed by a petition of 800,000 signatures.

It was the same story in other industrializing nations. The US Temperance movement, supported by religious and business groups, had started officially in 1826 and over the decades came to influence federal policy on liquor control, culminating, of course, in Prohibition from 1920 to 1933.

The history of licensing laws can be seen as the history of the civil war in Britain between the forces of industry and the forces of laziness. Excessive drunkenness and hangovers interfere with the running of the strict work schedules introduced by the Industrial Revolution. Even today, hard work has the upper hand over laziness: licensing laws in the UK force pubs to shut at 11 p.m. on weekdays and Saturdays, and at 10:30 p.m. on Sundays. This reinforces the feeling of Sunday blues, familiar to all schoolchildren and employees; we're supposed to go to bed early on Sunday, the better to sleep and the better to serve our employers on the Monday morning.

The First World War galvanized the authorities into making efforts to control our drinking habits. Here is a brief history of licensing laws from the Campaign for Real Ale, which fights for their abolishment:

In October 1914 evening closing time in London became 10:00 p.m. instead of 12:30 a.m. In 1915 opening hours were reduced from 16–17 hours (19.5 hours in London) to 5.5 hours and evening closing was 9–9:30 p.m. In 1916 the Government via the Central Control Board (Liquor Traffic) took over the four breweries in Carlisle as well as 235 pubs in the Carlisle, Gretna and Annan area. The next year pubs in the Enfield Lock area of London and Invergordon in Scotland were taken over. In all these areas there were worries that the effectiveness of the munitions factories were being endangered by drunkenness amongst the workers.

For most of the last century, that great pleasure, sitting in the pub all afternoon, was not legally permitted. That was the reason for the rise in private drinking clubs. Pubs are now permitted, once again, to open in the afternoons, but this is not enough. Shouldn't opening hours be a matter for the individual landlord to determine? Eleven p.m. closing causes umpteen social problems. When pubs all close at the same minute, you witness the phenomenon, unseen in any other country in the world, of millions of drunken people spilling onto the streets at precisely the same time, tanked up and ready to go, frustrated that they've been forced to stop drinking, and therefore fighting, shouting and causing damage in order to expend their excess energy. If they had been allowed to stay in the pub for a further hour or two, they would all gradually make their way home in dribs and drabs, quietly and peacefully. No one likes walking through any British town at 11:15 on a Saturday night—it's simply scary. And the UK is one of the few countries in the world with such strict licensing laws. Why, one wonders. Is there perhaps a self-hatred in the English breast, a fear of responsibility, a certain childishness, even a masochistic desire to be told what to do?

Another attack on pub culture lately has come in the form of the flashy bar. In my late twenties, I became briefly seduced by the trendy, metropolitan bar, before realizing that such bars are in fact the enemy of fun. Where the *pub* exists for old-fashioned pints of ale, conversation, blazing fires, warmth, wood and cosiness, *bars* are about showing off and being at the cutting edge of fashionable society, and they are about paying £7.50 for a gin and tonic. Fashion took the drinking culture and made the licensed establishment a place to be seen rather than a place to talk and think. In fact, in most of these places it's actually impossible to talk or to think as the banging techno is at ear-splitting volume. What looks like a "buzz" from the outside is in fact a collection of half-drunk, lonely, insecure people trying to make themselves heard above the din. One becomes hoarse with shouting, and the conversation, such as it is, is punctuated by long periods of staring at the clientele simply because one can no longer be bothered to shout. I was once told that the reason for the high volume levels was profit: "if you're not talking, you're drinking" was the theory. Commerce killed the pub. Says Chesterton in *What's Wrong with the World*: "certainly, we would sacrifice all our wires, wheels, systems, specialities, physical science and frenzied finance for one half-hour of happiness such has often come to us with comrades in a common tavern."

Even in provincial English towns, the weaker pubs have forsaken cosiness for bar styles: zinc has replaced wood; comfort has been sacrificed to image; it's goodbye to candles and hello to uplighters. Town centres offer theme bars to the "fickle" under-25 consumer, and these places base their style on the trendy London establishments that celebrities endorse in popular magazines.

Let us add also that the urban pub has been fiercely undermined by the gym. Instead of heading straight to the pub after work, an increasing number of pleasure-hating lunatics appear to enjoy going to the gym, where instead of quaffing foaming pints of nut-brown ale in convivial company they run alone on treadmills while watching MTV on giant screens to distract them from their agony. If you really want to exercise, then why not find a pub that is a one-mile walk from the office or home? That way, you'll walk two miles every day *and* have a good time.

I have moved my old Dansette record player into my home-pub, The Green Man, and we play Noël Coward and The Ink

Spots on sunny afternoons. I find that sort of music accompanies ale and cigarettes rather well. Also, as I do not sell liquor I do not need a licence so I can close whenever I wish and I have no fear of the exciseman. But out on the streets it's 11 p.m. already. The cursed bell has rung, crashing through our peace, and the dreaded phrase "drink up now" has been bellowed by the landlord. The blood is up, our good old English resentment at being told what to do has been stirred. It's time to riot.

11 p.m.
Riot

Damn the King, damn the Government, damn the Justices!
Rioters' chant of 1760s London

Maggie, Maggie, Maggie! Out, out, out!
Rioters' chant of 1980s London

Riot is a weapon, but one of a quite different order from the weapons of the authorities, of king and state, of the botherers, of the ranks of the anti-idle. Paradoxically, idlers are given to riot. Our rulers tend to use relentless drudgery to create oppressing, grinding bureaucracies which stifle us with boredom. Every now and then brute force is wheeled out. The idler's modus operandi, on the other hand, is to sit around talking and thinking for months,

and then to act with impetuosity, with "rapid and violent" diligence, with a visible outburst of passion, a "rising." Plans are
hatched in the pub, then, many moons later, buildings are
attacked, Trafalgar Square colonized, a university building occupied. As a piece of spectacle, the riot is particularly effective.
Jesus was a rioter: he turned over the money tables, creating a
precedent for millions of idealistic visionaries thereafter.

Lord Byron encapsulates the paradox of the rioting poet, the
seditious idler, the laid-back revolutionary. As for his idler creden-
tials, his first collection of poetry, published in 1807 when he was
just 19 and an undergraduate at Trinity College, Cambridge, was
entitled *Hours of Idleness*. He was also an aristocrat, a member
of the idle rich. But, for him, this financial independence gave
him the necessary detachment to see the iniquities perpetrated
by the new middle class more clearly than those who were
scurrying around making money. In any case, according to the
nineteenth-century critic Matthew Arnold, he was enraged by
"British Philistinism" and enraged still more by his own class's
apparent acquiescence to the commercial economy. Writes
Arnold: "The falsehood, cynicism, insolence, misgovernment,
oppression, with their consequent unfailing crop of human
misery, which were produced by this state of things, roused
Byron to irreconcilable revolt and battle." Byron himself put it
like this: "I have simplified my politics into an utter detestation
of all existing governments. Give me a republic. The king-times
are fast finishing; there will be blood shed like water and tears
like mist, but the peoples will conquer in the end. I shall not
live to see it, but I foresee it."

It was Byron's politics that led him to support one of the best
known and most misunderstood radical groups of the Industrial

Revolution era: the Luddites. Led by the mythical King Ludd, the Luddites set about stealing into factories at night and breaking the machines. They struck right at the heart of the matter. It was the machine which was destroying their quality of life, and which threatened to drag them down with it and reduce men to automatons. The Luddites carried out a planned campaign of frame-breaking and other actions from 1811 to 1813. They may have been tanked up, I don't know. And it really doesn't make any difference.

Well, Byron, as a member of the aristocracy, was entitled to speak at the House of Lords, and he used this power to give a voice to the rioters. The government's response to the agitations had been to introduce a piece of legislation called the Frame-Breaking Bill in 1812, which made machine-breaking a capital offence. Byron was one of the few voices in Parliament against this savage piece of bureaucracy, using the argument that such desperate measures would only have been undertaken if the people were desperate. "[T]he perseverance of these miserable men in their proceedings," he thundered, "tends to prove that nothing but absolute want could have driven a large, and once honest and industrious, body of the people, into the commission of excesses so hazardous to themselves, their families, and the community."

Byron's words were to no avail: in 1812, in a shocking example of the ruthlessness of the judiciary and the power of the anti-idle, 27 men were tried and executed for machine-breaking, one of them reportedly just 12 years old. Anyone who had had any connection with machine-breaking kept very quiet about it for decades afterwards. In 1816, Byron wrote his "Song for the Luddites" in a letter to a friend. It is not generally studied in schools so I shall reprint it here:

As the Liberty lads o'er the sea
Bought their freedom, and cheaply, with blood,
So we, boys, we
Will die fighting, or live free,
And down with all kings but King Ludd!

When the web that we weave is complete,
And the shuttle exchanged for the sword,
We will fling the winding sheet
O'er the despot at our feet,
And dye it deep in the gore he has pour'd.

Though black as his heart its hue,
Since his veins are corrupted to mud,
Yet this is the dew
Which the tree shall renew
Of Liberty, planted by Ludd!

It was the enslaving nature of the new work ethic that the Luddites had protested about and for which crimes they were killed by the state. Liberty and idleness for me are practically synonymous. An idler is a thinker and a dreamer and is fiercely independent. He would rather not riot but when his right to be lazy is attacked, he may be roused to activity.

There is a long tradition of rioting in the British Isles. We are a riotous people. The extent of this truth was first made clear to me by the historian John Nicholson, who in the 1970s published a pamphlet called "The Primer of English Violence," listing every British rebellion and uprising since the year 1485. As he writes in his introduction:

The self-congratulatory nature of the English concerning their supposed moderation looks upon strikes, demonstrations, riots, insurrections, rebellions and assassinations as aberrations from the norm. This primer proves otherwise. The idea of a peaceable nation of modern gentlemen is a fallacy engendered by the misrepresentation of history.

Since 1485, he adds, "scarcely a year has passed when the authorities have not been challenged by rebels or dissenters and responded with the use of force." I will give a brief extract to make the point:

1649	Diggers and Levellers uprisings against state
1650	Nude messiah rides into Bristol
1650	Digger Rebellion in Wellingborough
1651	Fifth monarchists organize strike against nailmakers in Birmingham
1652–3	Fifth Monarchy Men control Parliament of Saints, Cromwell dissolves
1655	Penruddock's Uprising (monarchists against Cromwell)
1659	Riot at Enfield, commoners against soldiers

In *The Making of the English Working Class*, E. P. Thompson similarly provides a list of insurrections from the late eighteenth and early nineteenth centuries:

The eighteenth and early nineteenth century are punctuated by riot, occasioned by bread prices, turnpikes and tolls, excise, "rescue," strikes, new machinery, enclosures, press-gangs and a score of other grievances. Direct action on particular grievances

merges on the one hand into the great political risings of the
"mob"—the Wilkes agitation of the 1760s and 1770s, the Gordon
Riots (1780), the mobbing of the King in the London streets (1796
and 1820), the Bristol Riots (1831) and the Birmingham Bull Ring
riots (1839). On the other hand it merges with organized forms
of sustained illegal action or quasi-insurrection—Luddism
(1811–13), the East Anglian Riots (1816), the Last Labourers'
Revolt (1830) the Rebecca Riots (1839 and 1842) and the Plug
Riots (1842).

All these riots can be seen as the last desperate outcry against the
new dogma of work, the final spasms of a once-independent
nation before it caves in to the slavery of industrialism. In the
official propaganda, such noble efforts are reframed in negative
terms, the grievances dismissed. In accounts of the Wilkes Riots,
we see the pro-work authorities try to dismiss such risings as
the work "of a beggarly, idle and intoxicated mob without
keepers, actuated solely by the word Wilkes." So, who was this
man Wilkes, who had such power to stir the masses?

John Wilkes was a peculiar firebrand, very much a product
of the eighteenth century. After spending ten years of his youth
carousing in London as part of the notorious Hellfire Club, he
became bored with pleasure-seeking and turned to radical politics. At this he was a great success. He became Member of
Parliament for Aylesbury in 1757. One of his first actions as MP
was to criticize King George III for appointing a crony, the Earl
of Bute, as Prime Minister. His attacks on the administration
led to a prosecution against him for seditious libel. It was based
on the following visionary passage, published in his radical newspaper, the *North Briton*:

The government have sent the spirit of discord through the land, and I will prophesy, that it will never be extinguished, but by the extinction of their power. A nation as sensible as the English, will see that a spirit of concord, when they are oppressed, means a tame submission to injury, and that a spirit of liberty ought then to arise, and I am sure ever will, in proportion to the weight of the grievance they feel.

Although the government's prosecution was unsuccessful, and Wilkes remained free, the case turned Wilkes into a celebrity and stirred up public sympathy for him as a champion of liberty. In 1768, he was arrested, and a crowd of 10,000 people turned up at the London prison where he was held, chanting "Wilkes and Liberty!", "No Liberty. No King." Troops opened fire and killed seven people. This massacre led to further outbreaks of rioting across London. The twentieth-century leftist historian George Rudé argues in his study *Wilkes and Liberty* (1962) that, far from being an uncultured mob of yobs, the rioters were educated artisans who:

demonstrated in St. George's Fields, at Hyde Park Corner, at the Mansion House, in Parliament Square and St. James's Palace; who shouted, or chalked up, "Wilkes and Liberty" in the streets of the City, Westminster and Southwark; who pelted Sheriff Harley and the common hangman at the Royal Exchange when they attempted to burn No. 45 of the *North Briton*; who smashed the windows of Lords Bute and Egremont and daubed the boots of the Austrian Ambassador; who paraded the Boot and Petticoat in the City streets, and burned Colonel Luttrell and Lords Sandwich and Barrington in effigy outside the Tower of London.

These are elements whom contemporaries and late historians have—either from indolence, prejudice or lack of more certain knowledge—called "the mob."

A less taxing and burdensome form of protest is the strike, the refusal to do any sort of useful work until our grievances have been addressed and a settlement reached. Whoever came up with the idea of the strike was an idler of genius: what could be more irritating to our rulers than to simply stop? No work, no useful toil, working classes loafing, men standing around doing nothing all day, thinking: this is what our masters cannot stand. In the first Russian Revolution of 1905, the combination of uprisings and strikes created a revolutionary fervour which one of its central architects, Lenin, described excitedly as follows:

Jan 25, 1905: Blood is flowing in many parts of the capital. The Kolpino workers are rising. The proletariat is arming itself and the people. There are rumours that the workers have seized the Sestoretsk Arsenal. The workers are providing themselves with revolvers, they are forging their tools into weapons, they are procuring bombs for a desperate fight for freedom. The general strike is spreading to the provinces. In Moscow 10,000 people have already ceased work. A general strike is to be called in Moscow tomorrow. A revolt has broken out in Riga. The workers in Lodz are demonstrating, an uprising is being prepared in Warsaw, demonstrations of the proletariat are taking place in Helsingfors. In Baku, Odessa, Kiev, Kharkov, Kovno and Vilna, there is growing ferment among the workers and the strike is spreading. In Sevastopol the stores and arsenals of the Naval Department are ablaze. There are strikes in Reval and in Saratov.

In Radom, an armed encounter took place between the workers
and reservists and troops.

Lenin, though, was far from an idler in spirit; driven and cold,
he was a bureaucrat. And it has to be said that when the will to
riot becomes co-opted by humourless revolutionary leaders like
Lenin and Cromwell, we enter an altogether more depressing
state of affairs—the substitution of a despotic regime, which at
least wore its evil on its sleeve, by a lumbering bureaucracy that
commits terrible acts while purporting to be motivated by the
public good. A kingdom, a socialist state: both are equally repug-
nant to your idler. Although, given a choice, the idler would probably prefer to live under a King Charles II who was corrupt but
fun-loving and reopened the theatres than under the pious and
grim republic of a pleasure-hating Cromwell.

The substitution of an old order by a new order seems to
produce the same problems, which is a sense of powerlessness
on the part of the people. In Russia, the inherited authority of
the tsars was replaced by the intellectual authority of bourgeois
thinkers such as Engels, Marx and of course Lenin, who was
firmly of the patronizing belief that the peasantry and working
classes needed to be enlightened by the educated middle classes.
The Marxists also believed in work, the nobility of labour.

Today's enemy, in the West at least, is not so much the governments as a new authority: consumer capitalism. Once the rich
people were the aristocracy, themselves the heirs to the warriors.
Then it was the turn of the nineteenth-century industrialists.
Now it is the CEOs of global companies who exploit the world
for profit. As a cartoon in a recent *Private Eye* had it, the fat cats
used to send us into the mills to make their millions, and now

they send us to the shopping centres. This is why we have seen a trend towards riots on the steps of company headquarters, riots in Seattle against the World Trade Organization, always brutally put down by police. Rapacious big business and efficient government are a formidable enemy for the dreamy, dreadlocked defenders of liberty.

But is rioting, though undeniably enjoyable, and an expression of the spirit of liberty, really worth it? Surveying the successive failures of revolutions, uprisings and riots over the last thousand years to install more humane laws or less interfering governments, one might conclude sadly that a better place to effect change is in oneself and in one's own immediate surroundings. It's true that rioting may occasionally effect a small change in policy, as when the so-called Poll Tax Riots in the UK helped bring about the abolition of the tax and its replacement with the Council Tax. But all too often things tend to revert to normal: the boring people take charge, the paper-shufflers boss us about.

Perhaps the only sane thing to do is to create one's own paradise. The punk group CRASS, for example, whom we met in our Idle Home chapter, failed to overthrow the state, although they did give a very effective voice to thousands of anti-Thatcherites, but within their countryside commune, which still thrives today, they succeeded at becoming their own masters. Penny Rimbaud (real name Jeremy Ratter) and CRASS also created an inspiring example for others to follow, an example of independent living and refusal to become a mere consumer. Rimbaud is something of a modern-day William Cobbett, and I would love him to write the *CRASS Guide to Cottage Economy*, a practical handbook to living outside the mainstream.

The answer, perhaps, is in anarchism, not socialism. The poet, the anarchist, the freedom-seeker, the rioter, the idler, must surely agree with D. H. Lawrence in his poem "A Sane Revolution," where he calls for us all to be aristocrats, to create our own paradise, to destroy work and to have a revolution for "fun."

Midnight

The Moon and the Stars

Hartley fell down and hurt himself—I caught him up crying
& screaming—& ran out of doors with him.—The Moon caught
his eye—he ceased crying immediately—& his eyes & the
tears in them, how they glittered in the Moonlight!
Samuel Taylor Coleridge on his young son, 1798

And whithersoever I go, there shall I still find Sun, Moon,
and Stars; there shall I find dreams, and omens, and
converse with the Gods!
Epictetus, *The Golden Sayings of Epictetus*

The moon and the stars are soothing constants in an idler's life.
Too often cut off from a clear night sky by the barrier of urban

fumes, most of us only get the chance to do some serious gazing when we have managed to snatch a weekend in the country. Certainly, when we have visitors down here in Devon, the clarity and splendour of the stars is frequently remarked upon. Their contemplation seems to reconnect us with a childlike sense of wonder at the mysteries of the universe. They are literally other-worldly, and so remove us from the world and its cares; they lift us off the ground. I love the Coleridge story above, particularly because when I first read it, my own son, Arthur, was just two, and was similarly entranced by the moon. Indeed, "moon" was one of his first words. "Moon!" he would say as we stepped out in the evening, "moon!," pointing up at the sky and then looking at me. In fact, when Arthur cries at night, I often take him outside to look at the moon, and it usually soothes him.

Gazing at the stars opens our minds to another reality, a mysterious eternal world, beyond material struggle. Despite the attempts of the rationalists to explain the stars as merely a constellation of suns light years away, we still revere them and revel in their mysteries. The gods live up there; and so do UFOs. When we started the *Idler* in 1993, I became interested in UFO culture. At the time, the idea that there was something out there, and that it was planning a visit, was entering the mainstream. Two US professors, Dr. John Mack and Dr. David Jacobs, had compiled research into the stories of so-called "abductees," Americans who reported experiences of being transported onto alien crafts for examination. The alien influence had even entered fashion: the skateboarding label Anarchic Adjustment made liberal use of alien iconography, and later the image of the "grey," the archetypal big-eyed alien with the almond-shaped face, became a common motif on T-shirts, badges and stickers.

This swell of interest in the alien and the UFO to me indicated some sort of spiritual urge, a desire to believe in the existence of an alternative dimension. The UFO provided a convenient way of doing this, since in our rational and mechanical world, it is easier to believe in a UFO than to believe in God. "UFOs, the theory goes, are simply folk like us who evolved on another planet and have a more advanced technology," the late Terence McKenna once remarked. "It doesn't strain credulity in the way that hypothesizing that we're in contact with an afterworld or a parallel continuum challenges our notion of reality." The UFO connected science and God and even promised salvation. For Dr. Mack, the UFO represented hope: "You see the world and the universe from an alien perspective. When you experience a connection with source like that, the imbalance of the world becomes intolerable . . . it may be possible to liberate the human faculties and energies that are needed to address the major personal, institutional and global problems that now affect humankind."

Man wants to fly, to see the gods, to become a god. The NASA moon landings were of course the most spectacular demonstration of this urge. Despite the clinical science and practical nature of these moon flights, the wonder, mystery and magic of them was not killed. Space, indeed, has been the latest arena for the millennia-long battle between the materialists and the mystics. This conflict is superbly enacted in the Steven Spielberg film *Close Encounters of the Third Kind*. At the very heart of the movie is the tension between the wild-eyed wonder of the crazed visionary, played by Richard Dreyfuss, and the sinister, hyper-organized, efficient, militaristic response of the authorities to the alien visitation. We all remember the orange-suited, anonymous-faced troops filing into the spacecraft, as if it were just another boring job rather than the most mind-blowing experience of their lives, and how they contrast with the raggedy figure of Dreyfuss, crouching behind a rock. These two poles—wonder and seriousness, the child and the adult—are combined in the ambiguous figure of François Truffaut, the scientist, who is employed by the authorities but who clearly has misgivings about their sterile approach to the landing.

A few years ago, I encountered a London-based organization called the Association of Autonomous Astronauts. A loose-knit affiliation of Marxists, futurists and revolutionaries on the dole, they created what they called a Five-Year Plan to get into space. Their radical idea of what constituted space travel, mixed with their hostility to official organizations such as NASA, was subversive and original. For the AAA, space travel was synonymous with a freedom from "gravity," from the earnestness, the seriousness, the heaviness that habitually keeps us locked to the floor. Rebelling against the traditional parental admonishment to the dreaming child—"keep your feet on the ground"—they were turning their gaze heavenward and dreaming of flying. They believed that space travel could be achieved by sitting in front of the fire at home and using the imagination to enter strange realms.

Essentially the AAA's mission was to reclaim the idea of space travel for the common man, democratize it, steal it back from the white-coated experts who baffle us with their science. For them, space represented an ideal of freedom. While they resisted the idea that they were merely creating metaphors, to me their insistence that space travel was possible even for unemployed layabouts was a way of making a plea for possibilities;

don't feel trapped and constrained, they were saying. You may have been told that you are an earth-bound mortal, but in fact you can do anything you want to do. In making this connection, between the stars and liberty, the ΛΛΛ were working within a long tradition. Robert Burns, for example, connects the two in his poem "Libertie: A Vision" (1794). Here the poet sits outside at midnight and is visited by a vision in minstrel's dress:

> As I stood by yon roofless tower,
> Where the wa'flower scents the dewy air,
> Where the howlet mourns in her ivy bower,
> And tells the midnight moon her care;
>
> The winds were laid, the air was still,
> The stars they shot alang the sky;
> The fox was howling on the hill,
> And the distant echoing glens reply;
>
> The stream adown the hazelly path
> Was rushing by the ruined wa's
> To join yon river on the strath,
> Whase distant roaring swells an' fa's;
>
> The cauld blue north was streaming forth
> Her lights wi' hissing eerie din;
> Athwart the lift they start an' shift,
> Like fortune's favours, tint as win;
>
> By heedless chance I turned mine eyes,
> And, by the moonbeam, shook to see
> A stern and stalwart ghaist arise,
> Attired as minstrels wont to be;

> Had I a statue been o' stane,
> His daring look had daunted me;
> And, on his bonnet graved was, plain;
> The sacred posy—LIBERTIE!

Freedom is out there, somewhere, glittering, almost visible, but just out of our reach. In Burns's poem, Liberty is represented as a spectral presence, lit only by moonlight, appearing as an ideal at that witching hour, midnight, when the "real world" of the day has receded. The stars are a tantalizing mystery. And the great thing is that the stars are free, in that they cost nothing to watch, and can be seen from anywhere by anyone. They can even shine through in the city sometimes, and indeed the night sky was an important resource for the young Coleridge, who, while trapped in Charterhouse School deep in the City of London, used to climb up on to the roof at night:

> For I was reared
> In the great city, pent 'mid cloisters dim,
> And saw nought lovely but the sky and stars.
> ("Frost at Midnight," 1798)

Contemplation of the heavens takes us beyond speech and language to another place, to somewhere magical, in the sense of mysterious and unknowable and full of wonder, and to breathe in the sight can provide us with a whoosh of pleasure which I find quite impossible to describe. So I will hand over to that infinitely wise American, the great idler poet Walt Whitman:

There is, in sanest hours, a consciousness, a thought that rises, independent, lifted out from all else, calm, like the stars, shining eternal. This is the thought of identity—yours for you, whoever you are, as mine for me. Miracle of miracles, beyond statement, most spiritual and vaguest of earth's dreams, yet hardest basic fact, and only entrance to all facts. In such devout hours, in the midst of the significant wonders of heaven and earth (significant only because of the Me in the center), creeds, conventions, fall away and become of no account before this simple idea. Under the luminousness of real vision, it alone takes possession, takes value. Like the shadowy dwarf in the fable, once liberated and look'd upon, it expands over the whole earth, and spreads to the roof of heaven. ("Democratic Vistas," 1871)

We feel small under the stars, yet paradoxically we feel more ourselves. We are who we are.

The stars are everywhere in our language. We even call our celebrities "stars," which symbolically elevates them to the level of gods. Indeed, today's celebrity culture has something in common with the deistic culture of ancient Rome. The Romans looked up to their gods, but also loved to write and talk about their fallibilities and scandals. The gods were above ordinary mortals, but were subject to baser instincts, too. How different from the infallible Christian mono-God, who is perfectly faultless to an extent that just makes us feel guilty. It's no wonder we love reading about celebrity divorces and drug problems in newspapers and magazines: we envy them, but we love to see reflected in their behaviour our own weaknesses. In the early twentieth century and before, this role was fulfilled by the aristocracy; it was they who somehow seemed to be above the level of ordinary mortals, and it was their doings, their bad behaviour, love affairs and bankruptcies, that were chronicled in the gossip columns of newspapers and magazines. It's the same old question: what sort of creature is a man? Is he noble and godlike or a snuffling beast imprisoned by base desires?

But the celebrity-stars, while they might satisfy a yearning for modern myths and good stories, are no substitute for the real twinkling diamonds that come out every night, everywhere, and have inspired our philosophers and poets to dream of better worlds on earth. Epictetus, who provides our epigram at the start of this chapter, was a stoic philosopher, a slave-turned-free-man, whose starry-eyed visions led him to fight for the rights of the common man. In AD 89 he was banished from Rome by the Emperor Domitian.

But gazing heavenward is seen as a waste of time by our practical-minded rulers. Our very language makes a virtue of being stuck on the earth, and criticizes those with loftier aspirations. Bad: head in the clouds, starry-eyed, losing grip, not living in the real world, moon-faced loon, lunatic, airy-fairy, space cadet, away with the fairies, moonstruck, on another planet. Good: feet on the ground, anchored, down-to-earth, grounded, keeping your head down, getting a grip.

We need to defend the stargazers, and this is what Oscar Wilde did in *Lady Windermere's Fan* (1893), with the classic line, "We are all in the gutter, but some of us are looking at the stars." Here he neatly inverted the modern prejudice that ground is good—solid, healthy—and that looking heavenward is somehow foolish, or time-wasting, for lunatics.

It's strange, in fact, that the moon should have become associated with lunacy when one considers that in Chinese philosophy it is seen as a force for good. Here is one of the epigrams of the mid-seventeenth-century writer Chang Ch'ao:

> To listen to a Buddhist lesson under the moon makes one's mental mood more detailed; to discuss swordsmanship under the moon makes one's courage more inspired; to discuss poetry under the moon makes one's personal flavour more charming in seclusion; and to look at beautiful women under the moon makes one's passion deeper.

Full moon is supposed to signify an auspicious night to hold a party, and camping out beneath the stars is always a pleasure. A camping holiday is a way of reconnecting with our primitive selves; we enjoy it because it lights a dormant memory of how we once lived. If one could get the hang of it, the wandering outdoor life would be a good one. Round here we like nothing better than sitting around a campfire.

1 a.m.

Sex and Idleness

According to the actor David Garrick, when Dr. Johnson was asked what were the greatest pleasures in life, he "answered fucking and the second was drinking. And therefore he wondered why there were not more drunkards, for all could drink tho' all could not fuck."

From Burns to Byron and from Bohemians to hippies, the history of riotous, easy living and the quest for liberty has been bound up with the pursuit of sexual freedoms. It is no accident that many of our outstanding radicals have also been pornographers. But, as one of the great idle pleasures, sex appears to be surrounded by an awful lot of problems and anxieties.

The pleasures of sex have long been attacked by the prudes and bureaucrats who tend to run countries and large institutions. Solo pleasuring has been a particular victim. In common with other forms of non-reproductive sex such as homosexuality or bestiality, the nineteenth century saw a widespread and concerted attack on masturbation from priests, schoolteachers, doctors and scientists. "The sooner he sinks to his degraded rest the better for him and the better for the world which is well rid of him," was how Maudsley, founder of the mental hospital which bears his name, wrote of the masturbator in 1868.

You can imagine the huge burden of guilt everyone must have been carrying around with them as a result of the moral campaign against the sin of onanism. Here is an extract from the guilt-torn diary of a certain Victorian do-gooder, written in 1850:

March 15: God has delivered me from the greatest offence and the constant murder of all my thoughts.

March 21: Undisturbed by my great enemy.

June 7: But this long moral death, this failure of all attempts to cure. I think I have never been so bad as this last week.

June 17: After a sleepless night physically and morally ill and broken down, a slave—glad to leave Athens. I have no wish on earth but sleep.

June 18: I had no wish, no enemy, I longed but for sleep. My enemy is too strong for me, everything has been tried. All, all is vain.

June 21: My enemy let me go and I was free.

June 24: Here too I was free.

June 29: Four long days of absolute slavery.

June 30: I cannot write a letter, can do nothing.

July 1: I lay in bed and called on God to save me.

(You may be surprised to learn that the owner of this towering libido was none other than Florence Nightingale.)

Masturbation among Victorian ladies was the cause of much hand-wringing for contemporary moralists, who associated the vice with idleness (the devil finds work for idle hands to do, I suppose). Here's an extract from a medical guidebook of the time:

> The symptoms which enable us to recognise or suspect this crime are the following: a general condition of languor, weakness and loss of flesh; the absence of freshness and beauty, of colour from the complexion, of the vermilion from the lips, and whiteness from the teeth, which are replaced by a pale, lean, puffy, flabby, livid physiognomy; a bluish circle around the eyes, which are sunken, dull and spiritless; a sad expression, dry cough, oppression and panting in the least exertion, the appearance of incipient consumption.

At the root of the opposition to "useless" sex was the new practical approach to life which saw sex as useful for the production of children and nothing more. Pleasure for its own sake was forbidden. The medical establishment came to help with a vast array of horrifying instruments designed to prevent masturbation in boys and girls. Catalogues of the time offered a whole panoply of steel girdles fitted with spikes for which only parents had the key. At the same time, sports such as tennis were promoted as healthy activities for young ladies, and a means of removing themselves from the seductions of self-love.

In the modern West we like to congratulate ourselves on having a more open-minded attitude to sex. We are free and easy about it, or so we like to think. But sex, like so many other pleasures, has been caught up in the striving ethic. It has become hard work; something we have to "perform" at; a competitive sport. The journalist Suzanne Moore made this point in the *Idler* in 1995. In her article, "Labour of Love," she recalled her school-friend Janice, who taught the young Suzanne various sexual tricks:

> What Janice tried to impress on me was that sex was an activity that you had to work at, practise, evolve techniques for: one vast exercise in self-improvement. I had never liked sports of any description. I was lazy. I couldn't be bothered . . . *Cosmopolitan* and all the other women's magazines . . . are full of endless lists of what makes people good in bed, lists of activities that we should explore, experiment with.

This vast effort is all wrong. Sex becomes something we have to learn. The magazines give us homework. And if we get it wrong, if we get low marks, then we feel guilty and useless. Fitness-freak pop stars like Geri Halliwell contribute to this sort of suffering, as does Madonna, who, as Moore says, "is of course living proof that you can try too hard. She has made sex as sexy as aerobics and, like step classes, something that has to be slotted in to an already tight schedule."

It seems to me that the situation is critical in the US, where sex has been elevated into a cross between a religion and a sport. Hard work and healthy sex: those are the pillars of the main-stream American economy. And spare us, please, the humour-less tantric-sex workouts of Sting. Moore makes a passionate appeal for the hard work to be taken out of sex. But the question remains: what is idle sex? With what shall we substitute the modern ideal of athletic power-shagging? Well, Suzanne has one answer:

> To be frank, I have never understood what was so wrong with lying back and thinking of England . . . when sex becomes such major toil, a labour of love, let me tell you that it is your revolutionary duty to phone in sick.

Oh, to lie back and be used and abused! This is surely the secret wish of the sexual slacker. Sex for idlers should be messy, drunken, bawdy, lazy. It should be wicked, wanton and lewd, dirty to the point where it is embarrassing to look at one another in the morning.

And idle sex should be languid. Men are characterized as wanting to get straight to the point when it comes to intercourse, and women complain that all men want to do is thrust it in. But in my own case, I find I have a slight sense of disappointment when the messing around comes to an end and the final act begins. It means that the mechanical element has taken over, the useful bit, the part which actually makes babies. A part of me would like simply to toy with my mistress for days on end under the lotus tree or on an enormous pile of velvet cushions, while smoking, drinking and laughing.

People criticize drunken sex but in my experience it tends to be better than sober sex. Drink and drugs improve sex by removing all the performance anxiety and guilt and concern about having a crap body, as well as certain, ahem, *inhibitions*. No—languor, not self-regarding athleticism, that is the key. And that is the motivating force behind the great sex/love poems the Song of Solomon and the twelfth-century *Rubáiyát of Omar Khayyám*.

Both were written—mercifully—before the advent of Alcoholics Anonymous, and both celebrate sex as a druggy, hazy, sensual experience, preferably to be enjoyed outdoors surrounded by the heady perfumes of vines and pomegranates. This is from the Song of Solomon (7:8–13):

8   I said, I will go up to the palm tree, I will take hold of the boughs thereof: now also thy breasts shall be as clusters of the vine, and the smell of thy nose like apples;

9   And the roof of thy mouth like the best wine for my beloved, that goeth down sweetly, causing the lips of those that are asleep to speak.

10   I am my beloved's, and his desire is toward me.

11   Come, my beloved, let us go forth into the field; let us lodge in the villages.

12   Let us get up early to the vineyards; let us see if the vine flourish, whether the tender grape appear, and the pomegranates bud forth: there will I give thee my loves.

13   The mandrakes give a smell, and at our gates are all manner of pleasant fruits, new and old, which I have laid up for thee, O my beloved.

The Rubáiyát of Omar Khayyám makes a similar plea for following pleasure and living in the moment. Let's grab our paradise now, it says, why wait?

> Some for the Glories of This World; and some
> Sigh for the Prophet's Paradise to come;
>   Ah, take the Cash, and let the Credit go,
> Nor heed the rumble of a distant Drum!

Ah, my Beloved, fill the Cup that clears
To-Day of past Regrets and future Fears:
  To-morrow!—Why, To-morrow I may be
Myself with Yesterday's Sev'n thousand Years.

Omar Khayyám is arguably the first poet to sing in praise of sex, drugs and rock'n'roll. It's just that he calls the sensualist's holy trinity "girls, wine and music." Khayyám also makes pleas to his beloved to "stop chattering," which reminds me of the following subtle love-verses by contemporary rocker-poet Zodiac Mindwarp:

You talk too much
Button your lip
Just take a trip
Behind my zip

But total sexual freedom, while a laudable ideal, turns out to be more difficult in practice. Guilt tends to creep in. And jealousy rears its ugly head. And promiscuous men have to deal with the general wrath of women (who could be accused of hypocrisy, since they slept with the promiscuous men in the first place). Wives and girlfriends are generally not up for open relationships, and it is a rare man who doesn't mind if his girlfriend or wife sleeps around. And there's always the problem of what happens if you embrace sexual freedom only to find that sexual freedom doesn't want to embrace you. That would be a bit of a blow. For sure, free love seems to come with a high price-tag.

How, then, can we enjoy sex without the effort and without the guilt? Modern civilization, ever since it was invented by the Greeks 500 years before the birth of Christ, has always had recourse to the two Ps: prostitution and pornography. Pornography is sometimes characterized as the symptom of a degenerate society, but anyone even noddingly familiar with Greek vases or statues on ancient Hindu temples will know that so-called unnatural sex acts, orgies and all manner of complex liaisons have for millennia past been represented in art for the pleasure and inspiration of the viewer everywhere. The desire to ponder images of love-making is clearly innate in the human—perhaps particularly the male—psyche.

Perhaps pornography holds the answer. Certainly it has the advantage of involving no one else, no possibility of judgement on our performance. Endless fantasy and no one to please except yourself. Porn removes the nagging anxiety that can sometimes spoil our erotic liaisons: is the other person enjoying it? Am I doing it right? Who cares.

It was Hugh Hefner's mission in *Playboy* to remove the guilt from masturbation. His genius was to connect this mission with a quest for a Bohemian lifestyle, and associate sex with upward mobility. Looking at 1960s *Playboy*s today, it's extraordinary how radical, thoughtful and avant-garde much of the content was. Hefner published Ray Bradbury, Jack Kerouac, Truman Capote, Henry Miller, Vladimir Nabokov, Kenneth Tynan and Philip Roth. He promoted Lenny Bruce and Woody Allen, and he ran long interviews with Malcolm X, Martin Luther King Jr., Bob Dylan and Fidel Castro. There were celebrations of the jazz scene and of drugs, and of doing it all together. A typical article, entitled "Sex, Ecstasy and the Psychedelic Drugs," examined "the delights and hazards of chemically enhanced or induced eroticism."

The flaw in the *Playboy* lifestyle was that it seemed to demand an absurdly high income. Although Hefner insisted that "gear and gadgetry were only accessories to the more important point of it all: an optimistic, romantic exploration of all the possibilities life had to offer," the magazine was aspirational and therefore tended inevitably to make the common man feel unhappy with his lot. But despite this, anyone could take heart in *Playboy's* fresh and joyful approach to living.

Another solution to the problem of where to find guilt-free sex has traditionally been found in prostitutes, courtesans and concubines. Most dads have experienced the transformation of their girlfriend from lover to mother, and the dampening effect that the demands of small children have on a wife's libido. Suddenly the young dad finds he is living the life of a monk with burdensome childcare duties. The wife has her children; the man has fulfilled his function as sperm-provider, and now she doesn't seem interested in useless sex. So what can a man do? He doesn't want to have an affair (too much hassle) but he does want sex. I often wish I lived in Paris in the nineteenth century when visits to luxurious brothels staffed by liberated courtesans, skilled practitioners in the art of love, were culturally acceptable. In my mind, Parisian brothels are full of fun, laughter and pleasure. The only brothels that seem to exist today in the UK masquerade as massage parlours and always look terribly seedy and off-putting. I understand, too, that the custom of taking a mistress still survives in France. But sadly, being constitutionally honest, I would find the deception and guilt very hard to deal with. I sometimes wish I were more deceptive by nature.

Perhaps the answer, for anyone of a similar disposition, is the festival. Many cultures enjoy the tradition of an annual bacchanal where all the normal rules are suspended. One such celebration, the Devil's Carnival, takes place every year in the Quebrada de Humahuaca region of Argentina, and according to a recent account in *La Nación* newspaper, for two weeks, free love is the order of the day:

> According to popular belief, chaos must reign once a year—at Carnival time, to be precise—for the denizens of heaven and hell to remain in harmony with the universe. At Carnival, the devil rises from the bowels of the earth and gives everyone permission to do as they please. But only for two glorious weeks . . . drinking and celebrating go on from morning to night. Marital ties are set to one side and, for several days, men and women become single again. "During Carnival, the devil is on earth, so no one can protest," they say, as they shake their sprigs of basil, the Carnival flower.

What a splendid idea! And it could be argued that this custom exists in the UK and elsewhere, albeit in an informal way. I have often heard the phrase "festivals don't count" as a way of excusing extra-relationship flings during a three-day bash. However, I have the feeling that if I came home after a three-day sex-fest, shaking a sprig of basil at my girlfriend by way of explanation, I would never be forgiven.

The last great problem with sex is that, as the very thing we think is going to free us, it can end up enslaving us, rather like other idle pleasures such as drinking and drugs. Seduced by its pleasures, we can become addicted. William Blake's poem "Song" from 1783 presents just such a warning:

How sweet I roam'd from field to field,
And tasted all the summer's pride,
'Till I the Prince of Love beheld,
Who in the sunny beams did glide!

He show'd me lilies for my hair,
And blushing roses for my brow;
He led me through his gardens fair,
Where all his golden pleasures grow.

With sweet May dews my wings were wet,
And Phoebus fir'd my vocal rage;
He caught me in his silken net,
And shut me in his golden cage.

He loves to sit and hear me sing,
Then, laughing, sports and plays with me;
Then stretches out my golden wing,
And mocks my loss of liberty.

Blake warns against that terrible and unfair paradox by which the very pleasures that we chase in order to express our desire for liberty—drugs, sex, alcohol—are the ones that can turn into an addiction and therefore imprison us.

One answer might be found in moderation, in the vices *and* the virtues. Is it possible to be moderately faithful, moderately good? Could we allow ourselves to be a little bit bad? To be naughty occasionally? It seems sensible to let the devil out of his cage once in a while, otherwise he might pop up when you're not expecting him.

2 a.m.
The Art of Conversation

Un véritable ami est le plus grand de tous les biens.
La Rochefoucauld, *Maxims*, 1665

I love the correspondence of *viva voce* over a bottle with
a great deal of noise and a great deal of nonsense.
Joshua Reynolds (1723–92)

The idler enjoys earthy pleasures. Not for him or her the strict
self-denial of the monk or the teetotalling, gym-going, routine-
adhering habits of the twenty-first-century striver. Talking,
sharing ideas and stories with friends old and new, this is the
lifeblood of the loafer. He loves company, he loves to chat and
be chatted at. He loves to sit around the table and to be so lost

in the moment that he completely loses all sense of time. Suddenly someone will say, with surprise, "It's two!" Time flies by. But how differently time moves when we are at our workplace. The worst offenders are those endless hours between two and six in the afternoon. They are the hours of death, the dragging hours. When I worked in a shop, that afternoon period was sheer agony. When it was finally over and we could cash up and lock up, we would go to the pub and four or five hours would pass in a flash. Then the pub would close and we would still be thirsty for more.

If I love the eighteenth century, it is because it was then above all eras that conversation was elevated to an art form, by Joseph Addison, Richard Steele, Dr. Johnson, Richard Savage, Oliver Goldsmith, Reynolds, Boswell and many others. It was the era of the club and the coffee shop. Boswell's *Life of Samuel Johnson* is above all a celebration of the joys of conversation. Hogarth mocked the clubs in his ironically titled *Midnight Modern Conversation*, which shows a scene of depravity, drunkenness and lechery. What called itself "conversation" was often in fact an unappealing collection of vomiters, gropers, brawlers and floppers. But that's fun, too.

Today we seem to have lost the art. We seldom remark on someone's "conversational eloquence" (as De Quincey did of the legendary Victorian loafer Walking Stewart). People now praise someone's energy and achievements, and focus on the final result rather than the process. (David Beckham, not noted for his powers of conversation, is a global hero.) Then it's back to the grind.

This is not a twenty-first-century phenomenon. Lin Yutang bemoaned the death of the art of conversation in the 1930s. For him, the acceleration of modern life was eroding the leisure time required for proper conversation. Central heating was one of the culprits:

> I believe . . . that the distortion of the home into an apartment without a log fire began the destruction of the art of conversation, and the influence of the motor car completed it. The tempo is entirely wrong, for conversation exists only in a society of men imbued in the spirit of leisure, with its ease, its humor, and its appreciation of light nuances. For there is an evident distinction between mere talking and conversation as such. This distinction is made in the Chinese language between *shuohua* (speaking) and *t'anhua* (conversation), which implies the discourse is more chatty and leisurely and the topics of conversation are more trivial and less business-like.

Like conversation, the log fire, by the way, is an idle pleasure. Its preparation, its contemplation, all delight. To sit beside a fire is to loaf. As has been often remarked, its role as the focus of the sitting room has been replaced today by the television, which, diverting and brilliant though it can occasionally be, is hardly conducive to leisurely discourse. Being at ease is the key, says Yutang:

> We can engage in a true conversation only when we meet our intimate friends and are prepared to unburden our hearts to each other. One of them has put his feet on a neighboring table, another is sitting on a windowsill and still another is sitting on the floor, upholstered by a cushion which he has snatched from the sofa, leaving one-third of the sofa seat uncovered.

Sharing is at the heart of conversation: sharing ideas, entertainment and stories. This is how the great eighteenth-century revolutionary Tom Paine's lifestyle around 1790 was described by a friend:

> Mr. Paine's life in London was a quiet round of philosophical leisure and enjoyment . . . At this time he read but little, took his nap after dinner, and played with my family at some game in the evening, as chess, dominoes, and drafts, but never at cards; in recitations, singing music, etc., or passed it in conversation; the part he took in the latter was always enlightened, full of information, entertainment and anecdote. Occasionally we visited enlightened friends . . . frequently lounging at the White Bear, Piccadilly, with his old friend, the walking Stewart, and other clever travellers from France, and different parts of Europe and America. When by ourselves we sate very late, and often broke in on the morning hours, indulging the reciprocal interchange of affectionate and confidential intercourse.

It was these exchanges, this period of wandering, talking and reading, that led to the publication in 1792 of his great work on human freedom, *The Rights of Man*. The whole of *The Rights of Man*, in fact, is a sort of conversation: the book is a spirited reply to Edmund Burke's attack on the principles of the French Revolution.

As well as giving rise to ideas, conversation gives a way of expressing them, and there is a long history of conversation as a literary form. Oscar Wilde's great essays on art and anarchy, "The Soul of Man under Socialism" and "The Critic as Artist," are written as dialogues as were, of course, Plato's Dialogues. In the *Idler*, we call our interviews "conversations," and they take the form of an edited transcript of a long rambling chat. The reason for this is twofold: first, when reading conventional magazine or newspaper interviews, I always skip to the bit where the subject is actually talking, and second, those conventional newspaper interviews are a con as they often attempt an objective Freudian psychological analysis on the basis of only an hour's meeting. (Details such as "he takes another sip of his Meursault" are somehow supposed to reveal the innermost depths of the celebrity's character.)

To me, the interesting thing is what someone has to *say*. Their character, their history, their ideas, their approach to life: these things will emerge through their conversation, their words.

And conversation should really take place at night. "Vote Hodgkinson, vote Conservative, vote go to bed early," jeered my friend John Moore one night when I announced at 10:30 p.m. that I was going to turn in. Dr. Johnson found people who went to bed early so irritating that he came up with the dictum "whoever goes to bed before midnight is a rogue." The earliest carriages should leave at 2 a.m. and anyone who wants to stay up later should be free to do so. For it is at night, free of the cares of the day, that the wine and the talk begin to flow. Hence the historical practice, long pursued in the UK, of drinking the most and staying up the latest as a matter of honour. "Drinking in particular was a universal practice," wrote the twelfth-century historian William of Malmesbury of the customs of the common people at the time of the Norman Conquest, "in which occupation they passed entire nights as well as days . . . They were accustomed to eat till they became surfeited, and drink till they were sick." Here is how Robert Burns describes this custom in his poem "Willie Brewed":

It is the moon, I ken her horn,
That's blinkin' in the lift sae hie;
She shines sae bright to wyle us hame,
But, by my sooth! she'll wait a wee.

Wha first shall rise to gang awa,
A cuckold, coward loun is he!
Wha first beside his chair shall fa',
He is the King among us three!

The first to go to bed is a coward and whoever falls down drunk
is the King! Splendid sentiments indeed. The practice persists
today in Scotland, I am relieved to say, and I remember many
happy evenings on the tiny and remote Isle of Eigg, where two
cases of McEwan's ale would be placed on the table, crab claws
would be smashed and eaten, and the chat would stretch out
till dawn, some of the participants taking short naps at the table
before waking to continue drinking and talking. One thinks too
of the laudable Irish custom of bringing a bottle of whiskey to
dinner, with nobody allowed to go to bed until it is empty. "Of
course, night is the best time for conversation, because there is
a certain lack of glamour in conversations during the daytime,"
writes Lin Yutang.

What is good conversation? It is certainly not about showing
off or shouting louder than the others. Some can talk and do
not listen. Some listen without talking. Both are equally irritating. The great conversationalist can do both in equal measure.
Indeed, if you talk without listening you become, in the phrase
of my friend Marcel Theroux, a "jukebox of monologues," await-
ing cues for rehearsed speeches.

Ideas emerge in conversation and are embellished, improved, contradicted or torn apart by the assembled company. Friends will come up with anecdotes that either affirm or disprove some notion. One's ideas are developed, modified. They are taken down from the museum shelf, dusted and put on view. And their true worth is revealed: the diamond turns out to be a piece of glass, the dusty stone a rare fossil.

Good conversation is a mark of generosity of spirit. I have met writers who refuse to talk, for example, about their work while in progress. They pompously excuse this mean spirit by saying something along the lines of "I don't want to jinx it by talking about it" or "if I talk it out I won't be able to write it"— which makes me think it must be a pretty fragile set of ideas that will evaporate into thin air if voiced. There is also the fear that one of the assembled company will perhaps steal the thoughts or ideas for their own work; an arrogant assumption indeed. Johnson, as we know, had no such prejudice. He didn't sit in the corner having great thoughts in silence, thinking, "I'll keep this to myself." He spewed forth, he showed off, he dogmatized, pontificated and disputed till the early hours. His love of company was also a fear of solitude; he was loath to go home where he would have to lie alone with his demons. It was this fear that led him to moderate Robert Burton's antidote to melancholy from "be not solitary; be not idle" into "when solitary, be not idle, and when idle, be not solitary."

For Johnson, good talk unified learning and experience. His biographer Walter Jackson Bate says he "prized activity of mind, a constant and ready exercise of the imagination in applying range of knowledge while simultaneously drawing upon acquaintance with 'the living world,' and he believed that these qualities were best formed in the energetic give-and-take of conversation."

Johnson was, however, a formidable opponent in conversation. Some of his friends were afraid to utter a word while in his company. Indeed, some complained that he would brook no opposition. "There is no disputing him," said the Rev. John Taylor. "He will not hear you, and having a louder voice than you, must roar you down." This brutality in conversation, however, is seen by G. K. Chesterton as a sign of an essentially democratic spirit. "The very fact that he wrangled with other people is proof that other people were allowed to wrangle with him. His very brutality was based on the idea of an equal scrimmage, like that of football. It is strictly true that he bawled and banged the table because he was a modest man. He was honestly afraid of being overwhelmed or even overlooked." In *What's Wrong with the World*, Chesterton compares Johnson's demagoguery with the refined polish of Addison, founder of the *Tatler* and the *Spectator*, who, he says, "was polite to everybody, but superior to everybody . . . a courteous superior [who] was hated."

In Plato's *Banquet* (*c*. 360 BC), Socrates talks all night until everyone has fallen asleep with the exception of Aristophanes and Agathon. The seventeenth-century thinker La Rochefoucauld, author of the *Maxims*, a short collection of reflections on human nature, developed his ideas and aphorisms over the course of attendance at many salons, particularly those of the literary hostess Mme de Sablé. The lines were the result of collective thinking, not of solitary reflection. The salons developed guidelines for conversational etiquette, and banned talk on religion or politics, as these subjects inevitably led to shouting, rudeness and a lack of harmony.

It is in the *Maxims* that we find La Rochefoucauld's admonition to self-centred conversationalists:

> One of the reasons why so few people are to be found who seem sensible and pleasant in conversation is that almost everybody is thinking about what he wants to say himself rather than about answering clearly what is being said to him. The more clever and polite think it enough simply to put on an attentive expression, while all the time you can see in their eyes and train of thought that they are far removed from what you are saying and anxious to get back to what they want to say. They ought, on the contrary, to reflect that such keenness to please oneself is a bad way of pleasing or persuading others, and that to listen well and answer the point is one of the most perfect qualities one can have in conversation.

It is for this reason, I think, that journalists often make good conversationalists. It is because (on the whole) they are curious about the world and about other people and about ideas. They want to learn; they do not think they have all the answers. It is this enquiring nature that led them to become journalists in the first place. A journalist is not a professional or an expert; he or she is an amateur, a wanderer, a seeker, and has none of the arrogance of the expert.

Conversation is an in-between activity; it takes place when the supposedly important business of the day is done. We see it as a reward for work; but in reality it leads to more and better work, as it is in conversation that our dreams and ideas are conceived and put forward. We come up with the idea; our friends moderate and develop it. When it comes to creating ideas, wrote the musicians Bill Drummond and Jimmy Cauty in *The Manual* (1990), their great work on creativity, it is a little-known fact that your best mate is a genius.

The idler's love of chat, sadly, is demonized by a society that prizes action above all else. "Don't talk about it—do it!" is the modern mantra. To which I reply, don't do it, talk about it. If the thing talked about is worth doing, then it will get done in its own time. But the talking is the best bit, the excitement of hatching plans and conceiving schemes. The talking, the bit before reality has hit, before the realization that some actual work will be involved in making this thing happen, when the possibilities are endless and our dreams of future schemes have not yet been dogged by practical demands; this part is when we can feel really free.

3 a.m.

Party Time

And, vow! Tam saw an unco sight!
Warlocks and witches in a dance!
Nae cotillon brent new frae France,
But hornpipes, jigs, strathspeys, and reels,
Put life and mettle in their heels.
Robert Burns, "Tam O'Shanter," 1790

We ain't beaten, man—we will beat this deluge.
Joe Strummer, Glastonbury Festival, 1997,
when the rain started coming

Bring together good drugs, good people and good music and you have a magical combination. At 3 a.m. we go beyond words.

I first experienced true hedonistic pleasure, of the sustained sort, in the early nineties, when the late, great journalist Gavin Hills introduced me to ecstasy and raves. What a revelation. At 22, I had assumed my partying days were over, but now it seemed the real hardcore nights out were all ahead of me. One of the great pleasures was the way this form of partying appeared to stretch out the night, to extend that 3 a.m. moment. One of the big hits of the day was the dance song "3 a.m. Eternal" by the KLF. I recently called the KLF's Bill Drummond and asked him about the thinking behind the song:

> 3 a.m. is the point in the day when the responsibilities and realities of the previous day have gone, and the responsibilities and realities of the next day haven't yet arrived. "3 a.m. Eternal" hit that point, as at that time, it seems that everything can be forever. It was an idea I had written on a bit of paper—3 a.m. Eternal. Then I discovered the Spanish word *madrugada*, meaning "the in-between time." At 2 a.m. you're wishing you'd gone home earlier; at 4 a.m. it's getting cold. But 3 a.m. has that magic about it. The rational intellect has vanished and you're in the moment. The doors of perception are open. Things happen. Like "Tam O'Shanter."

This is what being "out of it" means: being out of the everyday, dull, lifeless world, and in another world, full of surprise, warmth, magic and possibility. "Tam O'Shanter," written by Robert Burns in 1790, is about a farmer returning home late one night from the market, drunk. The inspiration for the poem came from a local tale that Burns had heard when working as a farmer and excise officer in Ayr. Here is how Burns described the legend:

> [I]t was the wizard hour, between night and morning . . . When he had reached the gate of the Kirk-yard, he was surprised and entertained, through the ribs and arches of an old Gothic window which still faces the highway, to see a dance of witches merrily footing it round their old sooty blackguard master, who was keeping all alive with the power of his bagpipe. The farmer, stopping his horse to observe them a little, could plainly descry the faces of many old women of his acquaintance and neighbourhood.

Central to the rave experience of the 1990s was, of course, the drug ecstasy, and reading Thomas De Quincey's *Confessions of an English Opium Eater*, I was struck by the many parallels between the ecstasy experience and De Quincey's description of opium. One of the similarities is the way the drug takes you to a different plane where you can remain for some hours. This contrasts with the less stable pleasure of drinking:

> The pleasure given by wine is always mounting and tending to a crisis, after which it declines; that from opium, when once generated, is stationary for eight or ten hours: the first, to borrow a technical distinction from medicine, is a case of acute—the second, the chronic pleasure; the one is a flame, the other a steady and equable glow.

A steady glow might also be a way to describe the ecstasy experience. This steadiness allows long periods of dancing and the experience of going into a trance; repetitive behaviour is encouraged, we are in the moment, there is no planning and no memory, just a simple joy of being. This is, or was, the attraction of ecstasy, and to someone like me, who had considered that at 22 it was time to "get real," knuckle down, have a career, the exhilaration brought by ecstasy, music and dancing all night was deeply liberating. This is how the radical chemist Alexander Shulgin describes the feeling:

> I feel absolutely clean inside, and there is nothing but pure euphoria. I have never felt so great, or believed this to be possible. The cleanliness, clarity, and marvelous feeling of solid inner strength continued throughout the rest of the day, and evening, and through the next day.

Mix this inner strength with music and you get hedonism, but for my generation the hedonism of those years was not mere escapism: it gave us an insight into how things could be, offering a glimpse of a more primitive state of being, free from hostility and desire and filled with the joy of living and of losing the ego in the collective. De Quincey made a similar point about opium, which, he said, "gives simply that sort of vital warmth which is approved by the judgment, and which would probably always accompany a bodily constitution of primeval or antediluvian health . . . a healthy restoration to that state which the mind would naturally recover upon the removal of any deep-seated irritation of pain that had disturbed and quarrelled with the impulses of a heart originally just and good . . . the opium-eater . . . feels that the diviner part of his nature is paramount."

The idle-minded are naturally of the belief that such states of intoxication are a human necessity and practised by all cultures around the world. They use such arguments to defend their habits. Indeed, it has often been argued that dancing while off your head can approximate to a spiritual experience. "A rabbi I interviewed said that young people s best chance of finding a mystical experience now is through taking drugs like LSD and ecstasy while dancing," remarked the late alternative thinker Nicholas Saunders, author of *E for Ecstasy* (1993), when I interviewed him in 1995. He said also that a Zen monk had seen God at raves. "First of all he couldn't stand the music, then he said: 'This is meditation. These people are completely in the moment. They've cut out the internal dialogue.'"

The music is, of course, absolutely central to the 3 a.m. experience. Music is the most magical of all the arts. Its power of transformation is nothing short of miraculous. Music can change our mood from misery to joy in a matter of seconds. It can send us into a trance for hours. It can help the body perform feats of physical dexterity unimaginable without it.

Dancing is unique among art forms in that it leaves no trace; it is done for its own pleasure; it is sublimely useless and non-egotistical. You cannot sign and sell it. Coleridge said that the three first art forms were architecture, cooking and clothes. But I think it more likely that dancing was the first. After all, you can dance naked and live in a cave, and when fruit weighed down the branches around you, there would not have been much need for cooking.

De Quincey was not a dancer but he wrote of the wondrous experience of listening to music while intoxicated; in his case, it was the opera on Saturday nights while on opium. "The choruses were divine to hear, and when Grassini . . . poured forth her passionate soul as Andromache at the tomb of Hector, etc., I question whether any Turk, of all that entered the Paradise of Opium-eaters can have had half the pleasure I had." De Quincey would also join "the poor" in their Saturday-night parties and then slowly wander through the back alleys of London on his journey home.

The authorities occasionally try to crack down on our right to party. Sex, drugs and rock'n'roll frighten our leaders. The nineties in the UK were marked by attempts by the bureaucratic botherers to legislate against raves and parties. These attempts tellingly stopped when they realized that our club culture was turning into a giant industry which attracted tourism and produced profits for poshies. The whole scene became increasingly bourgeois.

In the end, a compromise is generally reached: the party goes on.

The Church in the Middle Ages realized that parties were a human need, and that is why they allowed for them in the various celebrations of the year. The tradition persists in festivals such as the annual Glastonbury Music Festival, from which I returned three days ago and am still recovering. Glastonbury is a mind-blowing phenomenon: 150,000 people gather in a 400-acre site for three days or more to listen to music, drink, talk, dance and take drugs. It is essentially the 3 a.m. moment stretched out for 72 hours: no realities, just fun. The spectacle of so many people enjoying themselves is moving and uplifting. Those who dismiss it as mere hedonism have little understanding of the deep human need it fulfils. Glastonbury is about people talking to each other and dancing with each other free from the pressures of the commercial world. The necessities of life are readily available, so every fibre of one's being is devoted to enjoyment. It is a temporary return to a primitive state: no competition, no striving. You can talk and hang out, do nothing—for three days, which is a luxury indeed. The high spot of the 2003 festival was the Joe Strummer Memorial Camp Fire, organized by his widow Lucinda and other friends. Consisting of a fire that never went out, a ring of tree-trunk stools for people to sit on, a standing stone and a reggae sound system, it was a focus of security, fun and escape. It gave a little insight into how life should and could be.

Partying, wrote the philosopher Theodor Adorno in a 1953 essay, is wired into us. It's an instinct that we ought to indulge and not repress:

> If the satisfaction of instinctual urges is denied or postponed, they are rarely kept under reliable control, but are most of the time ready to break through if they find a chance. This readiness to break through is enhanced by the problematic nature of the rationality that recommends postponement of immediate wish-fulfilment for the sake of later complete and permanent gratifications.

In other words: you'll have plenty of opportunity to be miserable later, so why not enjoy yourself now. The finger-wagging, life-denying and patronizing "Just Say No" campaigns against pleasure-giving drugs, promoted by British and American governments, are always doomed to failure, not least because so many people just say "yes." We are a bewilderingly positive race. We are, in the phrase popularized by Oasis singer Liam Gallagher, "mad for it." We are equipped with a pleasure-seeking muscle that needs to be exercised.

The only problem with hedonism is that it is so enjoyable it can become addictive, and too-frequent debauches can seriously damage your health. After partying hard in my late twenties and early thirties, I became seriously concerned I might become an alcoholic. But I've found that circumstances have changed as I have grown older and that I party much less—not through an act of will but simply because that's the way things have gone. (And if there was ever one thing holding me back from drinking too much, it was a fear of becoming an AA person, never drinking again and being part of "the programme.") Certainly, when small children come on the scene, few people have enough energy (or staff) to get blasted all the time. Getting up at 6:30 a.m. and during the night is exhausting enough on its own without putting oneself through the rigours of hard living. I still have the odd binge, but it is much more occasional than in the past, perhaps just three or four a year. I try to build in a recovery period, too: plenty of sleep to restore body and mind to a comfortable condition. And that seems to be enough right now to satisfy the oblivion-seeker in me.

A life lived around parties can also make sober life seem dull by comparison, and leads to the unhealthy phenomenon of living for the weekend, while feeling depressed and powerless all week. The true idler wants to live a good life all the time, not just on Saturday nights, and the real lesson of hedonism is that we should attempt to enjoy *all* moments, not just those ones when we are out of our heads. Time should be savoured, not endured. Hedonism should provide ideas on how to live; it should not become a mode of living in itself, as it is unsustainable. William Blake's line "the road of excess leads to the palace of wisdom" is often used by habitual wasters to justify their behaviour. But too often they get stuck on the path and never reach the palace at the end of it.

I suppose too that a life lived around parties can become rather like hard work. The mental and physical effort involved in going out all the time becomes exhausting. You start to think you are missing out, and attend every social function that is offered to you just in case this one turns out to be legendary. Partying then becomes a chore—a habit rather than a pleasure.

Three a.m. is not all laughs. It is also the time when, if they so wish, the demons come to play. I have not experienced many dark nights of the soul, but when I have it was pretty terrifying. I remember one night very clearly. The 3 a.m. moment seemed to stretch into eternity. "In a real dark night of the soul it is always three o'clock in the morning," wrote F. Scott Fitzgerald in *Esquire*, in 1936. And this night was particularly long and particularly horrifying. Gruesome, grinning phantasms and goblins danced around in my head, making me sweat and sit up, terrified. The barriers in my mind had dissolved, and in flew the most frightful horrors. Luckily, my good 3 a.m. moments have outweighed my bad 3 a.m. moments, and no one said the path to idleness was going to be easy.

And when the party is over, we go home. That was the other great pleasure of the rave years—the chill-out session back at someone's house, where we would sit around as the sun rose, watching TV, drinking a goodnight beer, chatting or even just staring into space. We deserved it, after all the exertion of the previous eight hours. My friend James called it "the reward." And there was something special about the stillness of that moment, something akin to meditation, which is the form of idleness we will now turn to.

4 a.m.

Meditation

Numquam se minus otiosum esse, quam cum otiosus,
nec minus solum, quam cum solus esset.
Never less idle than when wholly idle;
Nor less alone than when wholly alone.

Cicero (106–43 BC), *De Officiis*

All day long no plans
And I remain at leisure
Wang Wei (698–759), "Reply to Chang Yin"

There is no purer form of idleness than meditation. It is where
doing absolutely nothing for hours on end is elevated to the
level of a spiritual quest.

Meditation is a way of connecting oneself with an inner dimension, a spirit, a soul, some sort of essence, which is largely ignored by the rational overmind. The *undermind* is what we're looking for when meditating, that part of our self which is beyond the intellectual, emotional and physical. We're trying to resist succumbing to mental flotsam, worldly care, anxieties of all kinds. The idea is that by nourishing the inner self in this way, we will build up reserves of strength which will make it easier to cope with life's problems and struggles. When our spirit is depleted and our soul undernourished, that is when the bastards can grind us down.

My father practises meditation with a group called the Brahma Kumaris, and for twenty years he has been getting up at 4 a.m. to do nothing for an hour before the day begins. I recently asked him why 4 a.m. was considered to be the best time to let one's soul roam around the cosmos:

Four a.m. might sound like a nightmare time to some, but provided that you have been to bed in good time and have had enough sleep, it can be the best time of day for filling with positive thought-energy. Actually, it's not even thought-energy, more a feeling of peace, and with that, a sense of well-being and good feelings towards others . . . When you nourish yourself well at that time it serves like a spiritual breakfast. You become much more likely to remain benevolent and less likely to become ratty, during the whole day. It's odd but it works. It's partly a matter of individual rhythm, setting the mind in that way while the brain's neurons are fresh and before the arousal hormones have started circulating—before you get going with the day's business.

Muslims are bound by a similarly strict routine. As part of the morning prayer, which takes place just before dawn, you must say "prayer is better than sleep" twice, presumably because your whole being would rather creep back into bed, and so a certain amount of convincing it otherwise is necessary. The argument for this early rising is that it helps to put you in a religious frame of mind for the whole day. "[C]elebrate (constantly) the praises of thy Lord, before the rising of the sun, and before its setting; Yea celebrate them for part of the hours of the night, and at the sides of day: that thou mayest have (spiritual) joy," says Al-Qur'ān.

Unfortunately, to me, sleep is better than prayer. My father's routines are a little too strict; getting up at 4 a.m. is my idea of pure hell. Most mornings, as it is, I am woken before 7 a.m. by the shrill bustle of small children, and I am nearly always grumpy about it, however cute their little faces are as they jump on my head. My father's calling demands other routines: in the Retreat Centre where he lives, piped music is played in all the corridors and halls for five minutes at regular intervals, every few hours, during which time everyone has to stop any activity and reflect for a while. All very lovely and good, but far too formal and disciplined for your idler, who would rather grab the moment when it presents itself.

I would argue for a far more informal approach. For me, meditation can occur at odd moments. It can come (and often does come) when staring out of the window of a train, always one of the true idle pleasures. But it's not always easy. People now conduct their business on the train, and you are forced to overhear their tedious jargon and self-bigging-up. The other day I had to listen to a young woman asking her boss whether her credit on a particular project could be upgraded from "researcher" to "senior researcher," because, she said, "I've contributed more to the project than the other girls." On the same journey, I listened also to a bore calling all his friends to tell them how well his job interview had gone. He used a phrase that I often hear in really boring business, "really exciting." It's hard to drift off into nowhereland when your arousal hormones are circulating wildly as a result of your rage at mobile-phone users. Fantasies of hurling their mobile phones from the train window tend to disturb the search for inner calm.

But if you try, you can take advantage of those lost moments of time in everyday life—waiting at the bus stop, sitting in a café when your friend is late, stuck in a car in a traffic jam—to meditate. It's not easy to drift off into nirvana while standing on a subterranean, airless, underground station platform, to be sure, but it is *possible*. It is not beyond the realms of imagining. And the more one practises turning those frustrating empty moments into delicious reflective inactivity, the better one will get at it. I'm not saying I have the hang of this: far from it. I still submit to stomping, to muttered curses, to the raising of my eyes heavenward and audible sighing when suffering travel delays. In my youth, I was known to punch bus stops in frustration. This was usually when I was late anyway. I knew, deep down, that my lateness was my own fault, but it was public amenities such as bus stops and benches which took the full force of my rage.

The way of the idler is a chaotic one. He attempts to escape from programmes, theories, formal spiritual practice, order, discipline. Routine irks him, as do rigid systems of thought. Bookshops are crammed with self-help books which promise that their particular theory will bring about all your worldly and spiritual desires. Get better at your job, at your relationship, your family; change your life in seven days. But the problem with alternative lifestyles is that they simply offer an alternative set of rules. One "ism" is replaced by another "ism." The Mind, Body, Spirit scene offers a bewildering choice of alternative leaders, for example, to whom weak people entrust their lives and money. If you look at alternative lifestyle magazines, the options are quite dizzying. Thousands of vitamin supplements, lifestyle gurus, meditation methods, ecstatic-dance therapies, ethical investments, mystic fayres, drumming workshops, complementary-health practitioners, spiritual paths, personal-growth techniques, hypnotists and self-awareness summer schools compete with each other for the attention of the poor lonely seeker of the truth. They all claim to offer the answer to your problems, they all cost money and they all simply encourage you to abandon one set of rules in favour of another, when surely the real solution is to abandon the whole idea of theories altogether. Rules are such a drag. I can never remember them, and then I break them, and then I feel guilty. Thank God I'm not a Muslim.

The idler's desire is to live with no rules, or only rules that have been invented by himself. He wants to develop the inner strength to have complete power over himself. He refuses to hand over that power to any authority whatsoever, however benign that authority may appear to be. And the fewer rules there are, the less potential there is for transgressing them all the time and therefore wasting energy in guilt. It is easy to become, in the words of Thoreau, a "slave-driver of yourself." We create sets of behavioural rules for ourselves and then feel bad when we fail to live up to them.

One of the myths that stops people meditating is that it's difficult. This myth is convenient to the various schools of meditation, in whose interest it is to present meditation as something that must be taught by experts and learned and therefore paid for. The confusing maze of meditation techniques puts further barriers between ordinary people and the art of reflection. Doing nothing, paradoxically, seems like such a hassle.

If we realized that meditation simply means staring into space, then it would be more accessible to more people. It's easy. A window is all you need. I remember being at school and being able to spend 20 minutes straight just staring out of the window. This is meditation, although my teachers called it daydreaming. Windows are free, and they are everywhere. They are on trains, on the top deck of buses, and most houses have loads of them. Read a poem, find a chair and sit by the window. That's all that's required.

The other key is to seize the moment. I was very impressed by Gavin Hills once when we were on holiday together. Hills was a beautiful mix of the cynic and the innocent, but I had not yet seen much of the innocent side. We were walking one day on the Isle of Eigg. We were surrounded by rocks, heather and mist. It was about lunchtime. Suddenly Gavin sat on a rock and said, "I'm just going to meditate for a bit." He then sat in silence for ten minutes. He had caught the moment; he didn't need a structure or a teacher in order to find moments of pure tranquillity. He knew them when he saw them. His other form of meditation was to get home from a rave in the early morning, take LSD and stare at the ceiling for hours.

If one does not like the idea of rising at 4 a.m. to meditate, then staying up till 4 a.m. may be an easier option. "To be up late is to be up betimes," as the old saying goes. And the chill-out culture, indeed, can encourage meditation. The phenomenon came into being when rave organizers realized it would be a good idea to provide rooms where clubbers, tired from dancing, could sit down and listen to ambient music, and take a break from the frenetic trance they had just been in. At the time, you would see pleasantly zonked-out ravers quietly chatting or simply staring into space or sitting peacefully with their eyes closed. The chill-out culture grew, and even spawned its own music. I remember sublimely happy times lying on my bed and listening to the great KLF album of 1990, which was itself called *Chill Out*, and remains the best of its kind. It was relaxing, inspiring and imaginative, all at the same time. Soon chill-out rooms grew as big or even bigger than the dance rooms in many clubs. There is now even an annual festival devoted to contemplation, with good music, in beautiful surroundings, called The Big Chill.

One of the best parts of the Glastonbury Festival experience is the 4 a.m. migration to the stone circle, which sits in a field overlooking the rest of the site. It's a spectacular sight at night, and there is a great spirit of fun and collective pleasure up there. You will also see many people simply lost in the moment, staring at the sky or at the scene below them, meditating, being, enjoying the sunrise.

Other readily available forms of meditation include hillwalking, sitting by the fire, listening to music with your eyes closed, fishing, smoking, and even "long periods of motorway driving" according to the writer Will Self. You can meditate on an aeroplane; in fact aeroplanes are ideal for contemplating the infinite mysteries of the universe since your head is literally in the clouds.

And Taoist wisdom teaches that it is wise to busy oneself with doing nothing:

> Whoever practises non-action
> Occupies himself with not being occupied

says Lao Tzu.

5 a.m.
Sleep

We are always hearing people talk about "loss of sleep"
as a calamity. They had better call it loss of time,
vitality, and opportunities.

Thomas Edison, "They Do What They Like to Do" (1921)

Along with Benjamin Franklin, the other great American enemy
of idleness was Thomas Edison, the inventor. Born in 1847, he
started work at 13 selling sweets and magazines to train travellers and spent his spare time reading books on science. His
love of money, machines and hard graft created the dynamic,
wealthy, productive captain of industry he later became. The
various inventions which poured forth from this hyperactive

character led him to co-found the Edison General Electric Company, which exists today as General Electric.

The great idlers of the time such as Oscar Wilde and Paul Lafargue had a vision of technology as freeing men from toil. Wilde, in "The Soul of Man under Socialism," wrote: "Machinery must work for us in coal mines, and do all sanitary services, and be the stoker of steamers, and clean the streets, and run messages on wet days, and do anything that is tedious and distressing." Lafargue, in "The Right to Be Lazy," wrote that "the machine is the saviour of humanity, the god who shall redeem man from the *sordidae artes* and from working for hire, the god who shall give him leisure and liberty." Edison, on the other hand, saw technology as a tool to increase productivity and efficiency. He used technology to enslave. The fact that he is portrayed as a great man, a paragon of American industriousness, tells us much about the decay of Western civilization in its journey from art and life to work and death.

Sleep, Edison believed, was a waste of time. It was unproductive, useless:

> Most people overeat 100 per cent, and oversleep 100 per cent, because they like it. That extra 100 per cent makes them unhealthy and inefficient. The person who sleeps eight or ten hours a night is never fully asleep and never fully awake—they have only different degrees of doze through the twenty-four hours.

This is clearly nonsense. If I have any less than eight hours' sleep—and I would prefer ten—I can't do anything. My treasured hours of sleep have been reduced lately as I have small children, who wake me at six or seven, and often during the night, too. If I haven't had enough sleep I find it very hard to do much work. I get angry, argumentative, unreasonable. I inflict cruel punishments for minor misdemeanours. I slam doors. I resent doing small tasks such as the washing-up. After a good night, however, I feel like a different person. I am cheerful, forgiving and helpful. I am also more efficient. I can do a day's work in three or four hours, leaving a lot more time for idling.

The very notion of cutting back on sleep is anathema to your idler, for whom sleep is one of the central pleasures of life. Sleep is a delicious procrastination, a putting-off, a giving-up, a Big Quit (to borrow a phrase from the writer Matthew De Abaitua). It is when we abandon the rational mind and give ourselves up to a greater power. Edison promoted the idea of "more work, less sleep." The idler's creed is "less work, more sleep."

It was Edison's anti-sleep philosophy that led him to invent that great enemy of idleness: the light bulb. This artificial sun was created so that we might no longer suffer the inconvenience of night, so unhelpful to hard work. With the invention of the light bulb, Edison enabled the workers to work at night. The light bulb brought in shiftwork, and Blake's prophecy in *The Four Zoas* (1797–1804) came true. It was the light bulb that managed

> To perplex youth in their outgoings & to bind to labours
> Of day & night the myriads of Eternity, that they might file
> And polish brass & iron hour after hour, laborious workmanship . . .

We are still bound to our labours today. In *Sleep Thieves*, Stanley Coren describes the effect of the light bulb on our sleep patterns:

[I]n one study conducted in our laboratory we looked at the amount of time the average young adult sleeps today and found that this was typically a bit less than 7½ hours a day. A similar study was conducted back in 1910. The timing is important because it was in 1913 that our modern tungsten filament light-bulb was introduced . . . Looking back at the sleep patterns that were common in the pre-tungsten-lightbulb era, we find that the average person slept 9 hours each night . . . In other words, Edison can claim to have added more than 500 hours of waking time to every year we live.

The invention of the light bulb was one of the greatest symbolic victories in the battle between industry and idleness. No excuse for slacking now! The attack on sleep has lately been taken up by the drugs companies peddling their sinister pills and potions. A recent television documentary on narcolepsy ran interviews with scientists claiming that they'd discovered a chemical in the brain, orexin, that keeps us awake, and the alternative US magazine *Utne* recently reported that drugs companies are hoping to harvest this chemical and use it to capitalize on our passion for work by creating drugs that increase alertness:

[D]rugs for specific disorders are finding wider markets. Provigil, a treatment for narcolepsy, a sleep disorder, is attracting attention as a possible alertness aid for healthy people . . . [Drug-industry critic Pat Mooney says]: "Mood-altering drugs that dispel discontent might be pressed upon workers."

This development was predicted by Dr. Michael Smith, writing in the *Idler* in 1995: "It's a safe bet that the hypnotic 'wonder drugs' of the future will be directed at reducing, rather than facilitating, our need for and enjoyment of slumber." I see ads on the London Underground for energy drinks and pills which claim to provide wakefulness to the user. One current ad runs the line: "Drained? You needn't be." It claims that such "daily fatigue" can be "beaten" by taking little capsules containing various vitamins. You don't get ads on the Underground saying: "Tired? Then Sleep More," as no one has figured out how to make money this way. Energy products are a clever idea, as we are all sleep-deprived. But who does this wakefulness serve? Our employers. Take this pill, say the ads, and we will help you to become more competitive, more alert, better able to work harder for your boss, less likely to lose your job. On the other hand, sleep-inducing drugs such as Valium and Temazepam, much beloved of druggies as a way of coming down after a night taking uppers, are beginning to become stigmatized. I foresee a Brave New World of drugged-up automatons, working round the clock, striving for efficiency and productivity targets.

The wise, on the other hand, have long praised sleep, this mysterious physical shutdown and friend to the afflicted. Dr. Johnson, a prodigious sleeper himself, saw sleep as a great leveller. If you're feeling down, he suggests, just imagine all the great men of our time curling up into a foetal position in bed as they wait to be transported to the Land of Nod:

> All envy would be extinguished, if it were universally known that there are none to be envied, and surely none can be envied who are not pleased with themselves. There is reason to suspect, that the distinctions of mankind have more shew than value,

when it is found that all agree to be weary alike of pleasures and cares; that the powerful and the weak, the celebrated and obscure, join in one common wish, and implore from nature's hand the nectar of oblivion.

The great Renaissance essayist Montaigne loved sleep; his only frustration was that when you are asleep, you are not conscious of its pleasures. He therefore instructed his servant to wake him in the middle of the night so that he could come into semi-consciousness in order to savour the feeling of sleepiness, and then enjoy the pleasure of going back to sleep. Sleep is a break from toil, a release of responsibility. Snuggled down under a duvet, we postpone our duties and give ourselves up to a greater force. Sleep can also have a magical effect on our worries. It can soothe away care, a function celebrated by the following sonnet by the Elizabethan songster Samuel Daniel:

> Care-charmer Sleep, son of the sable Night,
> Brother to Death, in silent darkness born,
> Relieve my languish, and restore the light,
> With dark forgetting of my cares return.
> And let the day be time enough to mourn
> The shipwreck of my ill-adventured youth;
> Let waking eyes suffice to wail their scorn,
> Without the torment of the night's untruth.
> Cease, dreams, the images of day-desires,
> To model forth the passions of the morrow;
> Never let rising sun approve you liars,
> To add more grief to aggravate my sorrow.

Still let me sleep, embracing clouds in vain;
And never wake to feel the day's disdain.

Heaven knows why—scientists still scratch their heads—but sleep can solve all our problems. When we are tired and fraught, our worries and duties can seem insurmountable. In the morning, things look better. John Steinbeck put it like this: "It is a common experience that a problem difficult at night is resolved in the morning after the committee of sleep has worked on it." Albert Einstein, whose achievements exceeded Edison's, made sure he had about ten hours' sleep a night.

In *Counting Sheep: The Science and Pleasures of Sleep and Dreams*, published in 2002, Paul Martin makes a compelling case for sleeping more. "The puritans and dull, workaholic sleep-deniers of this world would have us believe that sleep squanders our precious time that should instead be spent in fruitful labour," Martin complains. He argues that Edison, in fact, was a hypocrite, and, while he may not have slept long at night, he took frequent naps during the day. These naps, argues Martin, may even have led to the formation of many of his ideas. It is in that dozy halfway house between wakefulness and sleep, known as the hypnagogic state, that ideas are most likely to come to us. Sleep, therefore, is creatively useful. Martin also reveals the many scientific studies that have shown the benefits of long sleeping and napping to our health and happiness, and also shows how major disasters such as Chernobyl, and smaller ones such as train and motorway crashes, were caused by lack of sleep. Chasing profit leads to lack of sleep, and lack of sleep can lead to death.

Counting Sheep is a comforting read: it now seems that what we idlers are told are our refractory habits when it comes to slumber are actually healthy and normal. In being idle, all we are doing is crying out to live in a more ancient, natural and primitive fashion. Sleep is not for wimps; sleep is for the stronger breed, the great ones, the holders of the key to happiness—the idle.

Martin lists the following great thinkers who were also great sleepers and wrote in bed: Cicero, Horace, Milton, Jonathan Swift, Rousseau, Voltaire, Anthony Trollope, Mark Twain, Robert Louis Stevenson, Proust, Colette and Winston Churchill. I think it's fair to say that everyone on that list left the world a better place than they found it.

People who don't sleep much use their dynamism to bolster their self-righteousness, but they can do a lot of harm. They try to make other people feel bad. Mrs. Thatcher claimed to sleep only four or five hours a night. She used this fact to promote herself as a hard toiler and make others feel guilty, but in fact her chronic sleep deprivation probably contributed to her disastrous policies. I imagine she must have been in a zombie state when she conceived the Poll Tax. If you don't sleep you get mad, you get irritable, you get stupid, and you take it out on those around you.

I've fallen into the trap of sacrificing sleep to work myself. In order to make our deadline on an early edition of the *Idler*, we ended up working about 36 hours straight. Although I slightly enjoyed revelling in the heroic suffering after it was all over, to put ourselves through this pain was actually incredibly stupid. During the last 18 hours or so of this work bender, I worked at about one-tenth normal speed. It would have been more productive to go to sleep for nine hours and then resume work. Also, who cared if we were a day late on our deadline? Such masochistic punishment, born of a mixture of guilt and self-importance, must be resisted.

There is something unpleasantly controlling and brutal about people who claim not to sleep. Their desire to be in total control of their lives makes them afraid of oblivion. They fear sleep. Sleep is for the weak. A character in Jonathan Coe's novel *House of Sleep* (1998) puts it like this:

> Can you imagine what it must be like for a woman of Mrs. Thatcher's fibre, her moral character, to be obliged to prostrate herself every day in that posture of abject submission? The brain disabled, the muscles inert and flaccid? It must be insupportable.

Sleep itself can be seen as a radical act, something you have to fight for in a world that privileges action. John Lennon was a great defender of sleep. In "I'm Only Sleeping," he berates the botherers who call him lazy for sleeping so much, and calls them crazy for rushing around to no avail. What can be less harmful to the world than sleeping? Why do people always want to wake us up? Why can't they leave us alone? John Lennon is also proof that the sleepy lifestyle can produce great art. Who would you rather share a desert island with, Thomas Edison or John Lennon? Thatcher or Einstein? Who gives most and does least damage to the world, the sleepyheads or the half-crazed sleep-deniers?

In the sixties and seventies, there was a common belief that all household tasks would one day be performed by robots wearing artificial bow ties, leaving us free to lie around napping, as in Woody Allen's classic film *Sleeper*. But the reality is that technology has been a complete disaster when it comes to lightening the load. Labour-saving devices have not saved any labour. In his essential text "In Praise of Idleness," Bertrand Russell gives the example of a pin factory. In this pin factory, the workers work eight hours a day, and that produces enough pins for the world's needs. Then a technological advance appears:

> Someone makes an invention by which the same number of men can make twice as many pins: pins are already so cheap that hardly any more will be bought at a lower price. In a sensible world, everybody concerned in the manufacturing of pins would take to working four hours instead of eight, and everything else would go on as before. But in the actual world this would be thought demoralizing. The men still work eight hours, there are too many pins, some employers go bankrupt, and half the men previously concerned in making pins are thrown out of work.

A four-hour day is an eminently sensible way of operating our lives. It would give us a lot more time for sleep, as it is long working hours that eat into our sleep time. But in order to keep ahead in the office, we work later, skip lunch and maybe even work at home. After a late night, on perhaps just four hours' sleep, we drag ourselves into the office, sit there like zombies all day and say stupid things in meetings. Much better that we caught up on sleep and went into work after lunch. But this does not seem to be culturally acceptable. Heaven forbid we should have been enjoying ourselves midweek, and not at a sanctioned leisure time!

I implore scientists to come to our aid, and to stop inventing gadgets of empty promise. I implore employers to let their workers sleep. And I implore all readers to give mighty sleep the respect it deserves and submit to its power.

6 a.m.

On Holidays

I think if I had two or three quiet days of just sheer thinking I'd upset everything . . . I ought to go to the office one day and blow out my boss's brains. That's the first step.

Henry Miller (1891–1980)

Roll out of bed in the morning
With a great big smile and a good-good morning
Get out with a grin
There's a bright new day to begin
Wake up with the sun and the rooster
Cock-a-doodle like the rooster uster
How can you go wrong?
If you roll out of bed with a song?

Butlins "reveille jingle" from the 1950s,
played every morning at 7:30 a.m.

In the UK, 1936 saw a revolution in holidays. For the first time since the creation of the industrialized working class, the government, after countless committee meetings, studies and hand-wringing, cautiously introduced legislation that forced employers to give their employees one week's paid holiday per year. Presumably the legislators felt themselves to be great men, very generous and kind, for doing so. The "fun" entrepreneur Billy Butlin, who had been lobbying the government to introduce paid holidays, was in a position to capitalize on the new leisure time: his first camp, at Skegness, opened in 1936. By 1945, 15 million Britons were taking an annual holiday. If you compare this to the mere 8,000 people who, it is estimated, took holidays in the eighteenth century, it gives an idea of the massive expansion of the concept of the holiday as an organized collective pursuit, and of the commercialization of leisure.

The new annual holiday was justified in practical terms by a government committee. It would help efficiency: "It cannot, in our view, be denied that an annual holiday contributes in a considerable measure to workpeople's happiness, health and efficiency."

It was essential, however, that the holidays be filled with activity. They were not for loafing, since, as we have seen, idleness breeds sedition. Let them sit in the pub for a week, and the common people might get rebellious. In this, funnily enough, the new holidays had much in common with the first holidays of the eighteenth century, in that they were not simply "holidays for holidays' sake" and, at least ostensibly, had a practical purpose. In the eighteenth century the resort town of Bath was run by a man called Richard Nash, the Billy Butlin of his day, who as Master of Ceremonies welcomed jaded poshies for a week or two of healthful recreation. Nash offered a panoply of elegant diversions such as balls, book-borrowing, bathing, bands, lectures, dancing and horseback rides. The rich of the time were taking a break not from toil but from idleness. "Half of us come here to cure the bodily evils occasioned by laziness; the other half to remedy the mental disease of idleness and inoccupation, called *l'ennui*," wrote the famed letter-writer Elizabeth Montagu in 1749. Thus was born the activity holiday, which survives today, the only difference being that after 50 weeks of work we then have to suffer two more weeks of toil.

Billy Butlin was just the man to ensure that the twentieth-century toilers were kept busy, healthy and efficient when on holiday. A generation of workers had grown up who were so accustomed to constant labour and having their time controlled by another that they did not know how to make their own fun, and so had to have it arranged for them. A day at Butlins was a whirlwind of non-stop activity that your average seventeenth-century peasant would have found absurd. After reveille at 7:30 a.m., campers were subjected to a bewildering range of activities: "bathing, bowls, billiards, table tennis, gardens, lounges, dances, boating, tennis, cricket, concerts, beauty contests, physical training, the amusements of the fun fair, putting, riding, excursions, theatre." Rest was off the menu, as the American satirist and journalist Art Buchwald discovered on a visit to Butlins in 1957. At 5:30 p.m., he writes, after a day of jollity:

> We decided to sit down on a bench for a rest before dinner. A Redcoat came up with a worried expression on his face. "What's the matter, aren't you having a good time?"

Reflection, idleness, a pause for thought; such pursuits were not admissible in the world of Butlins. Non-stop amusement was the order of the day, in order to better return the masses to their posts in a cheerful state. The kids joined the Beaver Club, where the following moral code was taught:

B stands for: Be kind to animals.
E stands for: Eager always to help others.
A stands for: Always be clean, neat and tidy.
V stands for: Victory by fair play.
E stands for: Energetic at work and play.
R stands for: Respect for parents and all elders.

The Butlins holiday was the natural successor to the bank-holiday seaside trip. Bank holidays were introduced in 1871. Before the Industrial Revolution, days of leisure had been controlled by the church and were related to various saints' days. The "century of hard graft" had eroded these holidays, and now, in the early 1870s, the state decided graciously to intervene and provide a couple of secular days off. Again, the notion of a day off, as long as it was usefully spent, was defended in practical terms in a committee report, because they

> enabled so many operatives from time to time to visit our national exhibitions, and thus to acquire enlarged views, not only of the commercial greatness of their country, but of the important part which they are called upon to play in its promotion.

The "operatives," the authorities believed, would toil more happily and quietly in the mills if they knew they were contributing to "commercial greatness." The fact that "commercial greatness" means simply the vast wealth of a small ruling class was presumably shielded from the humble operatives. Big companies use the same tactics today: you are encouraged to be part of a "team" working for great things.

It was the bank holiday that led to that great British phenomenon, days out at the seaside, described as follows by a contemporary observer:

> one indiscriminate moving mass of cabs, cars, carts and carriages; horses, ponies, dogs, donkies, and boys; men, women, children, and nurses; and, the least and the biggest—babies and bathing machines . . . little boys with spades; nurses with babies; mammas with sewing; young ladies with novels; young gentlemen with Byron, canes, and eye-glasses; older ones with newspapers, sticks and spectacles.

We can detect in the above passage a whiff of snobbery. The cultured and sensitive of the day recoiled from the spectacle of the masses at play, the clerks and the factory workers gathering by rivers and at the seaside in vast numbers and enjoying the rare sense of being their own masters. Jerome K. Jerome, for example, called them "'arrys and 'arriets." And the realist writer George Gissing, writing in 1892, stood back in horrified awe:

> It is Bank Holiday today, and the streets are overcrowded with swarms of people. Never is so clearly to be seen the vulgarity of the people as at these holiday times. Their notion of a holiday is to rush in crowds to some sweltering place, such as the Crystal Palace, and there sit and drink, and quarrel themselves into

stupidity. Miserable children are lugged about, yelling at the top of their voices, and are beaten because they yell.

Gissing goes on to argue for a shorter working day; in other words, a better quality of life all year round:

> It is utterly absurd, this idea of setting aside single days for great public holidays. It will never do anything but harm. What we want is a general shortening of working hours all year round, so that, for instance, all labour would be over at 4 o'clock in the afternoon. Then the idea of hours of leisure would become familiar to the people and they would learn to make some sensible use of them. Of course this is impossible so long as we work for working's sake. All the world's work—all that is really necessary for the health and comfort and even luxury of manhood—could be performed in three or four hours a day. There is so much labour just because there is so much money-grubbing. Every man has to fight for a living with his neighbour, and the grocer who keeps his shop open till half an hour after midnight has an advantage over him who closes at twelve. Work in itself is not an end; only a means; but we nowadays make it an end, and three-fourths of the world cannot understand anything else.

Which passage seems to argue not for *more* wealth in the world, but more poverty. If we could be happier with less stuff, does it not then follow that we would have to work less, as we would need less money?

Our holidays today still suffer from the Butlins effect: they are over-organized, and it is a sin not to be cheerful. In the *Idler*, we once published a piece by the journalist Fiona Russell Powell on the all-in package holiday under the telling title "My Misery in Other People's Cheap Holidays." We wait at airports with the vulgar hordes, we get lost trying to find the holiday villa, we spend fortunes on rented cars, we lose our passports and have our bags stolen, we only realize on our last day that the local monastery sells fantastic cheap wine. Two weeks is no time at all; we are only beginning to acclimatize to the unfamiliar ways of another country by the time we have to go home. And then there is that absurd offspring of Butlins, the activity holiday, where various amusements such as skydiving, bungee jumping and banana-boating are encouraged, all designed to stop you thinking about how much you want to blow your boss's brains out.

We are still pitifully underserved when it comes to days off. In the last 70 years, the week's paid holiday has turned into four weeks in the UK, and, I understand, a paltry two weeks in the US (and even that meagre allowance is sometimes not taken by ambitious toilers). Is this civilization? Two weeks in the sun is surely scant recompense for fifty weeks of toil. The balance is all wrong. In ancient societies, there were far more rest days:

> In ancient Egypt popular supersititon forbade work on about one-fifth of the days of the year. In classical Athens there were fifty or sixty days of festival annually, and in Tarentum at its greatest period feast days outnumbered working days. In the old Roman calendar there were 108 days on which nominally for religious reasons no judicial or other public business could lawfully be transacted, while in the Julian calendar the number of such days was still greater.

So writes J. A. R Pimlott in *The Englishman's Holiday* (1947). It's incredible to me that with all our riches and machinery we have managed only to reduce the amount of leisure time enjoyed today compared with any time pre-1800. You might say we have weekends off, but weekends are when we do another sort of work—the shopping. It is when we play another of our allotted roles: that of the consumer. The supermarket, far from being cheap, quick and convenient, is expensive, time-consuming and a massive headache. What happened to lolling about and visiting local shops at our leisure?

At one time, work and play were more intermingled. The idea of a holiday as an escape from the hell of work is a relatively recent idea. The holiday came into being precisely when there was a need for it, when the notion of a job had settled down into a reality, and when the world of work became so unpleasant that it was absolutely necessary to take holidays to prevent us from going crazy. Before we all had jobs, there was less need to take an organized holiday as there were plenty of feast days, holy days and market days. And our leisure was mixed in with our work; for example, childcare and feeding pigs or chickens can be easily combined. Here is E. P. Thompson in *Customs in Common*:

> The term "leisure" is, of course, itself anachronistic. In rural society where small farming and the cottage economy persisted, and in large areas of manufacturing industry, the organization of work was so varied and irregular that it is false to make a sharp distinction between "work" and "leisure." On the one hand, social occasions were intermixed with labour—with marketing, sheep shearing and harvesting, fetching and carrying the materials

of work, and so on, throughout the year. On the other hand, enormous emotional capital was invested, not piecemeal in a succession of Saturday nights and Sunday mornings, but in the special feasts and festival occasions. Many weeks of heavy labour and scanty diet were compensated for by the expectation (or reminiscence) of these occasions, when every kind of social intercourse flourished, and the hardship of life was forgotten. For the young, the sexual cycle of the year turned on these festivals.

The development of the holiday has traditionally been viewed with suspicion by the authorities, who worry that the plebs will "waste" their leisure time in drinking rather than improving their minds or imbibing propaganda. The bank holidays of the late nineteenth and paid holidays of the twentieth centuries were different in one important respect from the old, pre-industrial feast days and saints' days—they were controlled from above. If the government could legislate for leisure, then the whole idea of the proles at play might become less threatening to the social order. Cromwell banned fun; the first act of Charles II in the Restoration was to restore the feast days that had been cancelled by the well-intentioned Republican. Daniel Defoe counted 6,325 maypoles erected in the five years after the Restoration. This gift of more free time was an extraordinarily liberal act on the part of the libertine monarch when you think that holidays, and in particular bottom-up, self-created holidays or holy days like May Day, have always been viewed as hotbeds of sedition.

"International May Day and American Labor Day: A HOLIDAY Expressing Working Class Emancipation Versus A HOLIDAY Exalting Labor's Chains" is an American socialist pamphlet published around 1913 which compares the natural, organic, people-created holiday of May Day with the officially sanctioned US Labor Day, created by the government in 1883. In the visionary prose characteristic of socialist writing of the period, the author interprets Labor Day as a lump of authoritarian sugar designed to make the capitalist pill easier to swallow. May Day, on the other hand, is a genuine, global festival of freedom. May Day's purpose is to

> demonstrate to the world that . . . [the workers] are all members of the same class, the proletariat—the propertyless, wage-earning class . . . in defiance of the capitalist class . . . When the police and cossacks of different countries appear on the scene on May Day it is always for the purpose of clubbing, maiming, arresting and killing working people; for the police and cossacks recognize that May Day is the drilling day of the Social revolution.

One might reflect that little has changed today: protests against global capitalism take place on May Day all over the world and are regularly dealt with by force. The author, Boris Reinstein, writes that by contrast Labor Day is merely a sort of sweetener for the workers:

> The American Labor Day, on the contrary, was a "gift" which the workers received from their masters . . . A vampire, when he settles down upon the body of a sleeping person and sucks its blood, is known to fan the victim with his wings, to soothe the victim's pain, and to prevent him from waking up and driving the vampire away. So was the Labor Day created by the political agents

of the American capitalists to fan the sleeping giant, the American working class, while the capitalists are sucking its blood . . . on that day the chains of wage-slavery are, figuratively speaking, taken off his limbs; he is made the hero of the day; his masters, the capitalists, stand before him in mock humility; their spokesmen in the press, pulpit and on their political platforms, overwhelm him with flattery; and the modern Silly Fool . . . throws out his chest and swells with pride. But, the day of mockery and of the Fool's Paradise over, the masters—who during this day are only slyly smiling—break out into sardonic laughter—though unheard by the slave—clap the chains back on his limbs and he again hears only the crack of the whip of Hunger and Slavery . . . May Day marshals the forces for the impending proclamation of Labor's Independence! It is the harbinger of Social Revolution!

This socialist revolution never happened, and now Americans work 2,000 hours a year, which I calculate to be around nine hours a day. In *The Overworked American*, Juliet Schor argues that Americans work a full month more each year than they did thirty years ago.

One problem, which underlies our meanness to ourselves when it comes to taking time off, is guilt, described by Nietzsche in *On the Genealogy of Morals* (1887) as a feeling of indebtedness (the word "guilt" has the same root as *guilder* and gold). We feel guilty at taking time off, as if we are not "doing our bit" for the social organism. The holiday has to have some use-value; it is not enough to take one for its own sake. "I really need a holiday," we say, and the implication is that we need to rest for a bit in order to return to our toil with renewed vigour. In 1882, Nietzsche condemned this emerging self-laceration and frugality in *The Gay Science*:

There is something in the American Indians, something in the ferocity peculiar to the Indian blood, in the American lust for gold; and the breathless haste with which they work—the distinctive vice of the new world—is already beginning to infect the old Europe with its ferocity and is spreading a lack of spirituality like a blanket. Even now one is ashamed of resting, and prolonged reflection almost gives people a bad conscience. One thinks with a watch in one's hand, even as one eats one's midday meal while reading the latest news of the stock market; one lives as if one "might miss out on something." "Rather do anything than nothing": this principle, too, is merely a string to throttle culture and good taste. Just as all forms are visibly perishing by the haste of the workers, the feeling for form itself, the era and the eye for the melody are also perishing. The proof of this may be found in the universal demand for gross obviousness in all those situations in which human beings wish to be honest with each other for once—in their associations with friends, women, relatives, children, teachers, pupils, leaders and princes: one no longer has the time and energy for ceremonies, for being obliging in a direct way, for esprit in conversation, and for any *otium* [leisure] at all. Living in a constant chase for gain compels people to expend their spirit to the point of exhaustion in continual pretence and overreaching and anticipating others. Virtue has come to consist of doing something in less time than someone else. Hours in which honesty is permitted have become rare, and when they arrive one is tired and does not only want to "let oneself go" but actually wishes to stretch out as long and wide and ungainly as one happens to be. This is how people now write letters, and the style of letters will always be the true "sign of the times."

If sociability and the arts still offer any delight, it is the kind of delight that our slaves, weary of their work, devise for themselves. How frugal our educated—and uneducated—people have become regarding "joy!" How they are becoming increasingly suspicious of all joy! More and more, work enlists all good conscience on its side; the desire for joy already calls itself a "need to recuperate" and is beginning to be ashamed of itself. "One owes it to one's health"—that is what people say when they are caught on an excursion into the country. Soon we may well reach the point where people can no longer give into the desire for a *vita contemplativa* (that is, taking a walk with ideas and friends) without self-contempt and a bad conscience.

Well, formerly, it was the other way around: it was work that was afflicted with the bad conscience. A person of good family used to conceal the fact that he was working if need compelled him to work. Slaves used to work, oppressed by the feeling that they were doing something contemptible. "Nobility and honour are attached solely to *otium* and *bellum* [war]," that was the ancient prejudice.

Nietzsche's point is: if we managed to remove our collective guilt about enjoying ourselves, then the culture of only taking time off when we are allowed by some outside force or by some inner self-controller might be damaged. The word leisure, incidentally, comes from the Latin *licere*, meaning "to be permitted." We have given responsibility for our free time to others, and we only have ourselves to blame.

Can we look to the trade unions to help in creating better lives? No. They're part of the problem. They believe the old myth "time is money." Their campaign for a "fair day's work for a fair day's pay" merely keeps the workers in check and limits their horizons to fractional wage increases or paltry improvements in working conditions. That's not freedom, that's merely a little bit of extra gold on the cage. The trade-union movement has done a lot of good over the last two hundred years—abolishing child labour was a good idea (although now I have young children of my own I'm inclined to lobby to bring it back), as was the gradual shortening of the working day (although they also invented the idea of overtime, which encourages the return of the 11-hour day as we try to earn some decent money. I remember as a removal man being delighted when we once did an 11-hour day, as it meant I would be paid 8 x £3 = £24 plus 3 x £4.50 = £37.50. But I had lost 11 hours of my life). Yet they still perpetuate a system of exploitation and alienation from the product of labour.

Certainly, we idlers should all be campaigning for more holidays. Jobs might be more bearable if we attended them only three or four days a week, and for three or four hours a day. Legislation in France, by the Socialist government of the late 1990s, which limited the working week to 35 hours led to a great increase in long weekends and trips to the seaside. Productivity, apparently, did not suffer. Jobs were created. But the 35-hour week was abolished by the new right-wing government in 2002. And this demonstrates the problem with legislative solutions: they can so easily be overturned by a new administration. The other problem with government-sponsored initiatives, however apparently benevolent, is that they are always another form of social control. They remove the spontaneity from festivity.

One solution may be found in the notion of off-peak living. This means you take your holidays in September, work odd hours, take trips during the week, stay at home on Fridays and Saturdays. Although I may counsel going with the flow in other areas of life, when it comes to travel and holidays, you are rewarded for going against the flow. Travelling on buses at 11 a.m. can be immensely pleasurable. If you avoid travelling around when the masses are on the move, you can bring a satisfying measure of control into your life. This would mean, of course, going freelance, a move rarely regretted by the former wage slave.

The management guru and friend to the idle Charles Handy invented the idea of chunking. This gives him one huge holiday every year. I went to interview him in 1993, when he explained the way that he divides his time: "I worked out that I need 100 days a year to make serious money. I do that by teaching at various seminars. I also need 100 days to write and read, and roughly 50 days a year for my causes and campaigns. That leaves 115 days which we can use for our own pursuits. By chunking it that way, we can spend 90 days sitting doing nothing—except eating, drinking and discovering Italy in Tuscany."

Theodore Zeldin has counselled the return of the sabbatical year, in *An Intimate History of Humanity* (1994):

> The weekend is only one half of the Sabbath. God also instructed the Jews to take a sabbatical holiday every seven years, in which they should stop tilling the land, cancel debts and release their slaves. The sabbatical year may become the human right demanded by the twenty-first century . . . Now that the expectation of life has been doubled, life cannot be viewed as offering just one chance, in one profession . . . The sabbatical year might offer a future, offering an opportunity to change direction or simply to

do what busy people do not have the time to do, namely think or take a long promenade.

The ancient Hebrew sabbatical year was the inspiration for the nineteenth-century working-class journalist William Benbow to propose his Grand National Holiday. Four weeks a year, in a row, in the summer—that was his proposal:

> Every seventh year, which was called the Year of Release, a continued festival was held among the Hebrews. Mark, a holiday for a whole year! How happy a people must be, how rich in provisions, to be able to cease from manual labour, and to culti-vate their minds during the space of a whole year! We English must be in a pretty state, if in the midst of civilization and abun-dance, we cannot enjoy a month's holiday, and cease from labour during the short space of four weeks!

Benbow was writing in 1832 when the newly created working class were toiling for ten or twelve hours a day, with only one day off a week, a handful of holidays such as Christmas and Easter, and no annual break. It is no surprise that his Grand National Holiday was never implemented, as it would doubtless have led to an opening of the eyes of the proletariat, and contributed to even more uprisings and riots than there already were.

The Grand National Holiday would also have led to the kind of overpopulation of holiday resorts that we see today. One good trick for those seeking the idle life is to move house to a holiday-type area and arrange to work in a flexible manner. Then you can grab the moment and go to the beach on a Wednesday rather than with everyone else at the weekend. Yesterday, for example, the sun was shining so we went to nearby Watermouth Castle, an eccentric North Devon theme park with no theme. I don't have to go there on a bank holiday when the rest of the world is there. Moreover, since I've been living in Devon I have not felt a desire to take a holiday. I work in the morning and have a holiday every afternoon. Trips, yes, long weekends and mini-breaks to see friends and go to weddings; but the idea of a fortnight in the sun each year holds less and less appeal. The expense and the hassle just don't seem worth it.

Another, more radical solution can be found in the idea of abandoning the notion of holidays altogether, and escaping the imprisoning work-versus-life mindset. When you are living an idle life, you have no toil to escape from. If your work is your fun, then why go away? The actor Keith Allen first put this idea to me in an interview in the *Idler*. He said: "Holidays mean nothing to me because I think I'm on holiday all the time." Similarly, the comedian, writer and broadcaster Arthur Smith, when asked "Do you take holidays?," replied: "My life is a holiday." This seems to me to be a wise solution. Even Billy Butlin had similar advice. "The secret of success in life is to enjoy your work . . . Have the confidence to strike out on your own, and start working for yourself as soon as you can." Which is a bit like Henry Miller blowing out the boss's brains.

Holidays, then, were originally saints' days when the peasants and nobility alike let their hair down for a few days. There was no travelling involved and the people created their own amuse-ments. There were a lot of these holidays. Then they turned into something healthy and good for you and filled with activity, but were restricted to the few. Then they became something healthy and good for you that was licensed and controlled by the state, available to the masses. They became secular and turned from holy days into holidays. And holidays became a lot more effort and a lot less fun than holy days. Having said this, I think it is well worth starting a campaign for more bank holidays. We should find out when all the old church festivals took place and lobby our powers to give us a new day off. Actually, we should forget about lobbying and just take the day off anyway—an unofficial bank holiday, an idler's day.

The problem with modern holidays is that they're such bloody hard work. My girlfriend, Victoria, has said that rather than blowing hundreds or thousands of pounds on a holiday she would rather hire a cook, cleaner and nanny for two weeks and stay at home, living in total luxury. It is no wonder that the true idler might recoil from the whole notion of the holiday, for isn't a holiday actually no more than the brother of work?

7 a.m.

A Waking Dream

"Father, O father! what do we here
In this land of unbelief and fear?
The Land of Dreams is better far,
Above the light of morning star."
William Blake, "The Land of Dreams," 1801

Full-time dreamer!
David St. Hubbins, in *This Is Spinal Tap*, when
asked what he would be were he not a pop star

How the idle at heart suffer for their dreaming. How cruel the
bureaucrats, teachers and usurers, who tell us our visions and
fancies are a waste of time. They tell us that we have our heads

in the clouds, they tell us to stop daydreaming, to stop staring out of the window. When we announce our extravagant schemes to our friends, they reply with a put-down such as "dream on" or "in your dreams." Dreams and idleness go together and are dismissed as "the children of an idle brain," as the sensible and grounded Mercutio says to the starry-eyed Romeo in *Romeo and Juliet*—meaningless, frivolous, silly and to be ignored. Dreamers are "away with the fairies." They are told to start living in "the real world."

We might ask, though: what is this "real world," exactly? Does "real world" mean toiling all day to produce useless objects that make other people poorer and less happy? Does "real world" mean office politics, insurance policies, pension plans, efficiency targets, Powerpoint presentations, debt collection, direct debit and corporate arse-licking? Is the "real world" joyless, sensible, punctual? Who is to say that all that stuff is not actually the fake world, the world we create in order to distract ourselves from the real world, which is the one we inhabit inside our heads? Both worlds are, after all, the products of imagination and language. I don't see why one should be privileged as being better than the other.

The real trick, indeed the duty of every serious idler, is to bring these two worlds together, to harmonize dreamworld and dayworld. It would be foolish to pretend that the Inland Revenue, electricity bills, service stations, mortgages and nappies don't exist. They do. I often try to avoid them, but they come and get you in the end. That pile of bills and duties and smells on the floor just does not seem to sort itself out.

We are reminded of the well-known story of Dr. Johnson, proving the harsh reality of matter, as recounted by Boswell:

[W]e stood talking for some time together of Bishop Berkeley's ingenious sophistry to prove the non-existence of matter, and that every thing in the universe is merely ideal. I observed, that though we are satisfied his doctrine is not true, it is impossible to refute it. I shall never forget the alacrity with which Johnson answered, striking his foot with mighty force against a large stone, till he rebounded from it, "I refute it thus."

The stone-kickers have a point, of course. But equally it is at our peril that we discount or ignore the world of dreams, for they exist too. By dreams I mean three related phenomena:

One: the strange visions and stories that come into our heads while asleep.

Two: the semi-conscious mind-wanderings referred to as daydreaming.

Three: our visions of a better world, as implied in the phrase "follow your dreams." Sometimes known as "madcap schemes."

In the journey towards living fruitfully with your dream-world, the first step is to stop ignoring the first type of dream. Dreamland is the original cyberspace, our own built-in spiritual virtual reality. Our dreams take us into other worlds, alternative realities that help us make sense of day-to-day life. Dreaming is a connection to our unconscious. It is to be treasured. Isn't it extraordinary that an activity which takes up so much of our lives is so often relegated to the realms of unimportance? We are based on dreams, they are at our centre. Listen to them.

Dreams make the world go round. Our dreams at night fill our subconscious with strange reflections of the day. In our dreams, our spirit roams free; we can fly, we can sing, we are good at things (I have dreams where I am brilliant at skateboarding, for example), we have erotic encounters with celebrities (I dream of Madonna; I used to, anyway), people's faces change as we look at them, one friend dissolves into another, as in a surrealist painting. Things are not what they appear. "It was my house but it wasn't my house." Reality, logic and reason fly out of the window. And this suspension of pedestrian rules, the total lack of self-policing, can be a huge inspiration to the creative spirit. The wise among us know this. Simone de Beauvoir, for example, wrote:

> I anticipate my nocturnal adventures with pleasure as I go to sleep; and it is with regret that I say good-bye to them in the morning . . . They are one of the pleasures I like best. I love their total unexpectedness and above all their gratuity . . . That is why in the morning I often try to bring them together again, to reform them from the shreds that float behind my eyelids, glittering but still fading fast.

For surrealist filmmaker Luis Buñuel, dreams were the highlight of his life:

> If someone were to tell me I had twenty years left, and ask me how I'd like to spend them, I'd reply: "Give me two hours a day of activity, and I'll take the other twenty-two in dreams . . . provided I can remember them." I love dreams, even when they're nightmares, which is usually the case.

The two hours a day, presumably, were when Buñuel would fashion some sort of art from his visions. Robert Louis

Stevenson used his dreams to create plots and characters for his stories. Little creatures which he called Brownies revealed stories to him. He said, "My Brownies do one half of my work while I am fast asleep." Stevenson's Brownies sound a bit like the "chattering elves of hyperspace" cited by Terence McKenna as one of the key elements of the experience of taking the drug DMT: mischievous, scampish, truth-giving sprites and fairies.

There are many examples of the creative power of dreams: "Kubla Khan" came to Coleridge in a dream, as did the tune for "Yesterday" to Paul McCartney. The idea for *Frankenstein* revealed itself to the young Mary Shelley in a waking dream; Einstein said that a breakthrough in his theory of relativity had come to him in a dream; Descartes had a dream that set him on the path towards his whole philosophical system (he said it was "the most important affair" of his life). Mendeleyev dreamt the Periodic Table after falling asleep at his desk. J. K. Rowling was staring out of the window on a train when the idea, plot and characters for *Harry Potter* came to her.

An outstanding example of the world of dreams entering our universe is Lewis Carroll's late-nineteenth-century "Alice" stories. Here is a masterpiece of the imagination where the everyday world is turned upside down and inside out. In the case of the "Alice" books, the idea was to show how absurd the adult world appears to a child, how full of crazy logic and pointless rules. Our great poets have been those who have broken down the barriers between dream and life—a definition of poetry might be "where dreams meet reality." Seeing a great band play fills us with the joy of the experience of another person's dreamworld entering the real world.

The art of living is the art of bringing dreams and reality together. This to me is the true spirit of anarchy; each feeds off the other in a happy circle of our own creation. There should be a dialogue between the two worlds, a harmony. The separation of the two into antagonistic fields of human experience, into mutually exclusive ways of living, is a tragedy and is reflected in "dissociations of sensibility" in other areas of life. Happy marriages have broken apart. Work and life have become divorced, art and science, too. People have become divorced from their thoughts; the specialists have taken over.

In the world of anti-dreams, the careerist experts have conquered small worlds and excluded others from them, unless they pay. The world of the mind is owned by psychoanalysts, the world of government by political parties, the world of food by supermarkets and their paid promoters, the celebrity chefs. One whole world has been split into millions of little ones, all competing with one another. This leads to a sense of powerlessness and stupidity. We follow someone else's rules and ask other people for help. We are helpless, and so we pay others for advice. But "dreaming is free," as Debbie Harry put it. It is completely outside of the commercial world. No one has managed to make money out of dreams, unless you include the fees paid to Sigmund Freud and his disciples. There are no dream gadgets, or dream-machine factories. Perhaps it is precisely because dreams are free that we put so low a value on them. We are more interested in our new cars than in the contents of our own heads.

Love, too, is a kind of dream, a fanciful imagining of a future state of perfection. When we are in love, we project on to the love object our hopes for a dream life. We believe that the other will help us to create the dream. Coleridge described this feeling as an "instinctive craving after this unknown bliss." Anyone who has been in love, even briefly, knows the elating and displacing effect it has on the spirit; it puts us into a sort of daydream, a delightful limbo land. It is also a state into which we can enter or from which (usually) we can withdraw. When we are in love, we can easily forget about it for some hours. Then we recall the feeling, bring it into our hearts, let it develop, flow, enjoy its presence. In this sense, it is like a dream in that it is a temporary state rather than a permanent one. We can choose to experience it, we can invite the feeling in and luxuriate in it. Then we can put it to one side and go and pay the gas bill. Relationships break down because neither side of love—the future bliss or the dreamy neverland—appears to happen in the long term. Perhaps if we realized that love is a dream we could enjoy it and live with it without letting it first enthral and then disappoint us.

Particularly relevant to the idler who is searching for rough creative material from which to hew his or her works is the hypnagogic state, the twilight world between sleeping and wakefulness, where the dreamer is conscious of dreaming, and may even have some control over the direction and content of the visions.

Coleridge was fascinated by his own "Reveries" and was the first writer to give them an identity distinct from normal dreams. In these reveries, he wrote in his *Notebook* around 1811, the mind orders the phantasms of sleep. "The Imagination, the true inward Creatrix, instantly out of the chaos or shattered fragments of Memory puts together some form to fit it." In other words, a sort of film director of the soul comes forward and starts to direct the progress of the vision. Coleridge wrote that we needed some sort of theory for this more active dream-state, in order to "explain and classify these strange sensations, the organic material Analagous (Ideas, materials as the Cartesians say) of Fear, Hope, Rage, Shame & strongest of all Remorse . . . The solution of this Problem would, perhaps, throw great doubt on the present dogma, that the Forms & Feelings of Sleep are always the reflections and Echoes of our waking thoughts, & Experiences."

The hypnagogic state Coleridge describes is more commonly referred to as "lucid dreaming." A lucid dream, writes Paul Martin in *Counting Sheep*, "is a special sort of dream in which the dreamer is fully aware at the time that he or she is dreaming . . . they are more vivid and more memorable than ordinary dreams . . . lucid dreams are more like acting out fantasies and desires."

The first step in encouraging lucid dreaming is the same as the first step on the long journey to idleness: throw out the alarm clock. You need to get plenty of sleep and then wake up naturally. Martin counsels: "Train yourself to think about your dreams first thing every morning when you wake up, before your memories evaporate and waking thoughts replace them." Learn to recognize when you are dreaming. And ask yourself, when awake, if you are dreaming. This habit will help you to hold on to your dreams. Lucid dreaming is a "freely available way of having fun and improving the quality of life. The adept lucid dreamer can enjoy delightful experiences across into the waking state, helping to bolster their mood during the day."

It works.

Waking dreams, lucid dreams and daydreams, as well as being

a source of pleasure in themselves, can also be of practical use in helping us create visions of our ideal life. Once the vision is in place, then the life will eventually follow. Be brave, idleheart! The difficulty is that we get ourselves caught in a double bind: we work so hard that we do not allow ourselves time to dream, and therefore we continue to work hard because we have not had the time to dream up an alternative. If you are ever sacked or made redundant, then I suggest you thank the good Lord above. It was while on the dole that I first conceived of the idea of the *Idler* magazine. As a dolie, I had long periods of lying in bed and then in the bath. But it was these luxurious (though admittedly guilt-torn) stretches of hypnagogia that gave me the foundations to create a work life for myself which I have thoroughly enjoyed. At a later period I used to lie in bed and imagine my ideal life. It went like this: live on the Isle of Eigg (a remote Scottish island and the most beautiful place in the world); read and write in the morning, chop logs in the afternoon, after a nap; spend the evening drinking in Dean Street, Soho. Obviously that's impossible. However, over the last seven months of writing this book, I have lived in a beautiful place, worked every morning, spent every afternoon in the garden, or on the cliffs or in the shed, and spent the evenings eating, drinking and talking. My dream, in essence, came true, even if the details may have changed.

Follow your dreams: this piece of advice is so often repeated that it has become a cliché. But it is worth reflecting on it for a moment. All too often, our consumer society equates following our dreams with making a lot of money, or being famous, or both. Money equals freedom is the myth. To be rich and famous is the dream of *Hello!* and *OK!* magazines. The money and fame, we are led to believe, or allow ourselves to be fooled into believing, will bring us the freedom and independence that we crave. We are naturally strong-willed creatures; anyone who has had children will know that little kids are imperious by nature. They will not be told what to do. That is why we have invented a series of tricks—punishments, threats, bribes, treats, no TV, no chocolate—designed to bend children to our will. "Break their wills betimes" were, we remember, the chilling words of advice from Methodist preacher John Wesley. In the same way, we adults have created a battery of techniques to oppress our own will and make it subservient. To be rich and famous seems like such a far-off dream that we are apt to give up completely and not even try to make tiny improvements to our life. The only effort we make to be idle is to enter the National Lottery each week. No, dreams are not about money. They are about you, and they are about quality of life and imagination. Perhaps the reason why we find this difficult to accept is fear—we are afraid of our dreams, and so we deliberately avoid them.

Another disgraceful misuse of the word "dream" is seen in its appropriation by modern marketing and company propaganda. During the dot-com boom, it always struck me as absurd how the new young companies such as boo.com spoke of themselves in almost visionary terms: *We have a dream*, they said. *Our staff share the dream. They are working hard to make the dream come true.* But what was this dream, exactly? A dream of selling large quantities of sensible sportswear to the youth of Europe? That's not a dream, that's merely a vision of large profits.

Real dreams are about seeing what others miss. If you have your head in the clouds, you can see the world more clearly. Maybe this is why so many poets and visionaries die young or drink heavily—it is painful when you can see the truth up close. It can be unbearable. The poet's response is to create things, to bring joy into the world and to report his vision to anyone who will listen, as Blake did in *The Four Zoas*, his astonishingly accurate prophecy of the harm that the Industrial Revolution and its agents would do to Albion:

> And all the arts of life they changd into the arts of death
> The hour glass contemnd because its simple workmanship
> Was as the workmanship of the plowman & the water wheel
> That raises water into Cisterns broken and burnd in fire
> Because its workmanship was like the workmanship of the
>   Shepherd
> And in their stead intricate wheels invented Wheel without wheel
> To perplex youth in their outgoings & to bind to labours
> Of day & night the myriads of Eternity. that they might file
> And polish brass & iron hour after hour laborious workmanship
> Kept ignorant of the use that they might spend the days of
>   wisdom
> In sorrowful drudgery to obtain a scanty pittance of bread
> In ignorance to view a small portion & think that All
> And call it Demonstration blind to all the simple rules of life

Or as Cicero wrote in *De Officiis*: "[W]e must regard as something base and vile the trade of those who sell their toil and industry, for whoever gives his labour for money sells himself and puts himself in the rank of slaves." Or again, as Charles Handy puts it: "It has always seemed to me slightly bizarre that we should queue up to sell our time to someone else. It's a form of slavery, voluntary slavery. We think it's great but it's crazy."

It is the same thought that Paul Lafargue, Bertrand Russell, Nietzsche and many hundreds of other writers and thinkers have articulated over the past two thousand years. It is the same thought that you and I have had.

I have a dream. It is called love, anarchy, freedom. It is called being idle.

Further Reading

A list of books and articles referred to, consulted
or of related interest:

Ackroyd, Peter, *Blake* (London: Minerva, 1996).

Adams, Jad, *Madder Music, Stronger Wine: The Life of Ernest Dowson, Poet and Decadent* (London: I. B. Tauris, 2000).

Arnold, Matthew, "Introduction," in *Poetry of Byron*, ed. Matthew Arnold (London: Macmillan, 1881).

Baker, Phil, *The Dedalus Book of Absinthe* (Sawtry: Dedalus, 2001).

Barrie, J. M., *My Lady Nicotine* (London: Hodder & Stoughton, 1901).

Bate, Walter Jackson, *Samuel Johnson* (London: Hogarth, 1984).

Baudrillard, Jean, *America*, trans. Chris Turner (London: Verso, 1988).

Benbow, William, "The Grand National Holiday and Congress of the Productive Classes" (London: National Union of the Working Class, 1832).

Benjamin, Walter, *The Arcades Project*, trans. Howard Eiland and Kevin McLaughlin (Cambridge, Mass., and London: Belknap Press, 2002).

Bernard, Jeffrey, "In Conversation with . . .," *Idler* 8 (1995).

Blake, William, *The Poetical Works of William Blake*, ed. John Sampson (London: Oxford University Press, 1914).

Boswell, James, *The Life of Samuel Johnson* (London: Dent, 1946).

de Botton, Alain, *How Proust Can Change Your Life* (London: Picador, 1997).

Brown, Pete, *Man Walks into a Pub: A Sociable History of Beer* (London: Macmillan, 2003).

Burns, Robert, *The Poetical Works of Robert Burns*, ed. J. L. Robertson (London: Henry Frowde, 1904).

Butlin, Billy, with Paul Dacre, *The Billy Butlin Story: "A Showman to the End"* (London: Robson, 1982).

Byron, George Gordon, Lord, *Poetry and Prose* (Oxford: Clarendon Press, 1962).

Caine, William, *An Angler at Large* (London: Kegan Paul, 1911).

Carroll, Lewis, *Alice's Adventures in Wonderland* (London: Methuen, 1965).

Carroll, Lewis, *Through the Looking Glass* (London: Methuen, 1955).

Cauty, Jimmy, and Bill Drummond, *The Manual: How to Have a Number One the Easy Way* (London: Ellipsis, 1998).

Chesterton, G. K., "The Ideal of a Leisure State," *Illustrated London News*, 21 March 1925.

Chesterton, G. K., "On Lying in Bed," in *Tremendous Trifles* (London: Methuen, 1909).

Chesterton, G. K., *What's Wrong with the World* (London: Cassell, 1910).

Cobbett, William, *Cottage Economy* (London: Peter Davies, 1926).

Cobbett, William, *Rural Rides* (London: Penguin, 2001).

Coe, Jonathan, *House of Sleep* (London: Penguin, 1998).

Coleridge, S. T., *Biographia Literaria* (London: Dent, 1939).

Coren, Stanley, *Sleep Thieves: An Eye-opening Exploration into the Science and Mysteries of Sleep* (London and New York: Free Press, 1996).

De Abaitua, Matthew, "The Big Quit," *Idler* 27 (1997).

De Quincey, Thomas, *Confessions of an English Opium Eater* (London: Penguin, 1986).

Doyle, Sir Arthur Conan, "The Man with the Twisted Lip," in *The Adventures and Memoirs of Sherlock Holmes* (London: Penguin, 2001).

Doyle, Sir Arthur Conan, "The Resident Patient," in *The Adventures and Memoirs of Sherlock Holmes* (London: Penguin, 2001).

Ehrenreich, Barbara, *Nickel and Dimed: On (Not) Getting By in America* (New York: Metropolitan Books, 2001).

Engels, Friedrich, *The Condition of the Working Class in England* (London: Penguin, 1987).

Frisbie, Robert Dean, *The Book of Puka-Puka* (Hawaii: Booklines Ltd, 1987).

George, Charles H. (ed.), *Revolution: Five Centuries of Europe in Conflict* (New York: Dell, 1962).

Glenn, Josh, "Cocktail Revolution," *Idler* 6 (1994).

Glenn, Josh, "The Sweetest Hangover," *Idler* 16 (1996).

Glenn, Josh, "Idle Idol: Henry Miller," *Idler* 19 (1997).

Goncharov, Ivan, *Oblomov* (London: Penguin, 1954).

Grahame, Kenneth, *The Wind in the Willows* (Oxford: Oxford University Press, 1999).

Handy, Charles, *The Empty Raincoat: Making Sense of the Future* (London: Hutchinson, 1994).

Handy, Charles, "In Conversation with . . .," *Idler* 3 (1993).

Hemingway, Ernest, *For Whom the Bell Tolls* (London: Penguin, 1955).

Hibbert, Christopher, *The Personal History of Samuel Johnson* (London: Pimlico, 1998).

Hirst, Damien, and Gordon Burn, *On the Way to Work* (London: Faber & Faber, 2001).

Hobsbawm, Eric, *Industry and Empire: From 1750 to the Present Day* (London: Penguin, 1999).

Hodgkinson, Tom, and Matthew De Abaitua (eds.), *The Idler's Companion: An Anthology of Lazy Literature* (London: 4th Estate, 1996).

Holmes, Richard, *Coleridge: Darker Reflections* (London: Harper-Collins, 1998).

Holmes, Richard, *Dr. Johnson and Mr. Savage* (London: Hodder & Stoughton, 1993).

Holmes, Richard, *Coleridge: Early Visions* (London: Harper-Collins, 1998).

Hughes, Ted, *River* (London: Faber & Faber, 1983).

Hutchinson, Robert J. (ed.), *The Book of Vices: A Collection of Classic Immoral Tales* (New York: Riverhead Books, 1995).

Huysmans, J.-K., *Against Nature* (London: Penguin, 1959).

Huysmans, J.-K., *With the Flow* (London: Hesperus Press, 2003).

Jayanti, B. K., *God's Healing Power: How Meditation Can Help Transform Your Life* (New York: Penguin, 2002).

Keats, John, *Poems* (Oxford: Oxford University Press, 1933).

Keats, *Letters*, ed. Robert Gittings (Oxford: Oxford University Press, 1970).

King James I, *A Counterblaste to Tobacco* (London: Rodale Press, 1954).

Knight, Joseph (ed.), *Pipe and Pouch: A Smoker's Own Book of Poetry* (Boston, Mass.: J. Knight Co., 1895).

Jerome, Jerome K., *Idle Thoughts of an Idle Fellow: A Book for an Idle Holiday* (London: Field and Tuer, 1886).

Jerome, Jerome K., *Three Men in a Boat (to Say Nothing of the Dog)* (Bristol: Arrowsmith, 1889).

Johnson, Samuel, *Rasselas, Poems and Selected Prose*, ed. Betrand

H. Bronson (New York and Toronto: Rinehart & Co., 1958).

Johnson, Samuel, *The Works: A New Edition in Twelve Volumes* (London: F. C. & J. Rivington, 1823).

Karmel, Miriam, "Drugs for All Reasons," *Utne* magazine, July/Aug 2003.

Kirsten, Sven A., *The Book of Tiki: The Cult of Polynesian Pop in Fifties America* (London: Taschen, 2000).

Klein, Richard, *Cigarettes Are Sublime* (London: Picador, 1995).

Krausnick, Helmut, and Martin Broszat, *Anatomy of the SS State*, trans. Dorothy Long and Marian Jackson (St. Albans: Paladin, 1970).

Lafargue, Paul, *The Right to Be Lazy, and Other Works*, trans. Charles H. Kerr (Charles H. Kerr & Co., 1907).

La Rochefoucauld, François, duc de, *Maxims*, trans. L. W. Tancock (London: Penguin, 1959).

Larrissy, Edward, *Rereading Literature: William Blake* (Oxford: Blackwell, 1985).

Lawrence, D. H., *Selected Poems*, ed. Keith Sagar (London: Penguin, 1972).

Leadbetter, Charles, *Up the Down Escalator: Why the Global Pessimists Are Wrong* (London: Penguin, 2003).

Le Goff, Jacques, *Time, Work and Culture in the Middle Ages*, trans. Arthur Goldhammer (Chicago and London: University of Chicago Press, 1980).

Loesser, Frank, (libretto) *How to Succeed in Business without Really Trying* (London: Frank Music Co., 1965).

Manning, Mark, *Collateral Damage: The Zodiac Mindwarp American Tour Diaries* (London: Creation, 2002).

Manning, Mark, *Fucked by Rock: The Unspeakable Confessions of Zodiac Mindwarp* (London: Creation, 2001).

Marvell, Andrew, *The Complete Poems*, ed. Elizabeth Story Donno (London: Penguin, 1972).

Martin, Paul, *Counting Sheep: The Science and Pleasures of Sleep and Dreams* (London: Flamingo, 2003).

Meades, Jonathan, "No self-respecting loiterer possesses any intent whatsoever, indeed loitering's very essence resides in its passivity," *The Times*, 7 September 2002.

Melville, Herman, "Bartleby, the Scrivener," in *The Complete Short Fiction* (New York: Random House Inc., 1997).

McKenna, Terence, "In Conversation with . . .," *Idler* 1 (1993).

Miller, Henry, *Tropic of Cancer* (London: Flamingo, 1993).

Montaigne, Michel de, *Complete Essays*, trans. M. A. Screech (London: Penguin, 1993).

Moore, Suzanne, "Labour of Love," *Idler* 9 (1995).

More, Thomas, *Utopia* (London: Penguin, 2003).

Nicholson, John, "Primer of English Violence," *Idler* 25 (1999).

Nicholson, Virginia, *Among the Bohemians: Experiments in Living 1900–1939* (London: Viking, 2002).

Nietzsche, Friedrich, *The Gay Science*, trans. Walter Kaufmann (New York: Vintage, 1974).

Nietzsche, Friedrich, *On the Genealogy of Morals*, ed. Walter Kaufmann, trans. Walter Kaufmann and R. J. Hollingdale (New York: Vintage, 1969).

Nietzsche, Friedrich, *Twilight of the Idols*, trans. R. J. Hollingdale (London: Penguin, 1968).

Orwell, George, *Down and Out in Paris and London* (London: Penguin, 2003).

Osborne, Andrew, "Work is three times as deadly as war, says UN," *Guardian*, 2 May 2002.

Paine, Thomas, *The Rights of Man* (London: Dent, 1915).

Paquot, Thierry, *The Art of the Siesta*, trans. Ken Hollings (New York: Marion Boyars, 2003).

Pascal, Blaise, *Pensées*, trans. A. J. Krailsheimer (London: Penguin, 1995).

Pearsall, Ronald, *The Worm in the Bud: The World of Victorian Sexuality* (London: Pelican, 1971).

Pimlott, J. A. R., *The Englishman's Holiday: A Social History* (London: Faber & Faber, 1947).

Playboy Enterprises Inc., *The Playboy Book* (London: Mitchell Beazley, 1994).

Porter, Roy, *Flesh in the Age of Reason* (London: Allen Lane, 2003).

Powell, Fiona Russell, "My Misery in Other People's Cheap Holidays," *Idler* 24 (1998).

Reid, Douglas, "Thank God It's Monday," *Idler* 31 (2002).

Reid, Douglas, "Weddings, Weekdays, Work and Leisure in Urban England 1791–1911: The Decline of Saint Monday Revisited," *Past and Present* 153 (1996).

Reinstein, Boris, "International May Day and American Labor Day: A HOLIDAY Expressing Working Class Emancipation Versus A HOLIDAY Exalting Labor's Chains" (New York: National Executive Committee, Socialist Labor Party, 1913).

Rimbaud, Penny, *Shibboleth: My Revolting Life* (Oakland, Calif.: AK Press, 1999).

Rogers, Cameron, *The Magnificent Idler: The Story of Walt Whitman* (London: Heinemann, 1926).

Russell, Bertrand, *In Praise of Idleness and Other Essays* (London: Routledge, 2004).

Russell, Bertrand et al, *Why Work? Arguments for the Leisure Society*, ed. Vernon Richards (London: Freedom Press, 1983).

Sartre, Jean-Paul, *Nausea*, trans. Robert Baldick (London: Penguin, 2000).

Saunders, Nicholas, *Ecstasy Reconsidered* (London: N. Saunders, 1997).

Saunders, Nicholas, *E for Ecstasy*, ed. Liz Heron (London: N. Saunders, 1993).

Saunders, Nicholas, "In Conversation with . . .," *Idler* 9 (1995).

Schlosser, Eric, *Fast Food Nation: What the All-American Meal Is Doing to the World* (London, Penguin, 2002)

Schor, Juliet B., *The Overworked American: The Unexpected Decline of Leisure* (New York: Basic Books, 1991).

Self, Will, "In Conversation with . . .," *Idler* 2 (1993).

Shulgin, Alexander, and Ann Shulgin, *PIHKAL: A Chemical Love Story* (Berkeley, Calif.: Transform Press, 1991).

Smith, Arthur, "Questionnaire," *Idler* 32 (2003).

Strathern, Paul, *Mendeleyev's Dream: The Quest for the Elements* (London: Penguin, 2001).

Stevenson, Robert Louis, "An Apology for Idlers" and "Ordered South," in *Virginibus Puerisque and Other Papers* (London: Kegan Paul, 1881).

Theroux, Louis, "Bed Lieutenant," *Idler* 7 (1994).

Thomas, Keith (ed.), *The Oxford Book of Work* (Oxford: Oxford University Press, 1999).

Thompson, E. P., *Customs in Common* (London: Penguin, 1993).

Thompson, E. P., *The Making of the English Working Class* (London: Penguin, 1991).

Todd, Olivier, *Albert Camus: A Life*, trans. Benjamin Ivry (London: Chatto & Windus, 1997).

Tomalin, Claire, *Samuel Pepys: The Unequalled Self* (London: Viking, 2002).

Trocchi, Alexander, *Cain's Book* (New York: Grove Press, 1960).

Twain, Mark, *The Adventures of Tom Sawyer* (London: Penguin, 1986).

Tzu, Lao, *Tao Te Ching: The Richard Wilhelm Edition*, trans. Richard Wilhelm (London: Penguin Arkana, 1988).

Tzu, Chuang, *Chuang Tzu: Taoist Philosopher and Chinese Mystic*, trans. H. A. Giles (London: Allen & Unwin, 1961).

Uglow, Jenny, *Hogarth: A Life and World* (London: Faber & Faber, 1998).

Uglow, Jenny, *The Lunar Men: a Story of Science, Art, Invention and Passion* (London: Faber & Faber, 2003).

Venables, Bernard, *Mr. Crabtree Goes Fishing* (London: Map Marketing Ltd, 2000).

Walton, Isaak, *The Compleat Angler* (London: Penguin, 1985).

Walton, Stuart, *Out Of It: A Cultural History of Intoxication* (London: Penguin, 2002).

Waterhouse, Keith, *The Theory and Practice of Lunch* (London: Michael Joseph, 1986).

Whitman, Walt, *Leaves of Grass*, ed. Malcolm Cowley (London: Penguin, 1976).

Whitman, Walt, *Democratic Vistas and Other Papers* (Amsterdam: Fredonia Books, 2002).

Wilde, Oscar, *Plays, Prose Writing and Poems* (London: Dent, 1955).

Wilson, Colin, *The Outsider* (London: Gollancz, 1990).

Wordsworth, William, and S. T. Coleridge, *Lyrical Ballads* (London: D. Nutt, 1891).

Yates, Chris, *The Secret Carp* (Ludlow: Merlin Unwin, 1992).

Yutang, Lin, *The Importance of Living* (London: Heinemann, 1938).

Zeldin, Theodore, *An Intimate History of Humanity* (London: Vintage, 1998).

Zeldin, Theodore, *Conversation* (London: Harvill, 1999).

A list of useful websites:

www.abebooks.co.uk
   Beautiful secondhand books at low prices.
www.anxietyculture.com
   Brian Dean's brilliant critique of liberal capitalism.
www.babyshambles.com
   For an insight into the mind of poet/rocker/freedom-seeker
      Peter Doherty.
www.bartleby.com
   Useful reference site.
www.camra.org.uk
   The home of the Campaign for Real Ale.
www.frugal.org.uk
   Spend less, work less.
www.hermenaut.com
   Josh Glenn's digest of heady philosophy.
www.idler.co.uk
   Website of the *Idler* magazine.
www.luxuriamusic.com
   For lovers of lounge music.
www.slowfood.com
   Website of the Slow Food movement, contains their inspiring
      manifesto.
www.spiralseed.co.uk
   How to grow vegetables and enjoy it.
www.whywork.org
   Home of the Creative Living Alternatives to Wage Slavery
      movement (CLAWS), a practical guide to free living.

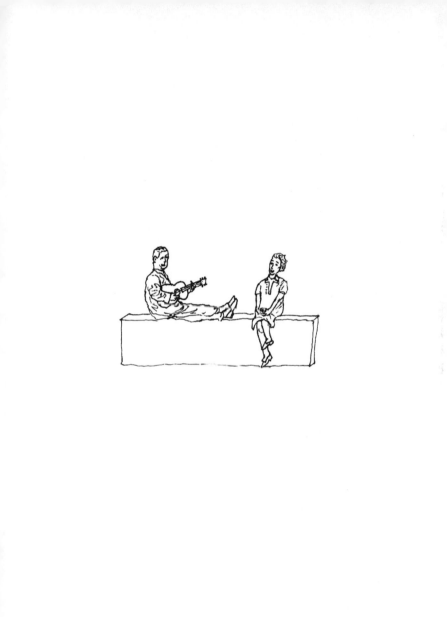

Acknowledgements

I'm eternally grateful to Simon Prosser, who suggested I write something like this in the first place, and then commissioned it and then edited it, beautifully. Thanks to Cat Ledger, my agent, and to the people at Penguin, particularly Juliette Mitchell, Anna Ridley, James Plummer and the meticulous Emma Horton and the two proofreaders, who saved me from making dozens of embarrassing mistakes. Thanks to Steve Marking, the designer, Roderick Mills for the illustrations and Belinda Lawley for the author photo. As for the content, there are so many people quoted and cited that I barely seem to have written the book at all. My greatest thanks go to the historian John Nicholson for introducing me to the radical history of England and to all sorts of work-related material. Also, in no particular order, all the people who have helped more or less directly, in conversation, writing or ideas: Penny Rimbaud, Matt ffytche, Matthew De Abaitua, Damien and Maia, Billy Childish, James Parker, Marcel Theroux, my mum, my dad, Neil Boorman, John Moore, Bill Drummond, Mark Manning, Louis Theroux, Fiona Russell Powell, Chris Yates, John Cooper Clarke, Pete Loveday, John Hull, Jason Skeet, Iain Aitch, David Brook, Simon Jameson, Will Hogan, Tom Shone, Josh Glenn, Greg Rowland, Will Self, John Michell, Charles Handy, Nick Lezard, Tony White, Arthur Smith, Keith Allen, Alan Porter, Sally

Agarwal, Jock Scot, the readers of the *Idler* . . . there are many, many others.

At the *Idler* I am always, constantly, grateful to my partner and friend Gavin Pretor-Pinney, and to co-workers Dan Kieran and Clare Pollard, and at home thanks to Claire Jordan and, last and most, Victoria Hull.

TOM HODGKINSON is still doing what he's always done, which is a mixture of editing magazines, writing articles and putting on parties. He was born in 1968, founded *The Idler* in 1993 and now lives in Devon, England.